"If slaughterhouses had glass walls,

everyone would be a vegetarian."

Paul McCartney

D1824370

In the name of the most merciful God

Special thanks to my mom

"Mrs Gohar Abdollah Pour"

And my sister

"Miss Sahar Khojasteh Farzad"

For helping me complete this book.

Vegans Assistant

(Persian Vegetarian Cookbook)

Vegetarianism Is Not Limitation

With

The Persian CookBook

By: Sajjad Khojasteh

Winter 2019

Published by:

GetBookOnline.com

Copyright©2018
SAJJAD KHOJASTEH FARZAD

All inquiries should be addressed to:

Sajjad.Khojasteh@LearnPersianOnline.com

ISBN: 9781795850056
Imprint: Independently published

Table of contents

Table of contents...13

About the author 17

To the readers..19

Description..20

Preface 21

Some notes related to the ingredients and style of making foods........ 22

Foods classification according to their unique features 24

The foods containing "grains" 24

The foods containing "garlic" 24

The foods made without "garlic" 25

The foods made without "oil"...27

The foods with a "sour taste" 27

The foods with a "sweet taste" 28

Some cooking terms 29

Iranian Cuisines...32

Âsh Resh'teh 34

A'das Po'low 38

Es'tân'bo'li Po'low 42

Fe're'ni 46

Ha'lim 50

Kash'k-e Bâ'dem'jân...54

Khu'râ'k-e A'da'si...58

Khu'râ'k-e Na'khod (Âb Na'khod) 62

Ku'ku Sab'zi 66

Ku'ku Sib Za'mi'ni (with baked potato).............................70

Ku'ku Sib Za'mi'ni(with raw potato) 74

Mâ'kâ'ro'ni-e Sab'zi'jât 78

Po'low...82

Po'low: Âb'kesh Method..84

Po'low: Ka'teh Method..88
Shir Be'renj..92
Sho'leh Zard..96
Gilanian Cuisines..100
Â'sh-e Ka'du..102
Â'sh-e Se'fid (Â'sh-e A'nâr)..106
Â'sh-e Torsh..110
Ash'ke'neh Ta'reh..114
Bâdem'jân Kabâb..118
Bâ'dem'jân Ta'reh..122
Bâ'dem'jân Va'ra'gheh Bâ Gou'jeh..126
Bâ'ghe'lâ Ghâ'togh..130
Bâ'ghe'lâ Po'low Bâ Pa'nir Be'resh'teh..134
Kho'resh't-e Ka'du..138
Khu'li Ou (Hâ'li Ou)..142
Ku'ku Bâ'dem'jân..146
Ku'ku She'vid..150
Ku'ku Sir..154
La'gad Da'mo'jey..158
Mâ'kâ'ro'ni Bâ Ja'fa'ri Vâ'ram'bu..162
Mir'zâ Ghâ'se'mi..166
Mor'ju Vâ'vij..170
Om'let Bâ Sir..174
She'vid Po'low Bâ Pa'nir Be'resh'teh..178
Sir Vâ'vij..182
Tah Bur'yân..186
Tor'sh-e Ta'reh..190
Iranian Side Items..194
Bu'râ'ni-e Es'fe'nâj..196
Dough..200
Mâs't-o Khi'yâr..204

Sâ'lâd Shi'ra'zi 208

Sâ'lâ'd-e Fasl 212

Gilanian Side Items 216

Bu'râ'ni-e Bâ'dem'jân 218

Kâl Ka'bâb 222

Zey'tun Par'var'deh 226

Pickles 230

Tor'shi-e Bâ'dem'jân Chu'châgh 232

Tor'shi-e Li'teh 236

Others 240

Da'lâr (Na'ma'k-e Sabz) 242

Ko'lo'bij Nân 246

So's-e Ger'du 250

Words you might not know 254

Foods ingredients at a glance 257

Table 1: Cooking Ingredients List 266

Table 2: Nutrition facts (Calories, Total fat, Protein and Sugar) .. 271

Table 3: Nutrition facts (Cholesterol, Sodium, Potassium and Carbs) ... 277

Table 4: Nutrition facts (Vitamins) 283

Table 5: Basic features (Timing Information) 289

Table 6: Basic features (Difficulty) 291

Table 7: Basic features (When should you eat the meals?) 293

Table 8: Common abbreviations 295

Table 9: Equivalent measures (Length) 295

Table 10: Equivalent measures (Volume) 296

Table 11: Equivalent measures (Weight) 297

Iranian main course images 298

Gilanian main course images 314

Iranian side item images 337

Gilanian side item images 341

Pickle images 345

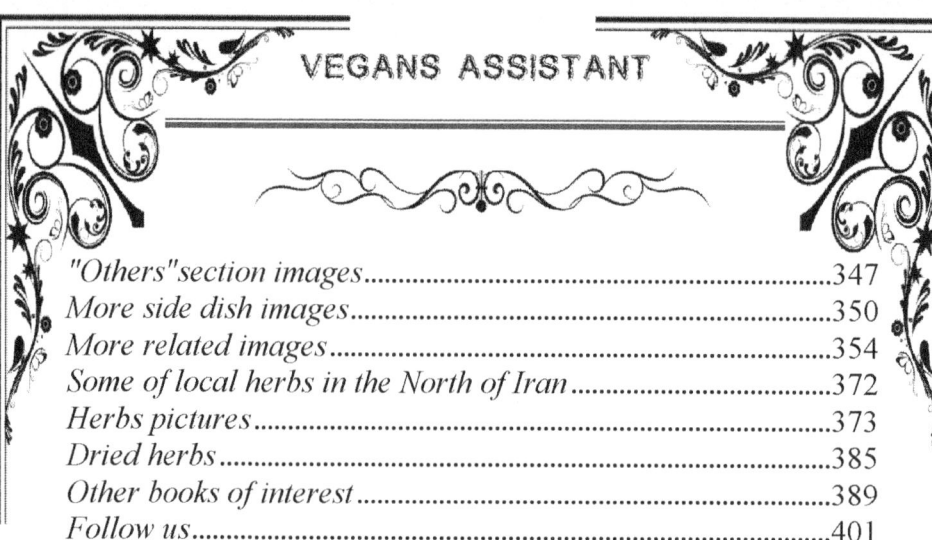

"Others"section images..347
More side dish images..350
More related images..354
Some of local herbs in the North of Iran................................372
Herbs pictures..373
Dried herbs..385
Other books of interest..389
Follow us..401

About the author

Sajjad Khojasteh is a Farsi teacher and author. He has been involved with language teaching since 2012. Sajjad has been succeeded to publish many Farsi and English books in the last 6 years with themes of Iranian culture, art, basic grammars, idioms, proverbs, food, poetry, etc. Some of his book's subjects are:

- ✓ "Fundamental Grammar Of Farsi Verbs: A Self-Study Verb Specifications Plus 202 Real Sentences Quizzes With Answers",

- ✓ "Persian Reading: 50 Iranian Vegetarian Food & Dessert Recipes: For Intermediate to Advanced Farsi Learners",

- ✓ "The Complete Book of Ghazals of Hafez: In Persian with English Translation",

- ✓ "Learn How to Read Hafez Poems: The Best Guide for Reading Hafez's Ghazals with Phonetics",

and some more.

If you want to be keep in touch with the author, join the conversation on his social media channels to stay up-to-date with him. Furthermore, you can find all the latest news about his new books, ask him questions, send him your comments and many more by following the links below:

E-Mail ⟶ Farsi.books@yahoo.com

Facebook ⟶ https://m.facebook.com/farsibookspublication

LinkedIn ⟶ http://linkedin.com/in/farsi-books-b7827563

Instagram ⟶ https://www.instagram.com/farsi.books

Twitter ⟶ https://twitter.com/farsibooks

Pinterest ⟶ https://www.pinterest.co.uk/farsibooks

Tumblr ⟶ Farsibooks

To the readers

The author attempted to introduce Iran's cuisine to the readers as much as possible but certainly the human writings need regular correction and revision. Therefore, if you find any problems during reading the book, please let me know through the following e-mail.

In addition, if you have any difficulties with the text understanding, you can send your questions to the following E-Mail to solve them. I would like to appreciate your cooperation in advance.

Direct message to the author:

Sajjad.Khojasteh@LearnPersianOnline.com

Description

Persian vegetarian food and dessert recipes are the ultimate comforting cuisine, full of robust and rich flavors. These recipes show you how to master the art of Persian cooking and illustrate how to prepare delicious, nice Persian foods from breakfast to dinner. The fresh and simple recipes will be available and perfect for everyday cooking. This book is for those who are vegetarians and interested in healthy foods. It is especially for people who want to put a fabulous dinner on the table for their Persian friends or just kids.

The cookbook explains the Persian traditions and the history that defines the way Iranian's eat. Ranging from traditional foods such as "Mirza Ghasemi" (a dish from Gilan province) and "Sabzi Po'low" (Herb Rice) to local foods in the North of Iran. The Persian recipes in this book highlight the Middle East cuisines.

Finally, with the help of this cookbook, you will not need to travel far to enjoy the authentic flavors of Persian.

"The Authors"

Preface

Nowadays there are increasingly more people worldwide who have chosen vegetarianism as their eating style. Thus, variety in vegan foods is a considerable issue. Therefore, the author has addressed the present book to the vegetarians to familiarize them with the Iranian vegan foods, especially Gilanian vegan foods. Moreover, besides the vegan food recipes, some unique side item recipes have been added which can bring more complete food table for the readers.

As the variation of Iranian vegan foods is high, 50 top recipes have been chosen and presented. There are kinds of vegetarianism but *"Lacto-Ovo Vegetarianism"* has been considered in this book. In other words, the book is related to the vegetarians who abstain from the consumption of animal meat.

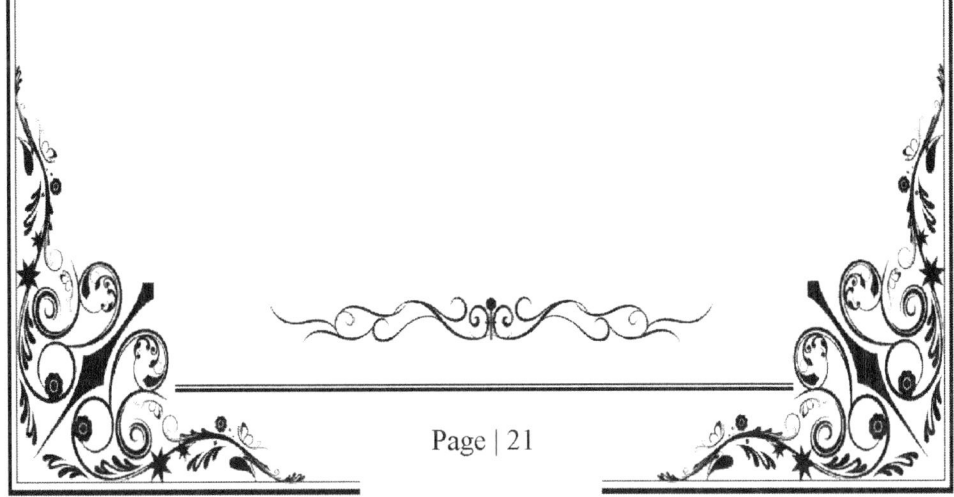

Some notes related to the ingredients and style of making foods

- All recipes are for 4 to 6 people.

- Each cup equals to 237 milliliters (equals to a regular glass)

- None of these foods are made by tools like microwave because they cause the foods to be less quality and harmful.

- About 60 % of the foods can be made without oil or at most with 3-4 tablespoons of oil which is very effective on health and keeps the ingredients value.

- About 80% of the foods are made of plants which is the evidence of the chosen foods high quality.

- Saffron gives better aroma and flavor to the food than turmeric does; but if saffron is unavailable or expensive, you can use turmeric instead even though saffron or turmeric is emphasized on a particular food.

- Not soaking the grains causes flatulence. To avoid this, drain the soaked grains and cook them with fresh water.

- To have a healthier food with high quality, cook and fry the food in the cast iron, copper and zinc pots and pans. Do not use non-stick cookware.

- As the readers' knowledge of cooking is unclear for the author, the instructions are explained in details, for instance, some details are presented for how to clean or chop the green bean. If you use cleaned or chopped green bean, just skip them.

- The suggested side items in each recipe may be set on an Iranian or Gilanian table and one can eat some of them along with their main courses.

- Some herbs in this book such as Ziziphora, Eryngium planum, Creeping wood sorrel[1] are known as aromatic local herbs in the North of Iran and maybe they are not found in other countries but certainly there are some other aromatic alternatives according to the climate of each country.

- Mincing the herbs indicates that they should be cut into the smallest pieces (you can use a food chopper), and grinding the herbs indicates that they should be crushed thoroughly (you can use a meat grinder).

- To deliver the book with the lowest price to the readers, the book is colorless.

---

[1] See page 372

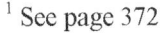

Foods classification according to their unique features

The foods are classified into the following criteria to help the readers regarding their tastes or special diets, then they can easily choose their favorite foods. The criteria are as the following:

The foods containing "grains"

Iranian cuisines

1.	Âsh Resh'teh	page 34
2.	A'das Po'low	page 38
3.	Khu'râ'k-e A'da'si	page 58
4.	Khu'râ'k-e Na'khod (Âb Na'khod)	page 62

Gilanian cuisines

5.	Â'sh-e Torsh	page 110
6.	Ash'ke'neh Ta'reh	page 114
7.	Bâ'ghe'lâ Ghâ'togh	page 130
8.	Bâ'ghe'lâ Po'low Bâ Pa'nir Be'resh'teh	page 134
9.	Kho'resh't-e Ka'du	page 138
10.	La'gad Da'mo'jey	page 158
11.	Mor'ju Vâ'vij	page 170

The foods containing "garlic"

Iranian cuisines

1.	Âsh Resh'teh	page 34
2.	Kash'k-e Bâ'dem'jân	page 54

Gilanian cuisines

3.	Â'sh-e Torsh	page 110
4.	Ash'ke'neh Ta'reh	page 114

5. Bâdem'jân Kabâb   page 118
6. Bâ'ghe'lâ Ghâ'togh   page 130
7. Kho'resh't-e Ka'du   page 138
8. Ku'ku Sir   page 154
9. Mir'zâ Ghâ'se'mi   page 166
10. Mor'ju Vâ'vij   page 170
11. Om'let Bâ Sir   page 174
12. Sir Vâ'vij   page 182
13. Tor'sh-e Ta'reh   page 190

Iranian side items

14. Mâs't-o Khi'yâr   page 204

Gilanian side items

15. Bu'râ'ni-e Bâ'dem'jân   page 218
16. Kâl Ka'bâb   page 222
17. Zey'tun Par'var'deh   page 226

Pickles

18. Tor'shi-e Bâ'dem'jân Chu'châgh   page 232
19. Tor'shi-e Li'teh   page 236

Others

20. So's-e Ger'du   page 250

The foods made without "garlic"

Iranian cuisines

1. A'das Po'low   page 38
2. Es'tân'bo'li Po'low   page 42
3. Fe're'ni   page 46
4. Ha'lim   page 50
5. Khu'râ'k-e A'da'si   page 58
6. Khu'râ'k-e Na'khod (Âb Na'khod)   page 62

7. Ku'ku Sab'zi page 66
8. Ku'ku Sib Za'mi'ni (with baked potato) page 70
9. Ku'ku Sib Za'mi'ni (with raw potato) page 74
10. Mâ'kâ'ro'ni-e Sab'zi'jât page 78
11. Po'low: Âb'kesh Method page 84
12. Po'low: Ka'teh Method page 88
13. Shir Be'renj page 92
14. Sho'leh Zard page 96

Gilanian cuisines

15. Â'sh-e Ka'du page 102
16. Â'sh-e Se'fid (Â'sh-e A'nâr) page 106
17. Bâ'dem'jân Ta'reh page 122
18. Bâ'dem'jân Va'ra'gheh Bâ Gou'jeh page 126
19. Bâ'ghe'lâ Po'low Bâ Pa'nir Be'resh'teh page 134
20. Khu'li Ou (Hâ'li Ou) page 142
21. Ku'ku Bâ'dem'jân page 146
22. Ku'ku She'vid page 150
23. La'gad Da'mo'jey page 158
24. Mâ'kâ'ro'ni Bâ Ja'fa'ri Vâ'ram'bu page 162
25. She'vid Po'low Bâ Pa'nir Be'resh'teh page 178
26. Tah Bur'yân page 186

Iranian side items

27. Bu'râ'ni-e Es'fe'nâj page 196
28. Dough page 200
29. Sâ'lâd Shi'ra'zi page 208
30. Sâ'lâ'd-e Fasl page 212

Others

31. Da'lâr (Na'ma'k-e Sabz) page 242
32. Ko'lo'bij Nân page 246

The foods made without "oil"

Iranian cuisines

1. Fe're'ni   page 46
2. Khu'râ'k-e Na'khod (Âb Na'khod)   page 62
3. Po'low: Ka'teh method   page 88
4. Shir Be'renj   page 92
5. Sho'leh Zard   page 96

Gilanian cuisines

6. Â'sh-e Ka'du   page 102
7. Â'sh-e Se'fid (Â'sh-e A'nâr)   page 106
8. Kho'resh't-e Ka'du   page 138

Iranian side items

9. Bu'râ'ni-e Es'fe'nâj   page 196
10. Dough   page 200
11. Mâs't-o Khi'yâr   page 204
12. Sâ'lâd Shi'ra'zi   page 208

Gilanian side items

13. Bu'râ'ni-e Bâ'dem'jân   page 218
14. Kâl Ka'bâb   page 222
15. Zey'tun Par'var'deh   page 226

Pickles

16. Tor'shi-e Bâ'dem'jân Chu'châgh   page 232
17. Tor'shi-e Li'teh   page 236

The foods with a "sour taste"

Gilanian cuisines

1. Â'sh-e Se'fid (Â'sh-e A'nâr)   page 106
2. Â'sh-e Torsh   page 110
3. Ash'ke'neh Ta'reh   page 114

4. Bâ'dem'jân Ka'bâb   page 118
5. Khu'li Ou (Hâ'li Ou)   page 142
6. Tah Bur'yân   page 186
7. Tor'sh-e Ta'reh   page 190

Iranian side items

8. Sâ'lâd Shi'ra'zi   page 208

Gilanian side items

9. Kâl Ka'bâb   page 222
10. Zey'tun Par'var'de`h   page 226

Pickles

11. Tor'shi-e Bâ'dem'jân Chu'châgh page 232
12. Tor'shi-e Li'teh   page 236

Others

13. So's-e Ger'du   page 250

The foods with a "sweet taste"

Iranian cuisines

1. A'das Po'low   page 38
2. Fe're'ni   page 46
3. Ha'lim   page 50
4. Shir Be'renj   page 92
5. Sho'leh Zard   page 96

Gilanian cuisines

6. Â'sh-e Ka'du   page 102

Others

7. Ko'lo'bij Nân   page 246

Some cooking terms
Alphabetical order

Absorb

To take in liquid, gas, or another substance from the surface or space around something. (Longman Dictionary)

Boil

To cook something in boiling water. (Longman Dictionary)

Boil over

If a liquid boils over when it is heated, it rises and flows over the side of the container. (Longman Dictionary)

Crush

To press something in order to break it into very small pieces or into a powder. (Longman Dictionary)

Cut sth into sticks

Cut something into long pieces in your desired thickness.

Dice

To cut food into small square pieces. (Longman Dctionary)

Drain

To make the water or liquid in something flow away. (Longman Dictionary)

Grind

To break something such as corn or coffee beans into small pieces or powder, either in a machine or between two hard

surfaces. (Longman Dictionary)

Liquid comes out

When the texture of a fruit or vegetable damaged, its liquid may come out.

Mash

To crush something, especially a food that has been cooked, until it is soft and smooth. (Longman Dictionary)

Settle

The food comes down and stays at the bottom of the pot.

Simmer

To boil gently, or to cook something slowly by boiling it gently. (Longman Dictionary)

Soak

If you soak something, or if you let it soak, you keep it covered with a liquid for a period of time, especially in order to make it softer. (Longman Dictionary)

Steam

To cook something in steam. (Longman Dictionary)

Steep

To put food in a liquid and leave it there, so that it becomes soft or has the same taste as the liquid, or so that it gives the liquid its taste. (Longman Dictionary)

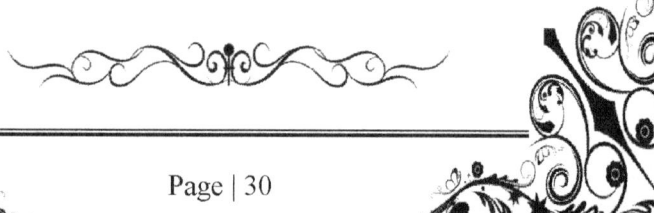

Stick at the bottom

If something sticks at the bottom, it becomes fixed and difficult to remove or burns due to lack of water or high heat.

Sticky

When Po'low cooks in too much water, the rice grains stick and clump together. At the end, Po'low looks terribly sticky.

Stir

To move a liquid or substance around with a spoon or stick in order to mix it together. (Longman Dctionary)

Stir-fry

To cook small pieces of food quickly by moving them around continuously in very hot oil. (Longman Dictionary)

Taste

To eat or drink a small amount of something to see what it is like. (Longman Dictionary)

Thin

Liquid. A liquid that is thin flows very easily because it has a lot of water in it. (Longman Dictionary)

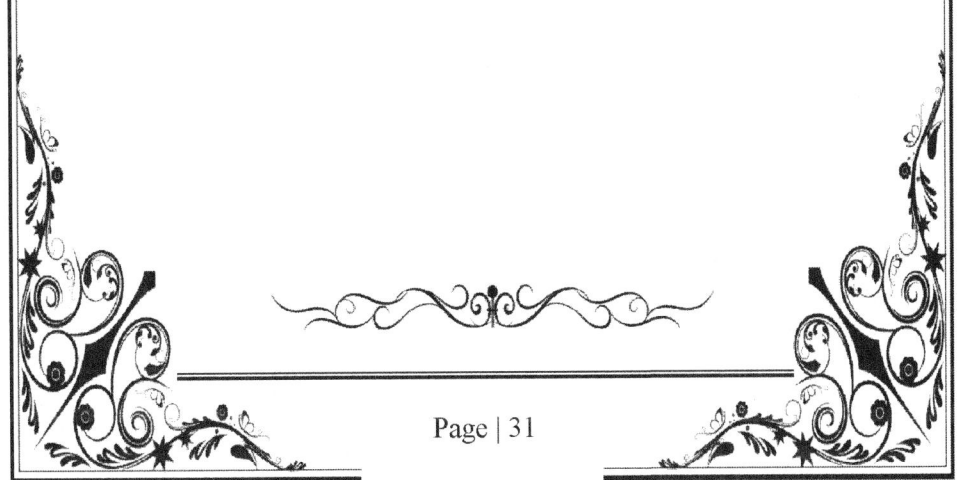

Iranian Cuisines

Iranian food names

Alphabetical order

1- Âsh Resh'teh   page 34

2- A'das Po'low   page 38

3- Es'tân'bo'li Po'low   page 42

4- Fe're'ni   page 46

5- Ha'lim   page 50

6- Kash'k-e Bâ'dem'jân   page 54

7- Khu'râ'k-e A'da'si   page 58

8- Khu'râ'k-e Na'khod (Âb Na'khod)   page 62

9- Ku'ku Sab'zi   page 66

10-1 Ku'ku Sib Za'mi'ni (with baked potato)   page 70

10-2 Ku'ku Sib Za'mi'ni (with raw potato)   page 74

11- Mâ'kâ'ro'ni-e Sab'zi'jât   page 78

12- Po'low   page 82

12-1 Po'low: Âb'kesh Method   page 84

12-2 Po'low: Ka'teh Method   page 88

13- Shir Be'renj   page 92

14- Sho'leh Zard   page 96

Âsh Resh'teh[1]

INFORMATION ABOUT THE MEAL

Basic Information:

Cuisine: *Iranian*

Course: *Main Dish*

Formal meal (for guest): *Yes, ~~No~~*

Recommend for: *~~Breakfast~~, ~~Lunch~~, Dinner*

Yield: *6 servings*

Level (From Iranian viewpoint): *Hard, Time-consuming*

Calories:

The meal: *~ 40 calories per 1 tablespoon*

The meal (with curd and fried onion): *~ 250 calories per cup*

Timing Information:

To soak: *~ 12 hours*

To prep: *~ 40 minutes*

To cook: *~ 6 hours*

Total time: *~ 6 hours 40 minutes*

---

[1] Vegetable and Noodle Thick Soup

Ingredients

~ 1 lb / ½ kg herbs including spinach, mint, leek, coriander and parsley

~ 1 lb / ½ kg pasteurized curd[1]   ~ ½ cup lentils

~ 11 oz / 300g thin noodles   ~ ¼ cup lima beans

~ 2 large onions   ~ ¼ cup pinto beans

~ 1 small garlic head   ~ ¼ cup red beans

~ 3 tbsp. dried mint   ~ ¼ cup mung beans

~ 16 cups water   ~ ¼ cup chickpeas

oil, salt, pepper and turmeric   ~ ¼ cup peeled wheat

Instructions before starting

- Soak all grains in water 12 hours ahead.
- Soak the peeled wheat in water 1½ hours ahead.
- Dice the onion.
- Crush the garlic.
- Mince the herbs.

---

[1] See page 254

To prepare

At first, rinse the soaked grains with cold water in a colander. Then fill ⅔ of the pot with mild water to boil on the stove. After boiling, it takes 4 to 5 hours for grains to cook. Do not put the lid on until water boils because with the lid on the water may boil over but after boiling you can put the lid on with the lowest heat.

During cooking the grains, you can fry the onions until golden, then take away the fried onions from the pan and fry the garlic. Fry the dried mint in another frying pan. Boil the curd in another pot for 20 minutes. Stir the grains every 45 minutes in order not to stick at the bottom. When the grains cooked, drain the soaked wheat in a colander and after removing the water, add it to the grains. Let the wheat simmer for 30 minutes, then add the herbs to the pot to simmer for 20 minutes. Next, add the thin noodles to Âsh and stir once to twice in order not to stick at the bottom. After boiling the thin noodles for 10 minutes, it is time to add the fried garlic and ¾ of fried onions with 90 percent of the boiled curd. It is worth mentioning that the heat should be at the lowest degree. Stir Âsh as you are adding the ingredients. At the end, add ¾ of the fried mint to the pot and stir once then turn off the heat. The food is ready.

Tips for this food

1. Âsh is an Iranian whole food and there is no need to serve with bread.
2. Garnish the food with the remaining curd, fried onions and mint.
3. Iranians eat the food with onion, pickles[1] and vegetables[2].

Bon Appétit

---

[1] See pages 351 and 352
[2] See pages 256 and 353

VEGANS ASSISTANT

A'das Po'low[1]

INFORMATION ABOUT THE MEAL

Basic Information:

Cuisine: *Iranian*

Course: *Main Dish*

Formal meal (for guest): *Yes, ~~No~~*

Recommend for: *~~Breakfast,~~ Lunch, ~~Dinner~~*

Yield: *5 servings*

Level (From Iranian viewpoint): *Medium, Time-consuming*

Calories:

The Food: *~ 40 calories per 1 tablespoon, ~ 240 calories per 1 spatula*

Timing Information:

To soak: *~ 3 hours*

To prep: *~ 30 minutes*

To cook: *~ 2 hours*

―――――――

Total time: *~ 2 hours 30 minutes*

―――――――――――

[1] Lentil Rice

Ingredients

- ~ 3 cups rice
- ~ 1½ cups lentils
- ~ 2 cup raisins
- ~ ½ cup of walnuts
- ~ 3 medium onions
- ~ 2 tbsp. tomato paste
- ~ ¼ cup steeped saffron
- ~ 15 cups water

oil, salt, pepper and turmeric

Instructions before starting

- Soak the rice in salted water 3 hours ahead.
- Soak the lentils in water 3 hours ahead.
- Dice the onions.
- Chop the walnuts into small pieces.
- Heat 1 cup of water.
- To make steeped saffron, dissolve a few threads in ¼ cup of warm water. See also "How to brew saffron?" on pages 255 and 365.

To prepare

Drain the soaked lentils and cook them with 2 cups of water (just to cover the surface of the lentils), some salt, pepper and turmeric. As soaked previously, the lentils take at least 20 minutes to cook. Then turn off the heat, and drain the lentils. In this step, fry ¾ of the diced onions until turn golden. Now add the drained lentils and 1½ cups of raisins to the golden onions, and stir-fry all ingredients, then turn off the heat.

Prepare the rice according to Âb'kesh method[1] until it reaches to the draining step. Then put the pot on the stove and pour 4 tablespoons of water, 3 tablespoons of oil and 2 spatulas of Po'low and steeped saffron or turmeric and mix them well. After 2 minutes, remove the pot from the heat and spread the ingredients to cover the pot bottom. At this moment, mix Po'low from inside the colander with fried ingredients in the pan and put all into the pot and place it over the low heat to cook. But before putting the lid on the pot, mix 2 tablespoons of oil and ½ cup of warm water and some salt and spread the mix over Po'low.

Until Po'low steams, fry the remaining onions with 3 tablespoons of oil, a little salt, pepper and turmeric in the frying pan. When the onions turned golden, add the walnuts and the remaining raisins to fry a little while. At this time, you can serve the steamed Po'low into a plate and put some of the fried ingredients over it. The food is ready to eat.

---

[1] See pages 84 and 310

Tips for this food

1. Iranians serve the food with onion, yogurt and olives.

Bon Appétit

Es'tân'bo'li Po'low[1]

INFORMATION ABOUT THE MEAL

Basic Information:

Cuisine: *Iranian*

Course: *Main Dish*

Formal meal (for guest): *Yes, ~~No~~*

Recommend for: *~~Breakfast~~, Lunch, ~~Dinner~~*

Yield: *6 servings*

Level (From Iranian viewpoint): *Medium, Time-consuming*

Calories:

The meal (combination):

~ 40 calories per 1 tablespoon

~ 240 calories per 1 spatula

Timing Information:

To soak: *~ 3 hours*   **To prep:** *~ 45 minutes*

                                           To cook: *~ 2 hours*

                            Total time: *~ 2 hours 45 minutes*

---

[1] Green Bean Rice

Ingredients

- ~ 4 cups rice
- ~ 1 lb / 450g soy protein
- ~ 1 lb / 450g green beans
- ~ 1 large onion
- ~ 4 tbsp. tomato paste
- ~ 2 cups milk
- ~ ¼ cup steeped saffron
- ~ 15 cups water
- oil, salt, pepper and turmeric

Instructions before starting

- Soak the rice in salted water 3 hours ahead.
- Soak the soy protein in the milk.
- Cut the excess parts of the green beans and chop them into small pieces (⅓ in / 1 cm each).
- Dice the onion.
- Heat 1 cup of the water.
- To make steeped saffron, dissolve a few threads in ¼ cup of warm water. See also "How to brew saffron?" on pages 255 and 365.

To prepare

At first, put the chopped green beans in a pot with 2 cups of water, then add some turmeric and pepper and place the pot on the stove with the medium heat for 40 minutes. Do not add salt now because the green beans get tough. Fry the diced onion in a pan with 3 tablespoons of oil, some salt, pepper and turmeric until the green beans get ready. When the onion turned golden, take the soy protein out of milk then put it in the pan to fry with other ingredients. Finally, add 4 tablespoons of tomato paste and stir to mix all together. If the green beans get ready, drain them to remove the excess water then add them into the pan. At this moment, stir the food gently because the green beans are easily crushed.

Prepare the rice according to Âb'kesh method[1] until it reaches to the draining step. Then put the pot on the stove with low heat and pour 4 tablespoons of water, 3 tablespoons of oil, 2 spatulas of Po'low and steeped saffron (or turmeric) at the bottom of the pot and stir. After 2 minutes, pick up the pot from the heat and spread the ingredients at the bottom of the pot to cover all the bottom. Now mix Po'low from colander with the ingredients of the pan, then put them in the pot. Place the pot on the stove again to steam but before covering the pot with a lid on, mix 2 tablespoons of oil, ½ cup of warm water and some salt and spread the liquid over Po'low. It takes 45 minutes to get ready.

---

[1] See pages 84 and 310

Tips for this food

1. You can mix and cook the ingredients in a rice cooker.

2. Iranians serve the food with onion, olives, Shi'râ'zi Sâ'lâd[1], yogurt and Dough[2].

Bon Appétit

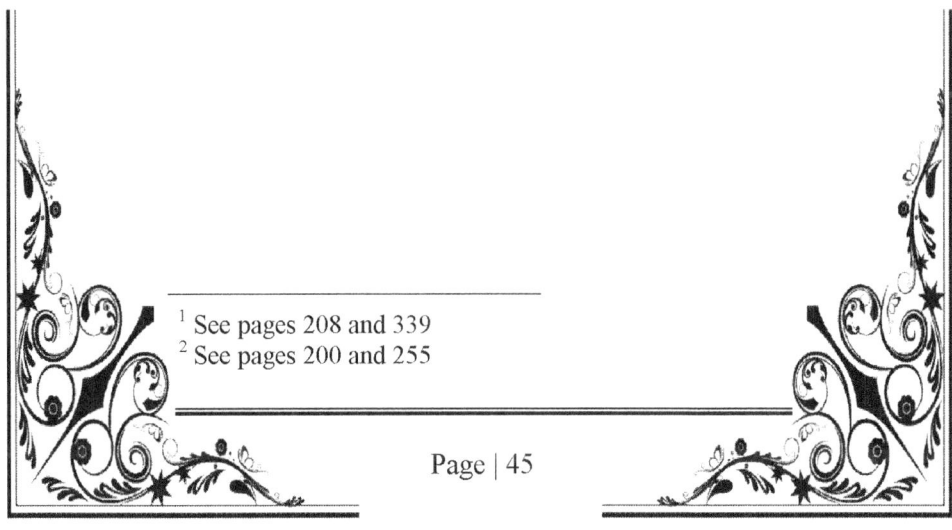

---

[1] See pages 208 and 339
[2] See pages 200 and 255

Fe're'ni[1]

INFORMATION ABOUT THE MEAL

Basic Information:

Cuisine: *Iranian*

Course: *First or main course*

Formal meal (for guest): *Yes (as a first course for dinner),* ~~*No*~~

Recommend for: *Breakfast,* ~~*Lunch*~~*, Dinner*

Yield: *5 servings*

Level (From Iranian viewpoint): *Easy*

Calories:

~ 200 calories per cup

Timing Information:

To soak: — **To prep:** —

To cook: *~ 20 minutes*

Total time: *~ 20 minutes*

[1] Rice Flour Pudding

Ingredients

~ 1 liter milk

~ 5 tbsp. rice flour

~ 5 tbsp. sugar

~ 3 tbsp. rose water

~ 1 tbsp. cinnamon

~ ¼ dessertspoon ground cardamom

~ ¼ dessertspoon salt

Instructions before starting

–

To prepare

Put the rice flour, milk, sugar, salt and ground cardamom into a saucepan and mix them well to dissolve in the milk. Then put the saucepan on the stove with medium heat, and from now on, keep stirring the whole ingredients. This should be continued until the milk boils. Then stop stirring and let it simmer for 15 minutes. After this time, add the rose water and stir once, then turn off the heat. Serve Fe're'ni in small bowls and garnish each bowl with cinnamon powder.

Note: Do not stop stirring until the milk boiling, otherwise the flour clumps together and Ferni sticks at the bottom of the saucepan.

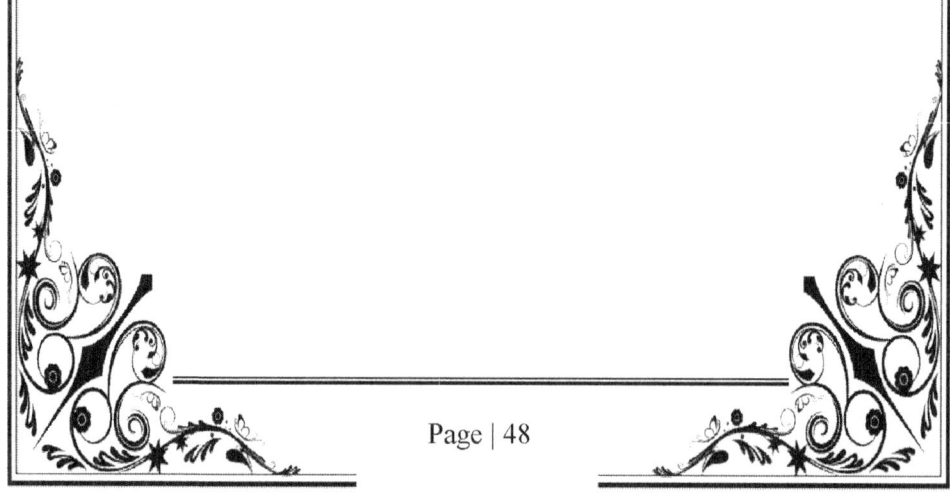

Tips for this food

1. This food is served without bread or rice.
2. This food is very nutritious and it is useful for sick people.

Bon Appétit

Ha'lim[1]

INFORMATION ABOUT THE MEAL

Basic Information:

Cuisine: *Iranian*

Course: *Main Dish*

Formal meal (for guest): *Yes, ~~No~~*

Recommend for: *Breakfast, ~~Lunch~~, ~~Dinner~~*

Yield: *4 servings*

Level (From Iranian viewpoint): *Hard, Time-consuming*

Calories:

~ 50 calories per 1 tablespoon

~ 180 calories per cup (without oil)

~ 300 calories per cup (with oil, a piece of bread and sugar)

Timing Information:

To soak: *~ 12 hours*

To prep: —

To cook: *~ 2 hours*

Total time: *~ 2 hours*

[1] Wheat Porridge

Ingredients

~ 12 oz / 350g peeled wheat

~ 5 tbsp. peeled sesame

~ 6 tbsp. sugar

~ 5 tbsp. sesame oil

~ ½ cup walnuts

~ ½ cup pistachios

~ 5 cups water

~ 2 tbsp. ground cinnamon

salt

Instructions before starting

- Soak the wheat in water overnight.
- Chop the walnuts and pistachios into small pieces.

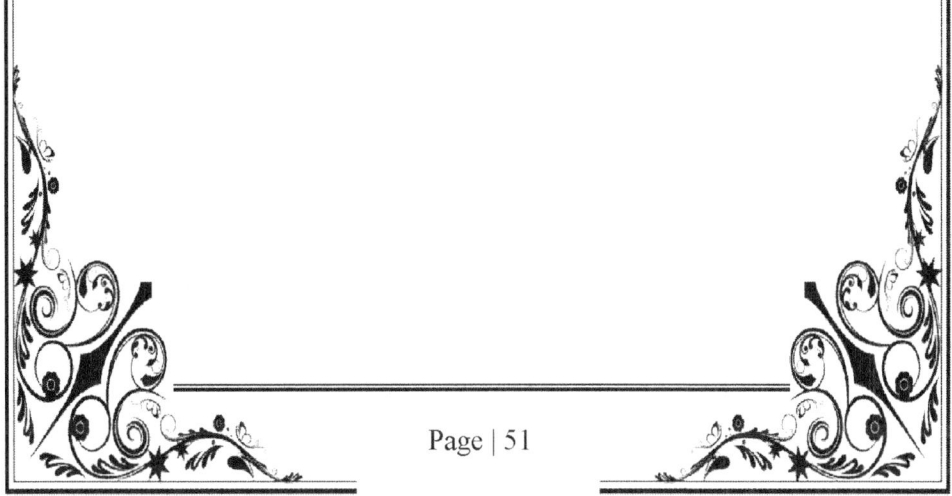

To prepare

Wash the wheat in a colander with cold water. Then put the wheat into a pot and add 5 cups of water and put the pot over the low heat to cook (you should not put a lid on the pot because the wheat boils over when the water reaches to the boiling point).

At this stage, grind the cooked wheat and pass it through a filter until the starch is separated. Now put the wheat passed through the filter into a pot and place it on the stove with low heat to boil. Then stir it regularly in order not to stick at the bottom of the pot. After 5 to 10 minutes, add sugar, 1 tablespoon cinnamon and 5 tablespoons of sesame oil, and keep stirring the food in order not to stick at the bottom. Turn off the heat after 30 minutes pour the food into a serving bowl, then garnish it with a little cinnamon, sesame, some chopped walnuts and pistachios. It's ready to eat.

Tips for this food

1. This food is usually served as a breakfast meal with hot Iranian breads like San'gak[1] or Bar'ba'ri[2].

2. Cinnamon is the main ingredient for this food. So, if cinnamon is not available, do not prepare the food because cinnamon has a strong effect on the flavor.

3. As no meat or poultry is used in this kind of Ha'lim, it is better not to eliminate walnuts, pistachios and sesame because they are very effective in the taste of this food.

4. While eating Ha'lim, some Iranians add a few teaspoons of sugar or salt to make it tastier.

Bon Appétit

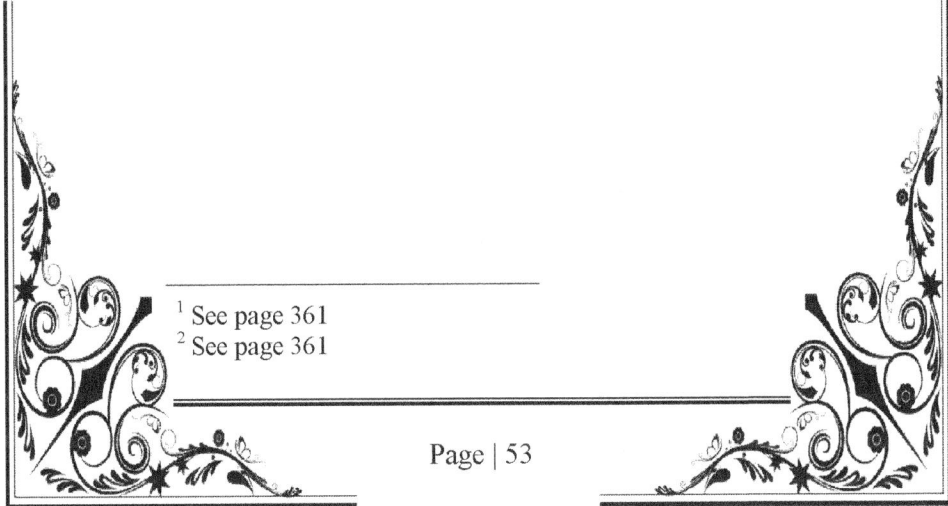

[1] See page 361
[2] See page 361

Kash'k-e Bâ'dem'jân[1]

INFORMATION ABOUT THE MEAL

Basic Information:

Cuisine: *Iranian*

Course: *Main Dish*

Formal meal (for guest): *Yes, ~~No~~*

Recommend for: *~~Breakfast~~, ~~Lunch~~, Dinner*

Yield: *5 servings*

Level (From Iranian viewpoint): *Medium, Time-consuming*

Calories:

The Curd: ~ *100 calories per 100g / 3½oz*

The meal: ~ *50 calories per 1 tablespoon, ~ 230 calories per serving*

Timing Information:

To soak: ~ *1 hour*

To prep: ~ *1 hour 15 minutes*

To cook: ~ *1 hour 45 minutes*

Total time: ~ *3 hours*

---

[1] Eggplant Dip

Ingredients

- ~ 3½ lb / 1½ kg medium eggplants
- ~ 1⅔ lb / 800g pasteurized curd
- ~ 1 medium garlic head
- ~ 2 large onions
- ~ 3 tbsp. dried mint

oil, salt and pepper

Instructions before starting

- Peel the eggplants and chop them. Soak them in salted water for 1 hour. After this time, drain the eggplants in a colander and wash them with cold water to rinse the salt. Let the eggplants dry, then fry them. Keep the fried eggplants in a dish.

- Boil the curd for 20 minutes.

- Dice the onions and garlic.

- Fry the dried mint.

To prepare

Fry the diced garlic and onions with some oil in the same frying pan which you have fried the eggplants. Then put the fried eggplants over the fried onions and garlic and add the fried mint with some salt and pepper to the frying pan. Now turn off the heat and mash all fried ingredients. Then pour the boiled curd over them and stir. Dish up the food, it is ready.

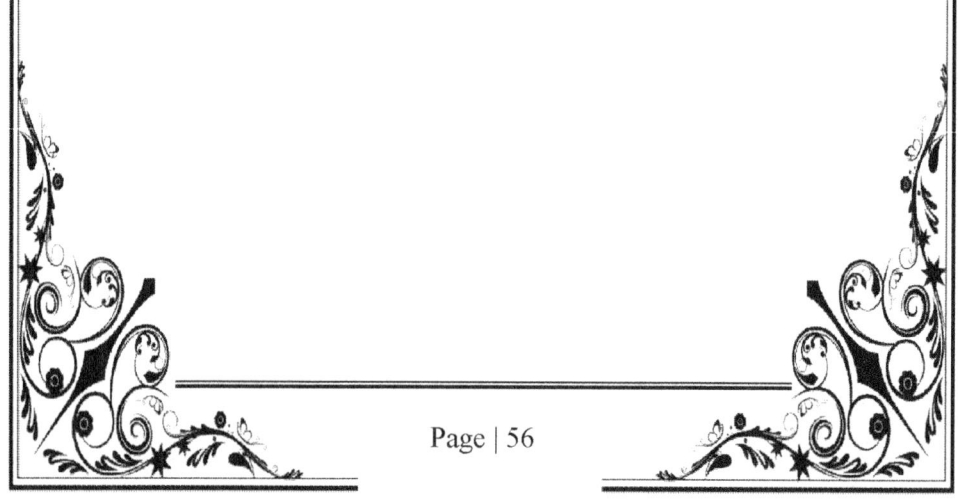

Tips for this food

1. The food is served with bread.

2. You can also replace the dried mint with ~ 12 oz / 350g fresh mint. In case of using fresh mint, mince it then fry and add to the food.

3. Iranians serve the food with vegetables[1] and onion.

Bon Appétit

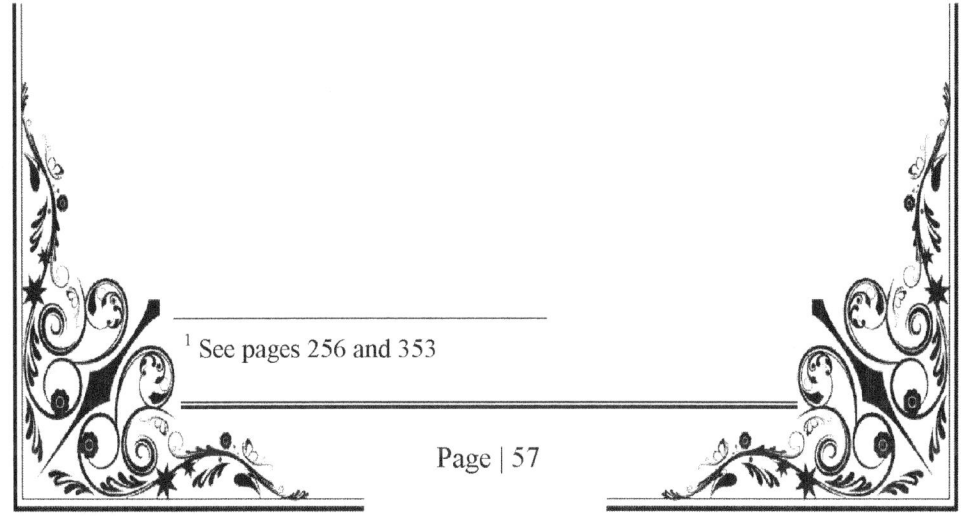

---

[1] See pages 256 and 353

Khu'râ'k-e A'da'si[1]

INFORMATION ABOUT THE MEAL

Basic Information:

Cuisine: *Iranian*

Course: *Main Dish*

Formal meal (for guest): ~~Yes~~, *No*

Recommend for: ~~Breakfast~~, ~~Lunch~~, *Dinner*

Yield: *5 servings*

Level (From Iranian viewpoint): *Easy, Time-consuming*

Calories:

~ *14 calories per 1 tablespoon*

~ *116 calories per 100g / 3½oz*

~ *185 calories per cup (with a little oil)*

Timing Information:

To soak: *~ 2 hours*

To prep: *~ 15 minutes*

To cook: *~ 1 hour 30 minutes*

———————————

Total time: *~ 1 hour 45 minutes*

———————————————

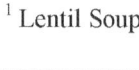

[1] Lentil Soup

Ingredients

~ 1 lb / 450g lentils

~ 2 large onions

~ 4 tbsp. tomato paste

~ 3 cups water

~ 5 tbsp. oil

salt, pepper and turmeric

Instructions before starting

- Soak the lentils in water 2 hours ahead.
- Mince the onions.

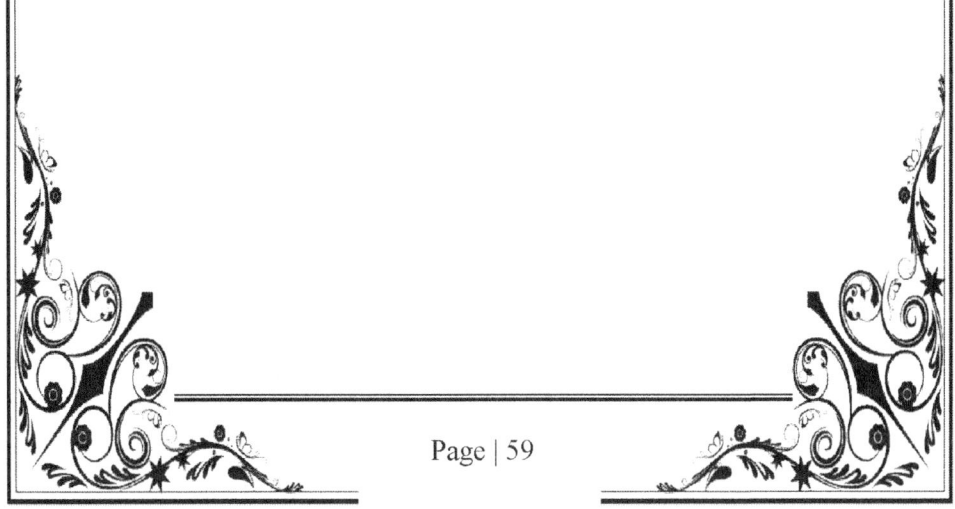

To prepare

Put the lentils with 3 cups of water, some pepper, salt and turmeric in a pot and place the pot over the heat. Until the lentils cook, fry the onions gently in a frying pan with 5 tablespoons of oil and when they are golden, add 4 tablespoons of tomato paste and stir-fry a little. After 3 minutes, add the frying pan ingredients to the lentils and stir them to mix well. Then cover the pot with a lid. After 30 minutes turn the heat off and the food is ready.

Tips for this food

1. The dish is served with bread.
2. Iranians serve the food with pickles[1] and onion.

Bon Appétit

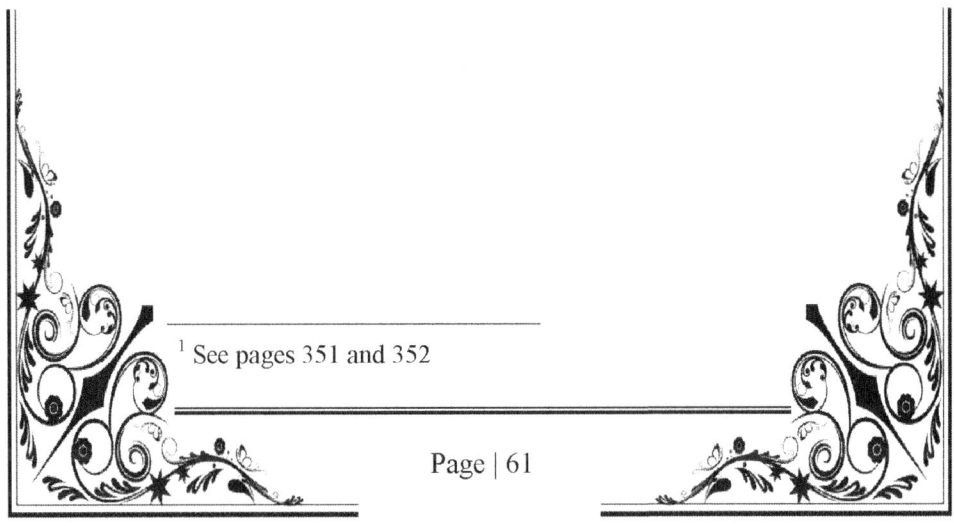

[1] See pages 351 and 352

Khu'râ'k-e Na'khod (*Âb Na'khod*)

INFORMATION ABOUT THE MEAL

Basic Information:

Cuisine: *Iranian*

Course: *Main Dish*

Formal meal (for guest): ~~*Yes*~~*, No*

Recommend for: ~~*Breakfast*~~, ~~*Lunch*~~, *Dinner*

Yield: *5 servings*

Level (From Iranian viewpoint): *Easy, Time-consuming*

Calories:

The chickpeas: *~ 1 calorie per 1 chickpea, ~ 120 calories per cup*

The meal (combination): *~ 45 calories per 100g / 3½oz*

Timing Information:

To soak: *~ 12 hours*   **To prep:** *~ 15 minutes*

                                      To cook: *~ 7 hours*

———————

Total time: *~ 7 hours 15 minutes*

Ingredients

~ 1 lb / 450g chickpeas

~ 1 medium onion

~ 1 medium potato

~ 18 cups water

salt, pepper and turmeric

Instructions before starting

- Soak the chickpeas in water overnight.
- Peel the potato and dice it.
- Dice the onion.
- Boil the water.

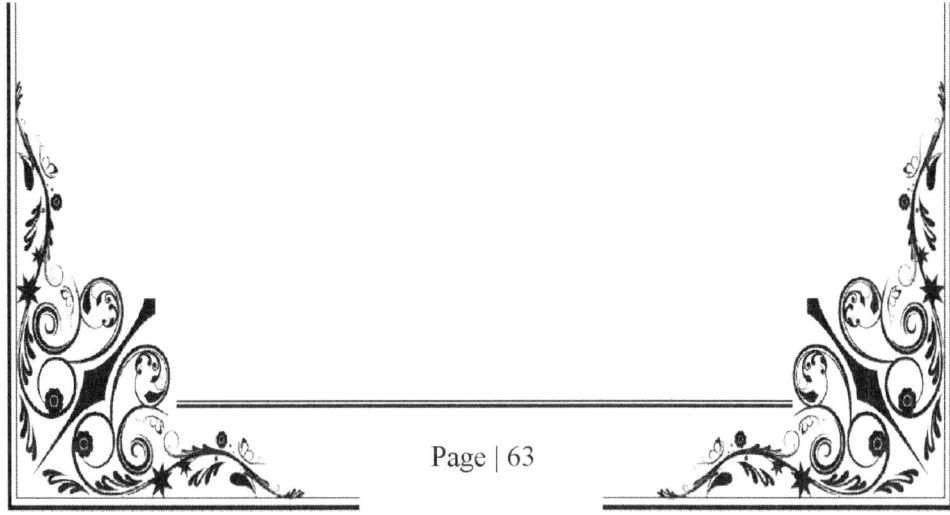

To prepare

Drain and rinse the soaked chickpeas and put them in a large pot. Add the diced onion, salt, pepper and turmeric and pour the boiled water over them. Put the pot on the stove, and wait for the water to boil again then turn the heat down. Cover the pot with a lid to simmer the chickpeas over low heat. Stir about every 45 minutes.

At the end and 30 minutes before turning the heat off, add the diced potato to cook. At this moment, check for salt, pepper and turmeric amounts and if necessary, add them to be absorbed by the food at the last 30 minutes. After this time, turn off the heat. Khu'râ'k-e Na'khod (Âb Na'khod) is ready. It takes 6-7 hours.

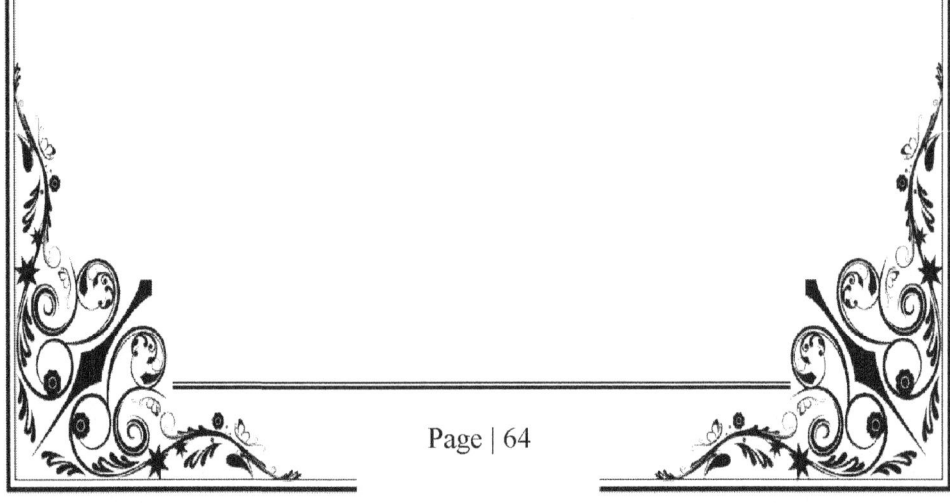

Tips for this food

1. This food is served with Iranian breads like San'gak[1] or Bar'ba'ri[2].

2. Iranians serve this food with onion, pickles[3] and some sour orange juice[4].

Bon Appétit

---

[1] See page 361
[2] See page 361
[3] See pages 351 and 352
[4] See page 366

VEGANS ASSISTANT

Ku'ku Sab'zi[1]

INFORMATION ABOUT THE MEAL

Basic Information:
Cuisine: *Iranian*
Course: *Main Dish*
Formal meal (for guest): ~~Yes~~, *No*
Recommend for: ~~Breakfast~~, ~~Lunch~~, *Dinner*
Yield: *4 servings*
Level (From Iranian viewpoint): *Easy, Time-consuming*

Calories:
The meal: *~ 306 calories per 100g / 3½oz*

Timing Information:
To soak: —   **To prep:** *~ 20 minutes*
                                 To cook: *~ 40 minutes*

_____

Total time: *~ 1 hour*

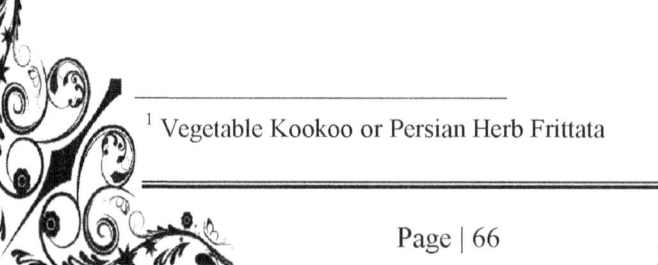

[1] Vegetable Kookoo or Persian Herb Frittata

Ingredients

herbs including:

~ 10 sticks coriander

~ 8 sticks fenugreek

~ 1 lb / 450g parsley and leek

and

~ 5 eggs

~ 1 tbsp. rice flour

oil, salt and pepper

Instructions before starting

- Mince the herbs.

To prepare

Put the minced herbs in a dish, then add the eggs, flour, salt and pepper and stir them to mix thoroughly. If you feel your mixed ingredients are too watery, you can lightly add rice flour.

For frying

Place a large frying pan on the stove and pouring 5-6 tablespoons oil into that to heat. Then make small patties, flatten them in an oval shape and carefully place them in the pan to fry. Where you see that the bottom and the edges are crispy, turn them over to fry the other sides. After frying all the mixed ingredients the food is ready.

Tips for this food

1. The food is served with bread.

2. As this food absorbs too much oil, use oil absorbent paper to soak up the excess oil after frying. So the food would be healthier.

3. Mâs't-o Khi'yâr[1] is more common side item with the food.

Bon Appétit

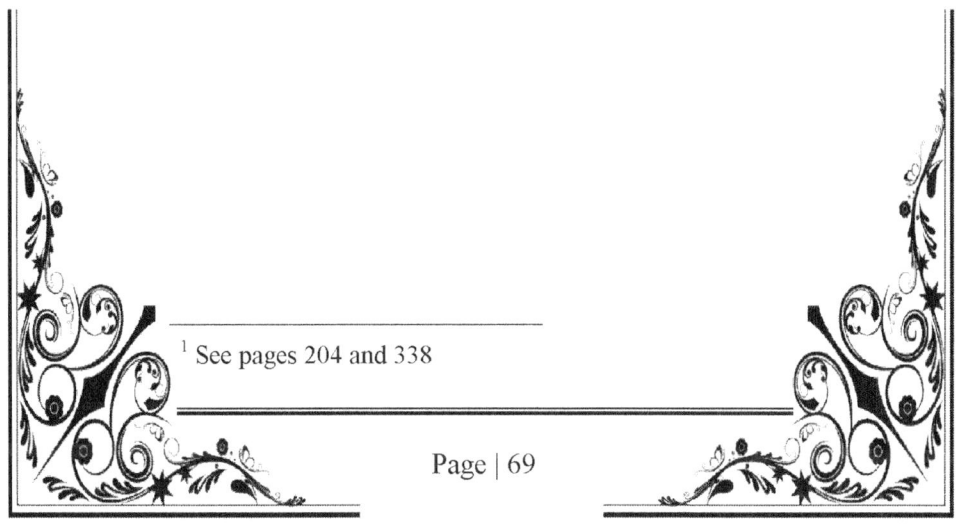

[1] See pages 204 and 338

INFORMATION ABOUT THE MEAL

Basic Information:

Cuisine: *Iranian*

Course: *Main Dish*

Formal meal (for guest): ~~Yes~~, *No*

Recommend for: ~~Breakfast~~, ~~Lunch~~, *Dinner*

Yield: *4 servings*

Level (From Iranian viewpoint): *Easy, Time-consuming*

Calories:

The meal: ~ *269 calories per 100g / 3½oz*

Timing Information:

To soak: —

To prep: ~ *10 minutes*

To cook: ~ *1 hour 40 minutes*

Total time: ~ *1 hour 50 minutes*

[1] Potato Patties

Ingredients

~ 5 medium potatoes

~ 3 eggs

~ 1 large onion

~ 2 tbsp. steeped saffron

~ 2 tbsp. thick yogurt

oil, salt and pepper

Instructions before starting

- Grate the onion (drain off the grated onion liquid by a spoon since it reduces the food quality).

- To make steeped saffron, dissolve a few threads in 2 tbsp. of warm water. See also "How to brew saffron?" on pages 255 and 365.

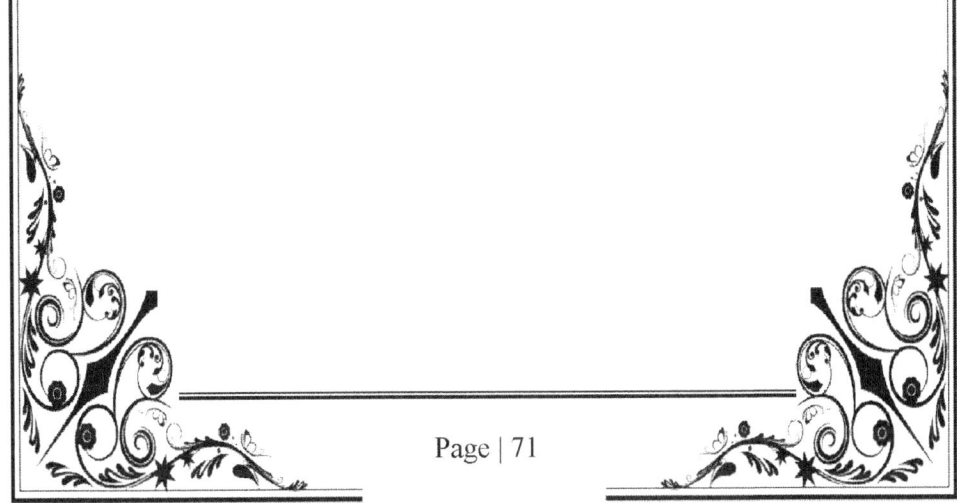

To prepare

Boil the potatoes, then peel them and mash them. Now put the mashed potatoes into a dish and add the onion, yogurt, saffron, eggs, salt and pepper and stir them to mix thoroughly. If you feel your mixed ingredients are too watery, you can lightly add rice flour.

For frying

Place a large frying pan on the stove and pouring 5-6 tablespoons oil into that to heat. Then make small patties, flatten them in an oval shape and carefully place them in the pan to fry. Where you see that the bottom and the edges are crispy, turn them over to fry the other sides. After frying all the mixed ingredients the food is ready.

Tips for this food

1. The food is served with bread.

2. If you have a problem with egg consumption, you can reduce its amount and make the food with 2 eggs.

3. As this food absorbs too much oil, use oil absorbent paper to soak up the excess oil after frying. So the food would be healthier.

4. This food can be served with side items like Dough[1] and "sliced onion, sliced tomato and parsely"[2].

Bon Appétit

---

[1] See pages 200 and 255
[2] See page 350

VEGANS ASSISTANT

Ku'ku Sib Za'mi'ni[1] *(with raw potato)*

INFORMATION ABOUT THE MEAL

Basic Information:

Cuisine: *Iranian*

Course: *Main Dish*

Formal meal (for guest): ~~Yes~~, *No*

Recommend for: ~~Breakfast~~, ~~Lunch~~, *Dinner*

Yield: *5 servings*

Level (From Iranian viewpoint): *Easy, Time-consuming*

Calories:

The meal: ~ *269 calories per 100g / 3½oz*

Timing Information:

To soak: —

To prep: ~ *30 minutes*

To cook: ~ *45 minutes*

Total time: ~ *1 hour 15 minutes*

[1] Potato Patties

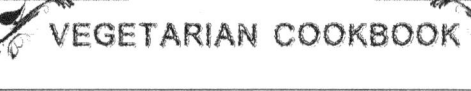
Ingredients

~ 6 medium potatoes

~ 2 small onions

~ 2 eggs

oil, salt, pepper and turmeric

Instructions before starting

- Peel the potatoes and onions, then grate them (if there is liquid after grating, it is better to remove it with a spoon because it reduces the quality of the food).

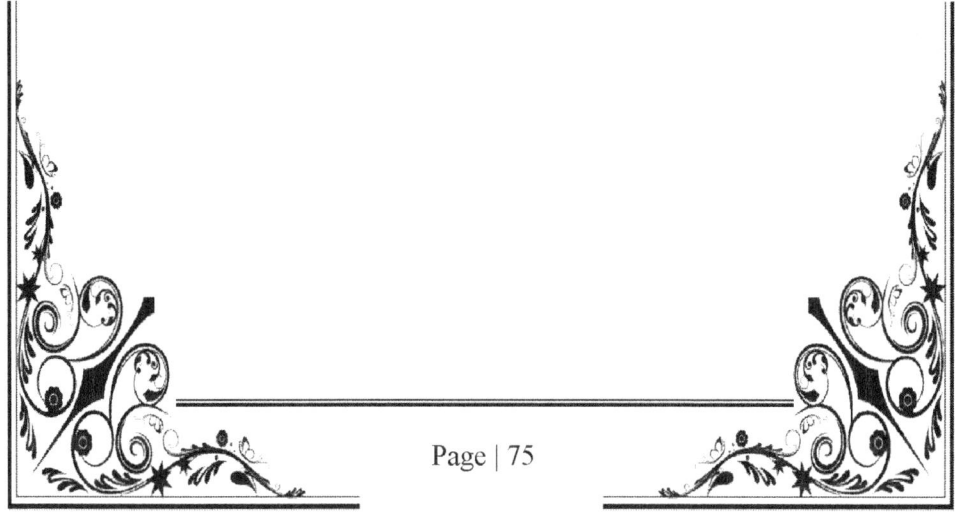

To prepare

Put the grated ingredients in a bowl, then add the eggs, some turmeric, salt and pepper and stir them well.

For frying

Place a large frying pan on the stove and pouring 5-6 tablespoons oil into that to heat. Then make small patties, flatten them in an oval shape and carefully place them in the pan to fry. Where you see that the bottom and the edges are crispy, turn them over to fry the other sides. After frying all the mixed ingredients the food is ready.

Tips for this food

1. This food is served with Po'low or bread.
2. It is better to grate potatoes and onions through tiny holes.
3. If you have a problem with egg consumption, you can reduce its amount and make the food with 1 egg.
4. As this food absorbs too much oil, use oil absorbent paper to soak up the excess oil after frying. So the food would be healthier.
5. This food can be served with side items like Dough[1] and "sliced onion, sliced tomato and parsely"[2].

Bon Appétit

---

[1] See pages 200 and 255
[2] See page 350

Mâ'kâ'ro'ni-e Sab'zi'jât[1]

INFORMATION ABOUT THE MEAL

Basic Information:

Cuisine: *Iranian*

Course: *Main Dish*

Formal meal (for guest): ~~*Yes*~~, *No*

Recommend for: ~~*Breakfast*~~, ~~*Lunch*~~, *Dinner*

Yield: *4 servings*

Level (From Iranian viewpoint): *Easy, Time-consuming*

Calories:

The pasta: *~ 182 calories per cup 140g / 5 oz*

Timing Information:

To soak: —

To prep: *~ 30 minutes*

To cook: *~ 1 hour*

Total time: *~ 1 hour 30 minutes*

[1] Vegetable Pasta

Ingredients

herbs including:

~ ½ lb / 200g coriander

~ 2 oz / 50g parsley, leek, lemon balm and spinach

and

~ 1 lb / 450g spaghetti

~ 1 medium onion

~ 2 tbsp. sour pomegranate seeds

~ 1 cup water

oil, salt, pepper and turmeric

Instructions before starting

- Dice the onion.
- Mince the herbs.
- Boil the water.
- Boil the spaghetti, then drain.

To prepare

First, stir-fry the onion with oil, salt, pepper and turmeric in a pot. Then add the herbs to the onion to fry. Now put the sour pomegranate seeds into the pot and after 5 minutes, pour the boiling water into the pot and put the lid on. Now reduce the heat to cook for 40 minutes, and the herbs soak up the water and get dry. At this moment, check the amount of salt and pepper, and if necessary, add a little to the food.

After this step, the drained spaghetti must be mixed with the ingredients from the pot. Put the lid on to cook for 20 minutes. Now the food is ready.

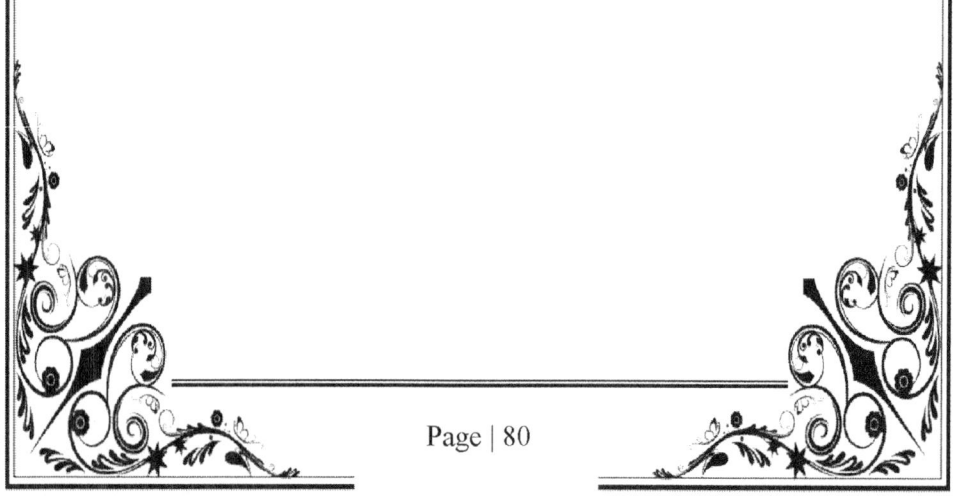

Tip for this food

1. This food can be served with onion, pickled garlic[1], olives, yogurt and Dough[2].

Bon Appétit

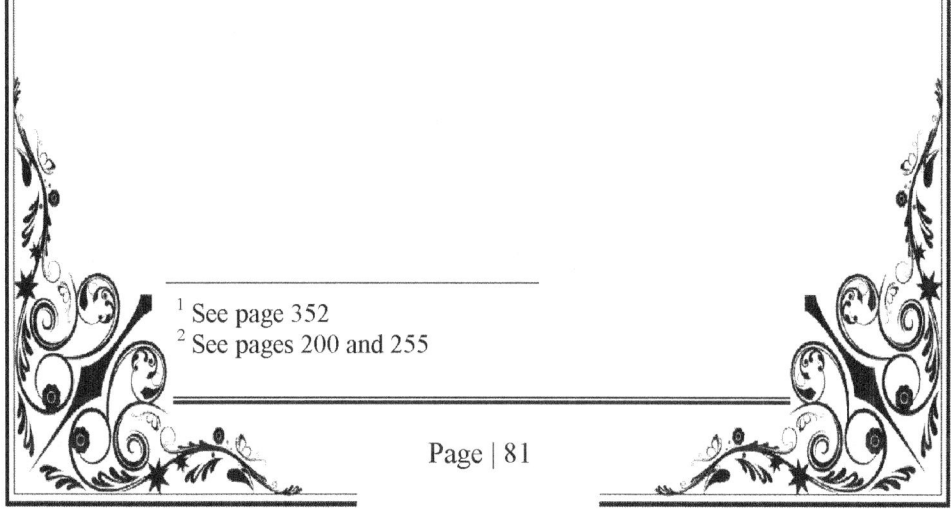

---

[1] See page 352
[2] See pages 200 and 255

Po'low[1]

INFORMATION ABOUT THE MEAL

Basic Information:

Cuisine: *Iranian*

Course: *Main Dish*

Formal meal (for guest): *Yes, ~~No~~*

Recommend for: *~~Breakfast,~~ Lunch, Dinner*

Yield: —

Level: —

Calories:

The Po'low (Âb'kesh method with Persian rice):

~ *35 calories per 1 tablespoon*

~ *210 calories per 1 spatula*

~ *120 calories per 100g / 3½oz (with oil)*

The Po'low (Ka'teh method with Persian rice):

~ *25 calories per 1 tablespoon*

~ *150 calories per 1 spatula*

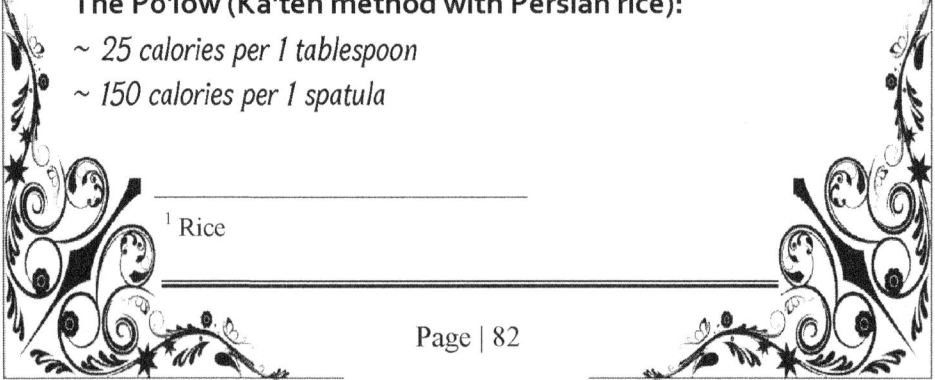

[1] Rice

To prepare

Before explaining about how to cook Po'low, you should know that most Iranaian stews are served with Po'low. In the following, there are two methods, "Âb'kesh[1]" and "Ka'teh[2]", which are common ways among Iranians. It is worth mentioning that Ka'teh is more healthier as it keeps rice starch which is full of nutrient materials. But in Âb'kesh method, Po'low loses its starch and valuable materials. Meanwhile, the advantage of Âb'kesh method is the Po'low appearance because at the end the rice grains are distinct and look nicer. But in Ka'teh method, besides Po'low higher quality, the rice grains look rather sticky.

It should be noted that Âb'kesh method is a conventional method among Iranians and Ka'teh method is common among some families and regions like the North of Iran.

---

[1] See pages 84 and 310
[2] See pages 88 and 311

VEGANS ASSISTANT

Po'low: Âb'kesh Method[1]

INFORMATION ABOUT THE MEAL

Basic Information:

Cuisine: *Iranian*

Course: *Main Dish*

Formal meal (for guest): *Yes, ~~No~~*

Recommend for: *~~Breakfast~~, Lunch, Dinner*

Yield: *5 servings*

Level (From Iranian viewpoint): *Easy, Time-consuming*

Calories:

Âb'kesh method with Persian rice:

~ *35 calories per 1 tablespoon*

~ *210 calories per 1 spatula*

~ *120 calories per 100g / 3½oz (with oil)*

Timing Information:

To soak: ~ *3 hours*   **To prep:** —

To cook: ~ *1 hour*

Total time: ~ *1 hour*

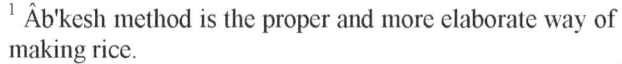

[1] Âb'kesh method is the proper and more elaborate way of making rice.

Ingredients

- ~ 4 cups rice
- ~ 1 tbsp. steeped saffron
- ~ 12 cups water
- ~ 3 tbsp. oil
- ~ 1 tbsp. salt

Instructions before starting

- Soak the rice in salted water 3 hours ahead, then drain.
- To make steeped saffron, dissolve a few threads in 1 tbsp. of warm water. See also "How to brew saffron?" on pages 255 and 365.

To prepare

Pour 12 cups of water in a pot and put it on the stove, then bring it to a boil. Now put 4 cups of the presoaked rice with 1 tablespoon of salt in the pot and stir the rice grains in order not to clump together. Then place a lid on the pot (but pay attention not to boil over) and let the rice grains get tender in the boiling water. (Note: The rice grains should be tender as each grain crushes easily between your two fingers or your teeth but its core is still tough). Up to that moment, stir them once every 4 minutes.

When the rice grains get a little tender, drain them in a colander immediately. Then place the same pot on the stove and turn down the heat. At this stage, mix 4 tablespoons of water, 3 tablespoons of oil, 2 spatulas of Po'low with steeped saffron (or turmeric) and spread the mix at the bottom of the pot. Then cover the pot with the lid for 2 minutes to make the pot hot. After that, put the rest of Po'low in the pot and mix 2 tablespoons of oil, ½ cup of water and some salt and spread the mix over Po'low and then put the lid on. It takes 40-45 minutes to steam Po'low.

Tips for this food

1. Po'low is the base of 90 percent of Iranian foods that you can serve it with stews explained in the following sections.

2. You can use a Dam'ko'ni[1] (a fitted fabric pot-lid cover) in the last step (steaming time). It causes steam drops to be absorbed by the towel and not to return to Po'low, then the rice grains are distinct and apart from each other.

3. In Âb'kesh method, if you soak the rice more in water and salt, it looks nicer. You can also use lemon juice to make Po'low whiter. To do so, add 1 tablespoon of lemon juice to boiling water.

4. You can also use a rice cooker for cooking Po'low in Âb'kesh method.

Bon Appétit

---

[1] See page 255

VEGANS ASSISTANT

Po'low: Ka'teh[1] Method

INFORMATION ABOUT THE MEAL

Basic Information:

Cuisine: *Iranian*

Course: *Main Dish*

Formal meal (for guest): ~~*Yes*~~, *No*

Recommend for: ~~*Breakfast*~~, *Lunch*, *Dinner*

Yield: *5 servings*

Level (From Iranian viewpoint): *Easy, Time-consuming*

Calories:

Ka'teh method with Persian rice:

~ *25 calories per 1 tablespoon*

~ *150 calories per 1 spatula*

Timing Information:

To soak: ~ *3 hours*

To prep: —

To cook: ~ *50 minutes*

Total time: ~ *50 minutes*

---

[1] Ka'teh is an easy Persian rice recipe

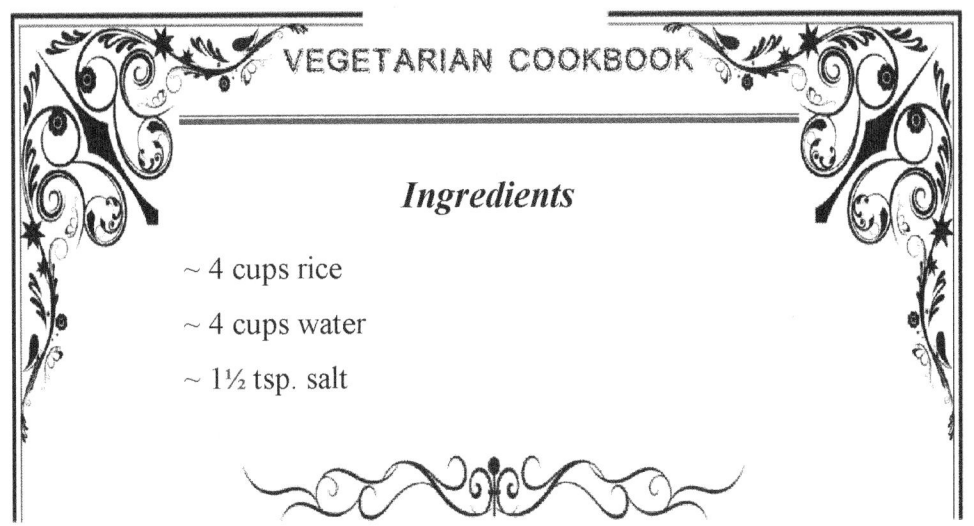

Ingredients

~ 4 cups rice

~ 4 cups water

~ 1½ tsp. salt

Instructions before starting

- Soak the rice in salted water for 3 hours in the same pot which you are going to cook the rice.

To prepare

Put the rice pot with the same water and salt over high heat and place a lid on. Then wait for the water to boil. Take care not to boil over. To prevent the boiling over, stir it twice and as there is a sign for boiling over, remove the lid. At this moment, let the water reach lower than the rice surface and then put the lid on in order to steam for 30-40 minutes.

Tips for this food

1. It seems that cooking Po'low in Ka'teh method is an easy way but, in fact, incorrect recognition and delay in cooking steps may lead to mushy or tough Po'low.

2. Being too sticky is related to excess water. Therefore, regarding people's tastes it is possible to cook rice with excess water, but Po'low looks bad.

3. Some people add a little butter or oil to the water at the beginning to make it more delicious but basically, there is not any kind of oil in Ka'teh method.

4. Experimentally, you can sprinkle some drops of water on the external sides of the pot and listen to the sound (like bizzz), the created sound and its intensity indicate whether Po'low is cooked or not (the stronger the evaporation sound is, the better Po'low is cooked and also the more likely it is going to burn).

5. You can also use a rice cooker for cooking rice in Ka'teh method.

Bon Appétit

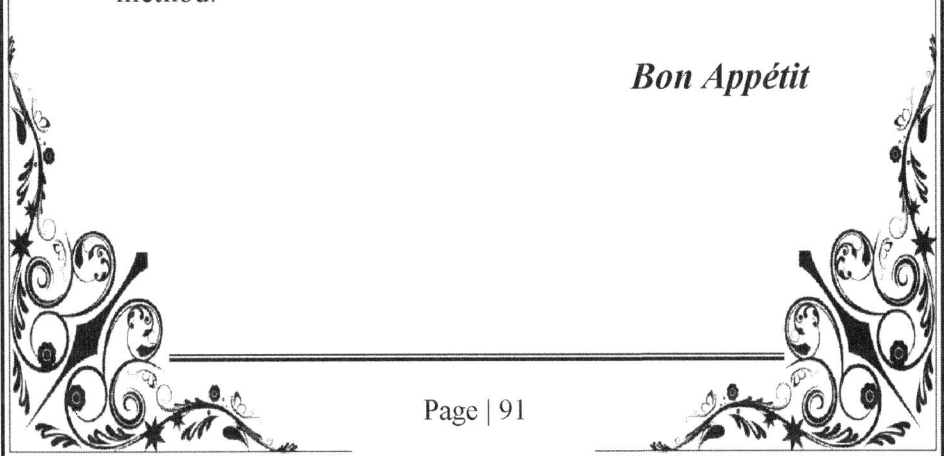

Shir Be'renj[1]

INFORMATION ABOUT THE MEAL

Basic Information:

Cuisine: *Iranian*

Course: *Main Dish*

Formal meal (for guest): ~~Yes~~, *No*

Recommend for: *Breakfast,* ~~Lunch,~~ *Dinner*

Yield: *5 servings*

Level (From Iranian viewpoint): *Easy*

Calories:

~ 111 calories per 100g / 3½oz

Timing Information:

To soak: *~ 3 hours*

To prep: —
To cook: *~ 50 minutes*

Total time: *~ 50 minutes*

[1] Rice Pudding

Ingredients

~ 4 cups milk

~ 2 cups rice

~ 2 cups water

~ ½ cup sugar

salt

Instructions before starting

- Soak the rice in salted water for 12 hours.

To prepare

Drain the rice after soaking, and put the drained rice along with 2 cups of water and a little salt in a pot and place the pot on the stove. Wait for the water to boil, then reduce the heat and place the lid in half way on the pot so that the water evaporates slightly. Then remove the pot from the stove and mash Po'low thoroughly with a masher. At this point, add milk and sugar to Po'low and mix them well. Place the pot on the stove again with the medium heat and wait for the ingredients to boil. During this time, it is necessary to stir the food regularly, so that it does not stick at the bottom. After boiling, reduce the heat to simmer for 30 minutes. The food is ready when it is thickened and looks mushy.

Tips for this food

1. Shir Be'renj is very beneficial for children and those who are sick or physically weak and need food supplements.

2. You can balance the required sugar according to your taste. For example, at the time of preparing this food for children, more sugar is usually used.

Bon Appétit

VEGANS ASSISTANT

Sho'leh Zard[1]

INFORMATION ABOUT THE MEAL

Basic Information:

Cuisine: *Iranian*

Course: *First or main course*

Formal meal (for guest): ~~Yes~~, *No*

Recommend for: ~~Breakfast~~, ~~Lunch~~, *Dinner*

Yield: *4 servings*

Level (From Iranian viewpoint): *Hard, Time-consuming*

Calories:

~ *25 calories per 1 tablespoon*

~ *250 calories per cup*

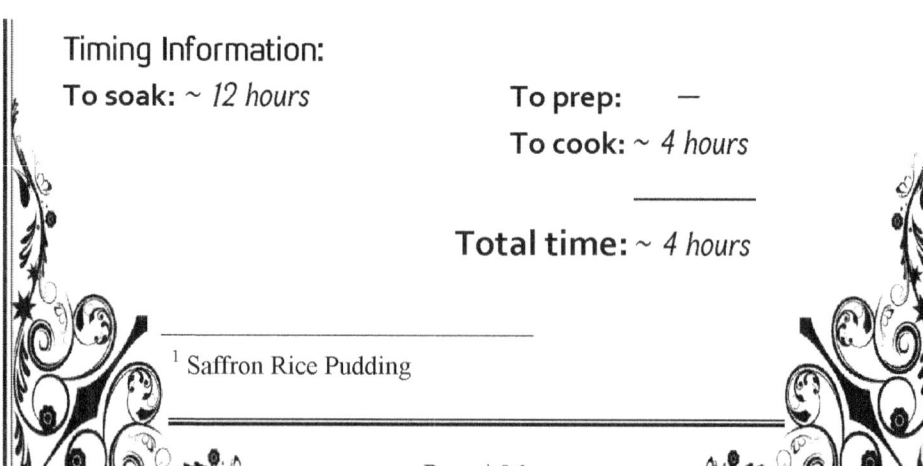

Timing Information:

To soak: *~ 12 hours*

To prep: —

To cook: *~ 4 hours*

Total time: *~ 4 hours*

---

[1] Saffron Rice Pudding

Ingredients

~ 2 cups rice

~ ½ lb / 250g sugar

~ ⅓ cup steeped saffron

~ ½ lb / 250g chopped almonds

~ 14 cups water

salt

Instructions before starting

- Soak the rice in water for 12 hours.
- To make steeped saffron, dissolve a few threads in ⅓ cup of warm water. See also "How to brew saffron?" on pages 255 and 365.

To prepare

Drain the rice after soaking and put it in a pot with 14 cups of water and some salt. Put the pot on the stove, then wait for the water to boil. After boiling the water, reduce the heat and put the lid half way on the pot. During cooking the rice, stir it several times to mash the rice and stop sticking at the bottom. Then add sugar and steeped saffron, respectively. when you feel the smell of saffron from the food, add 6 oz / 200g of chopped almonds, then stir them thoroughly. Check the amount of sweetness, then turn the heat off after 3 minutes. Put Sho'leh Zard in a special dish and garnish it with the remaining almonds.

Tips for this food

1. This dish is served without bread or rice.
2. If the cooked rice is not mashed after stirring, you can use a masher.

Bon Appétit

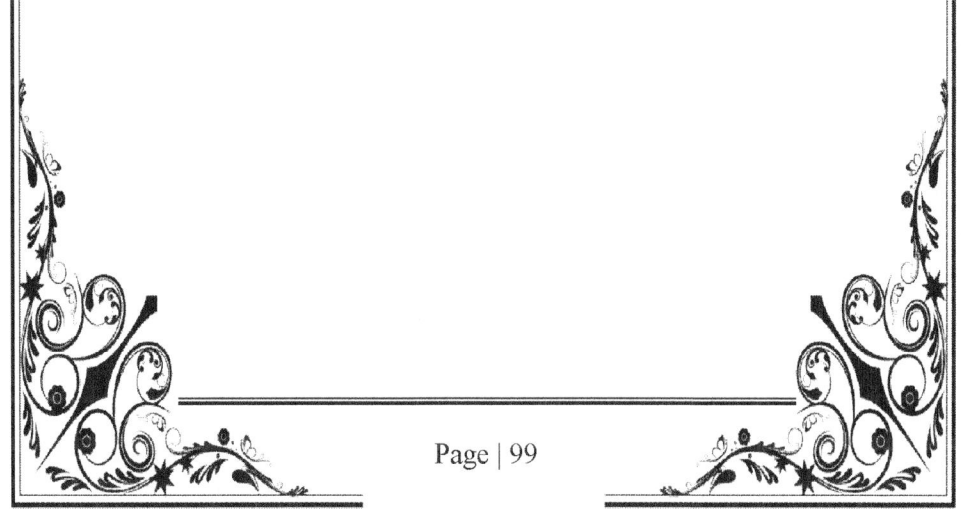

Gilanian Cuisines

Gilanian food names
Alphabetical order

15- Â'sh-e Ka'du   page 102

16- Â'sh-e Se'fid (Â'sh-e A'nâr)   page 106

17- Â'sh-e Torsh   page 110

18- Ash'ke'neh Ta'reh   page 114

19- Bâ'dem'jân Ka'bâb   page 118

20- Bâ'dem'jân Ta'reh   page 122

21- Bâ'dem'jân Va'ra'gheh Bâ Gou'jeh   page 126

22- Bâ'ghe'lâ Ghâ'togh   page 130

23- Bâ'ghe'lâ Po'low Bâ Pa'nir Be'resh'teh   page 134

24- Kho'resh't-e Ka'du   page 138

25- Khu'li Ou (Hâ'li Ou)   page 142

26- Ku'ku Bâ'dem'jân   page 146

27- Ku'ku She'vid   page 150

28- Ku'ku Sir   page 154

29- La'gad Da'mo'jey   page 158

30- Mâ'kâ'ro'ni Bâ Ja'fa'ri Vâ'ram'bu   page 162

31- Mir'zâ Ghâ'se'mi   page 166

32- Mor'ju Vâ'vij   page 170

33- Om'let Bâ Sir   page 174

34- She'vid Po'low Bâ Pa'nir Be'resh'teh   page 178

35- Sir Vâ'vij   page 182

36- Tah Bur'yân   page 186

37- Tor'sh-e Ta'reh   page 190

VEGANS ASSISTANT

Â'sh –e Ka'du[1]

INFORMATION ABOUT THE MEAL

Basic Information:
Cuisine: *Gilanian*
Course: *Main Dish*
Formal meal (for guest): ~~Yes~~, *No*
Recommend for: ~~Breakfast, Lunch,~~ *Dinner*
Yield: *5 servings*
Level (From Gilanian people viewpoint): *Medium, Time-consuming*

Calories:
The meal: *unknown*

Timing Information:
To soak: *~ 12 hours*   **To prep:** *~ 20 minutes*
                                    To cook: *~ 3 hours*

_____

Total time: *~ 3 hours 20 minutes*

_____

[1] Pumpkin Âsh

Ingredients

~ 4½ lb / 2 kg pumpkin

~ 1 cup of rice

~ 3 cups milk

~ ¾ cup sugar

~ 6 cups water

salt

Instructions before starting

- Soak rice in salted water for 12 hours.
- Peel the pumpkin and chop it into 1-2 in / 3-5 cm cubes.

To prepare

Drain the rice after soaking and put it into a pot with 5 cups of water and some salt then put the pot on the stove. Wait for the water to boil, then reduce the heat and put the lid on half way. During cooking, stir regularly to mash the rice.

At the same time, cook the pumpkin cubes in another pot with 1 cup of water and sugar until mash thoroughly. Then add the mashed pumpkin to the backed rice and stir them constantly in order not to stick at the bottom of the pot.

When the mashed ingredients are mixed together, add 3 cups of milk. From now on, it is necessary to stir regularly (once every 10 minutes) in order not to stick at the bottom and not to boil over. Before turning the heat off, taste if it is sweet enough. At least 2 cups of water disappear then the food is ready.

Tips for this food

1. This kind of Âsh is served without Po'low or bread.
2. While cooking the food, it is very likely that it sticks at the bottom. Therefore, you should stir it regularly.
3. Balance the sugar amount according to your taste.

Bon Appétit

Â'sh-e Se'fid[1] (_Â'sh-e A'nâr_)[2]

INFORMATION ABOUT THE MEAL

Basic Information:

Cuisine: *Gilanian*

Course: *Main Dish*

Formal meal (for guest): ~~Yes~~, *No*

Recommend for: ~~Breakfast~~, ~~Lunch~~, *Dinner*

Yield: *5 servings*

Level (From Gilanian people viewpoint): *Medium, Time-consuming*

Calories:

The meal: *~ 40 calories per 1 tablespoon*

Timing Information:

To soak: *~ 3 hours*   **To prep:** *~ 45 minutes*

                                   To cook: *~ 1 hour*

                          _____

                          Total time: *~ 1 hour 45 minutes*

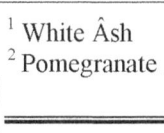

[1] White Âsh
[2] Pomegranate Âsh

Ingredients

~ 2 cups rice

~ 1 lb / ½ kg Da'lâr[1]

~ 2½ lb / 1 kg sour pomegranates

~ 3 tbsp. sour plum paste

~ 14 cups water

salt and ground angelica[2]

Instructions before starting

- Soak the rice in salted water 3 hours ahead.
- Deseed the pomegranates and then grind them.

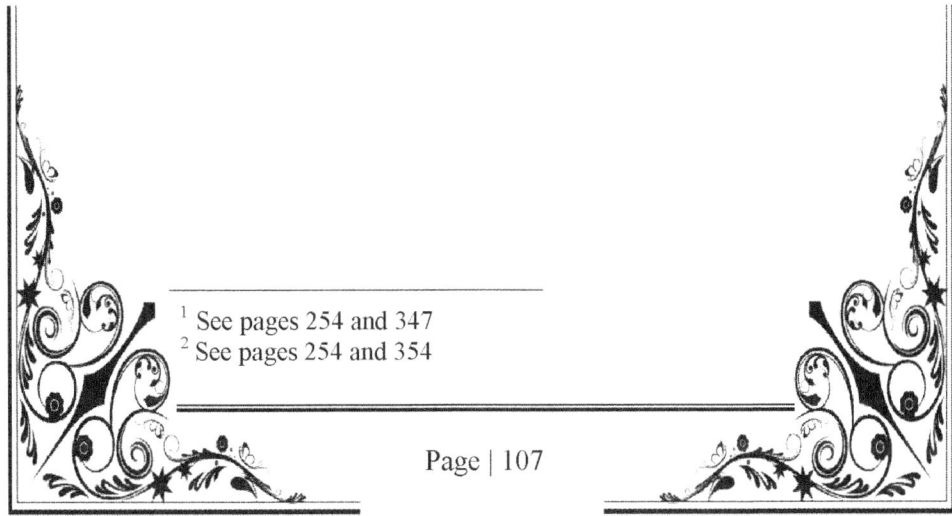

[1] See pages 254 and 347
[2] See pages 254 and 354

To prepare

Put the rice with 14 cups of water and some salt in a pot to cook on the stove. Stir regularly to mash the rice. When it is cooked, turn the heat off. Put the ingredients including Da'lâr, ground pomegranates, sour plum paste, ground angelica and cooked rice in separate dishes. Now you can serve some cooked rice in your plate and add these side dishes, then stir and eat.

Tips for this food

1. This kind of Âsh is served without bread or Po'low.

2. All ingredients in this Âsh are raw except rice. In fact, rice is an integral part of Â'sh-e Se'fid (Â'sh-e A'nâr) and other ingredients are mixed while eating the food.

3. If the rice is not mashed after regular stirring, you can use a masher.

Bon Appétit

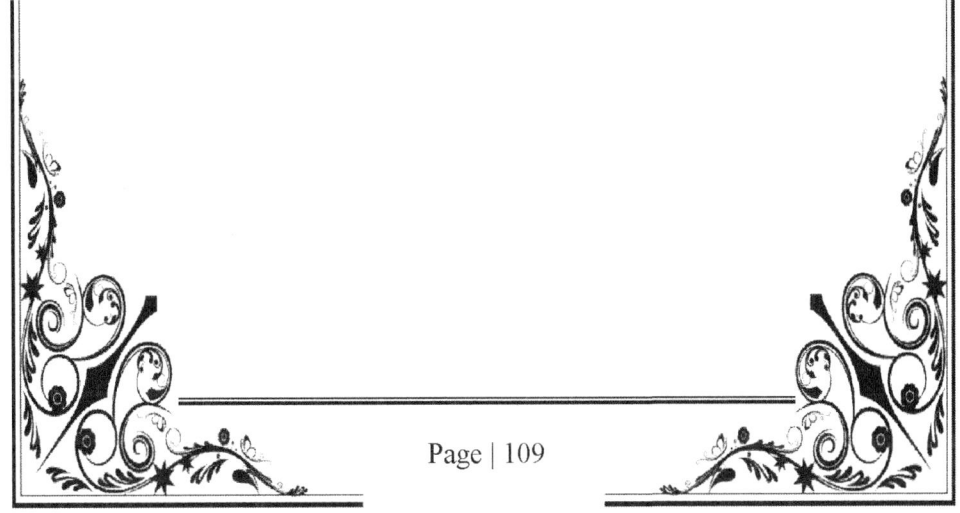

Â'sh-e Torsh[1]

INFORMATION ABOUT THE MEAL

Basic Information:

Cuisine: *Gilanian*

Course: *Main Dish*

Formal meal (for guest): ~~Yes~~, *No*

Recommend for: ~~Breakfast~~, ~~Lunch~~, *Dinner*

Yield: *5 servings*

Level (From Gilanian people viewpoint): *Medium, Time-consuming*

Calories:

The meal: *~ 429 calories per serving*

Timing Information:

To soak: *~ 3 hours*   **To prep:** *~ 40 minutes*

To cook: *~ 3 hours*

Total time: *~ 3 hours 40 minutes*

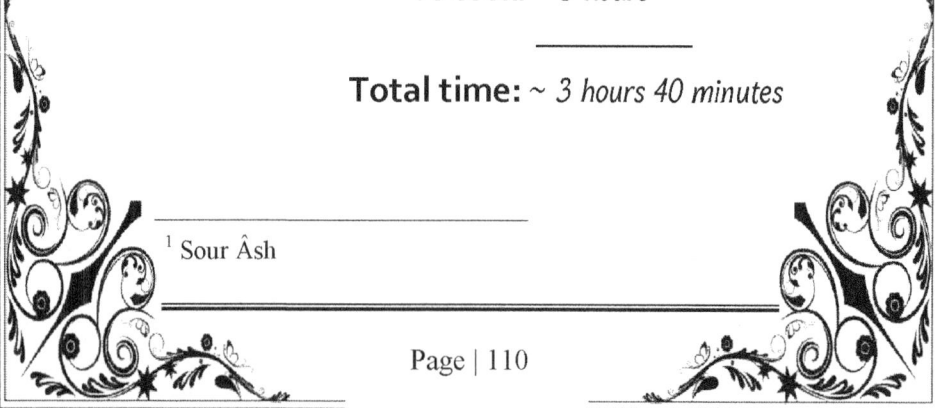

[1] Sour Âsh

Ingredients

herbs including:

first group: ~ 1 lb / ½ kg leek, parsley, beet greens, coriander, mint, ziziphora and eryngium planum

second group: ~ ½ lb / 250g coriander, mint, beet greens, creeping wood sorrel, ziziphora and eryngium planum

and

~ 1 cup rice

~ ½ lb / 200g deseeded fava beans

~ 1 lb / 450g sour greengage plums

~ 2 large onions

~ 5 garlic cloves

~ 7 cups water

oil, salt and pepper

Instructions before starting

- Soak the rice in salted water 3 hours ahead.
- Mince the first group of herbs.
- Fry the second group of herbs after mincing.
- Dice the onions and then fry them in the oil.
- Mince the garlic cloves after peeling and then fry them in some oil.

To prepare

Put the fava beens and greengage plums in separate pots to cook. Put the rice with 7 cups of water and some salt in another pot to boil on the stove. Then stir rice regularly to mash it. Then put the first group of herbs with the baked fava beens and sour greengage plums in the rice pot to mix with the rice. Stir the ingredients once every few minutes. In this stage, add some salt since herbs and fava beans absorb the food salt. Next, put the second group of herbs with fried onions and garlic into the pot and stir them again to mix all ingredients together and after 10 minutes turn the heat off.

Tips for this food

1. This Âsh is served without bread or Po'low.

2. If Po'low is not mashed after regular stirring, you can use a masher.

3. You can cook sour greengage plums with seeds or without seeds in this Âsh, but if you decide to cook them with seeds, be careful with your teeth while eating.

4. Gilanian people serve the food with vegetables[1] and white radish.

Bon Appétit

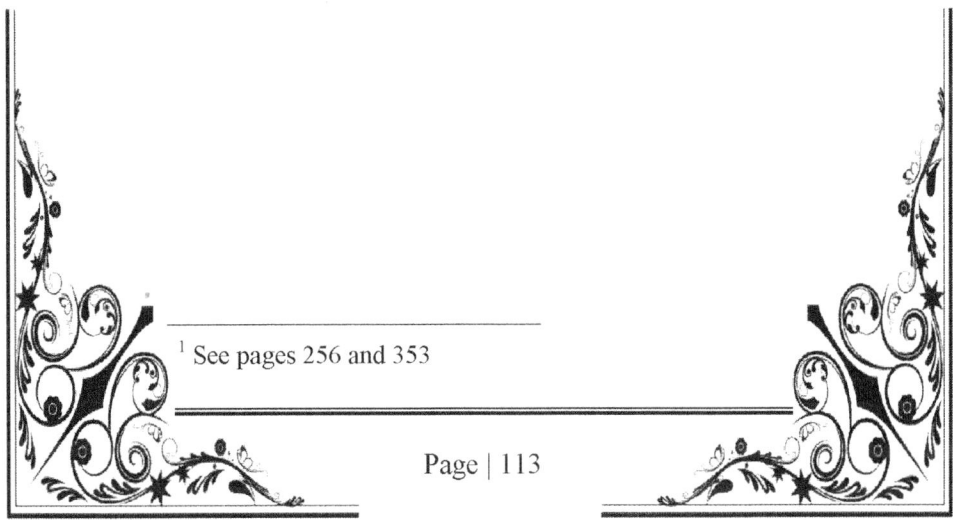

[1] See pages 256 and 353

VEGANS ASSISTANT

Ash'ke'neh Ta'reh[1]

INFORMATION ABOUT THE MEAL

Basic Information:

Cuisine: *Gilanian*

Course: *Main Dish*

Formal meal (for guest): ~~*Yes*~~, *No*

Recommend for: ~~*Breakfast*~~, *Lunch, Dinner*

Yield: *6 servings*

Level (From Gilanian people viewpoint): *Easy, Time-consuming*

Calories:

The meal: *unknown*

Timing Information:

To soak: —

To prep: *~ 15 minutes*

To cook: *~ 1 hour 15 minutes*

Total time: *~ 1 hour 30 minutes*

---

[1] Ash'ke'neh Tareh Stew

Ingredients

~ 1⅔ lb / 800g herbs including Ash'ke'neh (Chu'vâsh)[1],
   coriander, leek, parsley, scallion, ziziphora and mint

~ ½ lb / 250g fava beans

~ 2 garlic heads

~ ½ lb / 250g greengage plums

~ 4 cups water

~ 2 tbsp. oil

salt and pepper

Instructions before starting:

- Mince the herbs.
- If fresh fava beans are available, remove the first skins, but not the second ones, and if the fresh fava beans are not available (it means the fava beans are dry), the second skin should be removed, too.
- Peel the garlic cloves.

---

[1] Ash'ke'neh also called Chu'vâsh is a culinary herb in the spinach family. The local herb is used in the North of Iran cuisines. (See page 373)

To prepare

Put the minced herbs along with 5 cups of water and a little salt in a pot. Place it over the high heat to boil. Then add the fava beans and garlic. If herbs and beans are fresh, they cook in 1 hour (at this moment, the food smells of garlic). Next, put the greengage plums into the pot and add 2 tablespoons of oil to the ingredients. Cover the pot with the lid to simmer for 10 minutes, then the food is ready.

Note: As the food boils over very soon, do not put the lid on. But after a few stirring and turning the heat down or at the end, you can put the lid in half.

Tips for this food

1. This food is served with bread (for dinner) or Po'low (for lunch).
2. You can add the greengage plums with or without the seeds.
3. Gilanian people serve this food with garlic and cucumber.

Bon Appétit

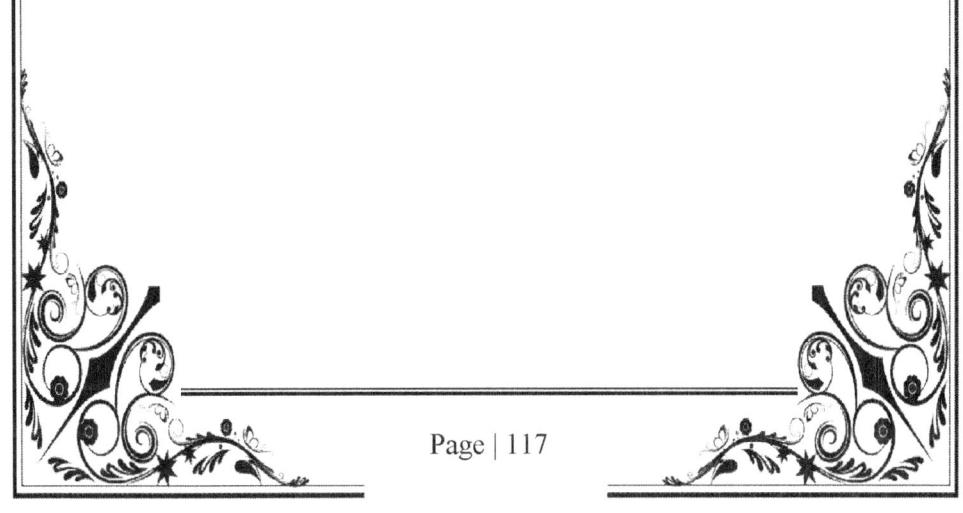

Bâdem'jân Kabâb[1]

INFORMATION ABOUT THE MEAL

Basic Information:

Cuisine: *Gilanian*

Course: *Main Dish*

Formal meal (for guest): *Yes, ~~No~~*

Recommend for: *~~Breakfast~~, Lunch, ~~Dinner~~*

Yield: *5 servings*

Level (From Gilanian people viewpoint): *Medium, Time-consuming*

Calories:

The meal: *unknown*

Timing Information:

To soak: *1 hour*   **To prep:** *~ 15 minutes*

To cook: *~ 1 hour 30 minutes*

Total time: *~ 1 hour 45 minutes*

---

[1] Eggplant Kebab

Ingredients

~ 5 oz / 150g herbs including coriander, pennyroyal, leek, parsley, eryngium planum and ziziphora

~ 2 lb / 1 kg eggplant   ~ 1 lb / 450g walnuts

~ 2 medium tomatoes   ~ 2 garlic cloves

~ 1 tbsp. pomegranate paste   ~ 1½ cups water

oil, salt and pepper

Instructions before starting

- Peel the eggplants and make a slit lengthwise with a knife in order to stuff them with the ingredients. Soak the eggplants for 1 hour in salted water. After this time, drain the eggplants in a colander and wash them with cold water to rinse the salt. Then let the eggplants dry.

- Cut the tomatoes in half.

- Grind the herbs with walnuts and garlic cloves, then mix them with the pomegranate paste. Then divide the mix equally into two dishes.

To prepare

First, stuff the eggplants with ½ of the premade mix and fry them in a frying pan. After that, fry the tomatoes and put all the fried eggplants and tomatoes into a dish.

Now mix the other half of the premade mix with 1½ cups of cold water to make a sauce and stir well. Pour the mix into the same frying pan, then add salt, pepper and a little turmeric. And bring it to a boil. After boiling, reduce the heat and put the fried eggplants and tomatoes into the sauce one by one. From now on you don't need to stir the stew because the ingredients are easily crushed. After about 1½ hours, the food is ready.

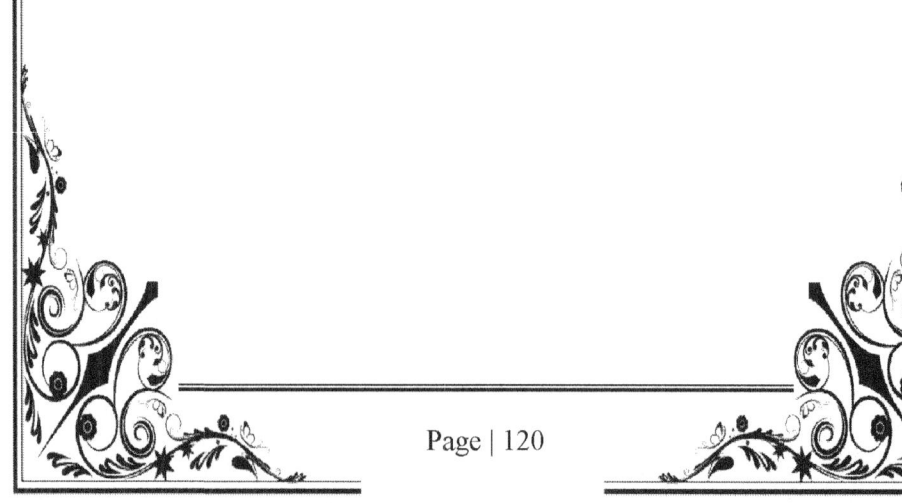

Tips for this food

1. Gilanian people serve the stew with Po'low.
2. It is better to pick thin, tiny and similar eggplants, so that you can fry them in a medium size pan.
3. Gilanian people serve the stew with onion, vegetables[1], and olives.

Bon Appétit

[1] See pages 256 and 353

VEGANS ASSISTANT

Bâ'dem'jân Ta'reh[1]

INFORMATION ABOUT THE MEAL

Basic Information:

Cuisine: *Gilanian*

Course: *Main Dish*

Formal meal (for guest): ~~Yes~~, *No*

Recommend for: ~~Breakfast~~, *Lunch, Dinner*

Yield: *4 servings*

Level (From Gilanian people viewpoint): *Easy, Time-consuming*

Calories:

The meal: *unknown*

Timing Information:

To soak: *~ 1 hour*

To prep: *~ 30 minutes*

To cook: *~ 45 minutes*

————————

Total time: *~ 1 hour 15 minutes*

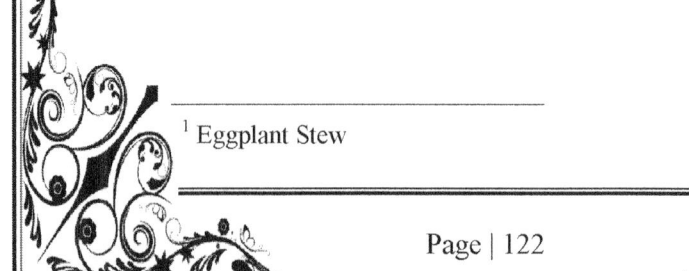

———————————

[1] Eggplant Stew

Ingredients

~ 4 medium eggplants

~ 4 medium tomatoes

~ 2 eggs

~ 1 large onion

oil, salt, pepper and turmeric

Instructions before starting

- Peel the eggplants and dice them. Soak them in salted water for 1 hour. After passing this time, drain the eggplants and wash them with cold water to rinse the salt. Then let them dry a little while.
- Dice the onion.
- Peel the tomatoes and then grate them.

To prepare

Place a frying pan on the stove with medium heat, then put the diced onion into that and fry it with some oil, salt, pepper and turmeric. Then add the prepared eggplants to the fried onion and stir-fry. After frying a little, add the grated tomatoes and stir them a few times until the tomatoes liquid disappears. Then wait for 20 minutes to cook the ingredients (stir regularly so as not to stick at the bottom). Beat the eggs in a dish and spread over the stew and put the lid on. When the eggs cooked, the food is ready.

Tips for this food

1. The stew is served with both Po'low (for lunch) and types of Iranian breads like San'gak[1] or Bar'ba'ri[2] (for dinner).

2. Gilanian people serve the food with olives, Bu'râ'ni-e Bâ'dem'jân[3], vegetables[4] and onion.

Bon Appétit

---

[1] See page 361
[2] See page 361
[3] See pages 218 and 341
[4] See pages 256 and 353

VEGANS ASSISTANT

Bâ'dem'jân Va'ra'gheh Bâ Gou'jeh[1]

INFORMATION ABOUT THE MEAL

Basic Information:

Cuisine: *Gilanian*

Course: *Main Dish*

Formal meal (for guest): ~~Yes~~, *No*

Recommend for: ~~Breakfast~~, *Lunch*, ~~Dinner~~

Yield: *4 servings*

Level (From Gilanian people viewpoint): *Easy, Time-consuming*

Calories:

The meal: *unknown*

Timing Information:

To soak: *~ 1 hour*

To prep: *~ 15 minutes*

To cook: *~ 1 hour*

Total time: *~ 1 hour 15 minutes*

---

[1] Eggplant Slices with Tomato

Ingredients

~ 4 medium eggplants

~ 4 medium tomatoes

~ 2 eggs

oil, salt, pepper and turmeric

Instructions before starting

- Peel the eggplants and slice them (~ ½ in / 1 cm thick), then soak them in salted water for 1 hour.
- Slice the tomatoes (~ ½ in / 1 cm thick).

To prepare

Drain the eggplants and wash them with cold water to rinse the salt. Let the soaked eggplants dry. Then fry the eggplants over low heat. When the eggplants are fried, pour 2 beaten eggs over them. Now put the lid on to bake the eggs, then turn off the heat after 5 minutes and remove them from the frying pan and keep them in a dish.

Heat some oil again in the frying pan then fry the sliced tomatoes (put the lid on while frying tomatoes). Turn the tomatoes over after 15 minutes to fry the other side. When the tomatoes liquid a little disappeared, turn the heat off. Dish up the fried eggplants and tomatoes in a serving dish beside each other. The food is ready.

Tips for this food

1. The food is served with Po'low.

2. Gilanian people serve the food with garlic, Kâl Ka'bâb[1], Zey'tun Par'var'deh[2] or types of side dishes made of yogurt such as Bu'râ'ni-e Bâ'dem'jân[3], Mâs't-o Khi'yâr[4], shallot yogurt and Dough[5].

Bon Appétit

---

[1] See pages 222, 342 and 343
[2] See pages 226 and 344
[3] See pages 218 and 341
[4] See pages 204 and 338
[5] See pages 200 and 255

Bâ'ghe'lâ Ghâ'togh[1]

INFORMATION ABOUT THE MEAL

Basic Information:

Cuisine: *Gilanian*

Course: *Main Dish*

Formal meal (for guest): *Yes,* ~~No~~

Recommend for: ~~Breakfast,~~ *Lunch,* ~~Dinner~~

Yield: *4 servings*

Level (From Gilanian people viewpoint): *Easy, Time-consuming*

Calories:

The stew:

~ *45 calories per 1 tablespoon*

~ *545 calories per serving*

Timing Information:

To soak: —

To prep: ~ *1 hour*

To cook: ~ *1 hour*

———

Total time: ~ *2 hours*

———

[1] Fava Beans Stew

Ingredients

~ 1 lb / ½ kg lima beans

~ 4 oz / 100g fresh dill or ~ 2 tbsp. dried dill

~ 2 eggs

~ 4 garlic cloves

~ 4 cups water

oil, salt, pepper and turmeric

Instructions before starting

- If the beans are dried, soak them in salted water overnight, then you can easily deseed them. But if the beans are fresh, remove their pods. Whether dried or fresh, split the seeds.
- Peel the garlic cloves and mince them.
- Boil the water.

To prepare

Put a frying pan with the beans inside over low heat. Now add dill, garlic, 5 tablespoons of oil, turmeric and salt and stir-fry all ingredients. Then pour the boiled water over them until the water covers the ingredients. Stir once and put the lid on to simmer for 40 minutes. Check the stew a few times but do not stir it a lot because the beans are easily crushed. 10 minutes before turning the heat off, crack 2 eggs over the stew. Do not put the lid on to make a nice- colored stew. The food is ready as soon as the eggs are baked.

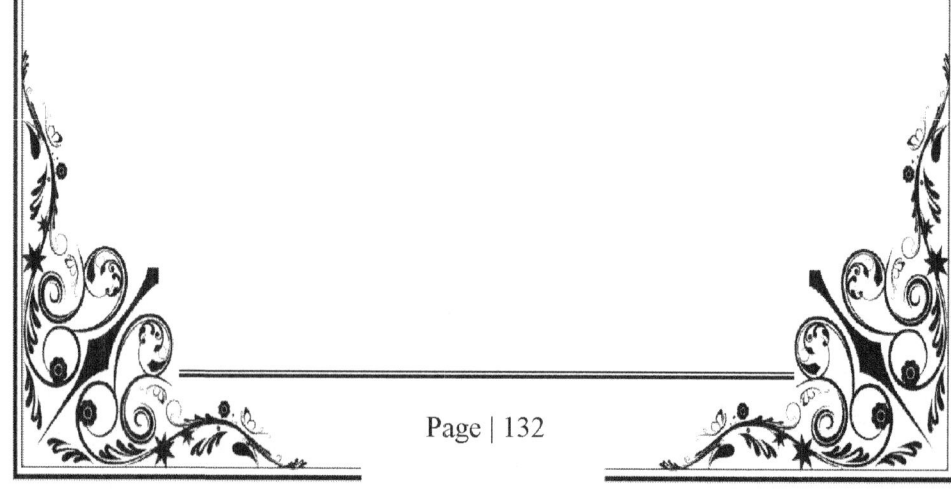

Tips for this food

1. The stew is usually served with Po'low (Ka'teh method[1]) in the North of Iran.

2. It is better to prepare the stew with fresh dill but if the fresh dill is not available, you can use dried dill.

3. After cracking the eggs over the stew, do not stir it.

4. It is better to use quail eggs because the stew looks nicer and the food is more nutritious.

5. Gilanian people serve the stew with pickled garlic[2].

Bon Appétit

---

[1] See pages 88 and 311
[2] See page 352

VEGANS ASSISTANT

Bâ'ghe'lâ Po'low Bâ Pa'nir Be'resh'teh[1]

INFORMATION ABOUT THE MEAL

Basic Information:

Cuisine: *Gilanian*

Course: *Main Dish*

Formal meal (for guest): ~~*Yes*~~, *No*

Recommend for: ~~*Breakfast*~~, *Lunch*, ~~*Dinner*~~

Yield: *5 servings*

Level (From Gilanian people viewpoint): *Easy, Time-consuming*

Calories:

The meal (combination): *~ 600 calories per serving*

Timing Information:

To soak: *~ 3 hours* **To prep:** *~ 30 minutes*

To cook: *~ 1 hour 30 minutes*

Total time: *~ 2 hours*

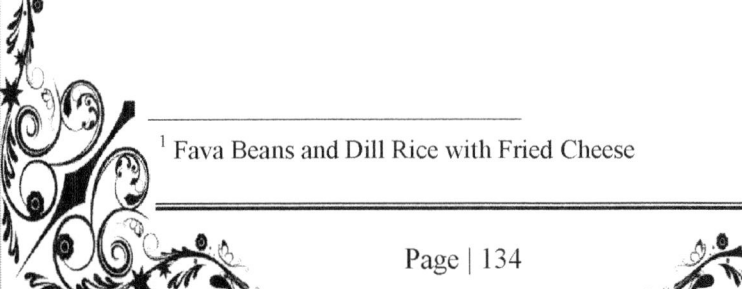

---

[1] Fava Beans and Dill Rice with Fried Cheese

Ingredients

- ~ 4 cups rice
- ~ 11 oz / 300g fava beans
- ~ ½ lb / 200g dried dill or ~ 1 lb / 450g fresh dill
- ~ ½ lb / 250g breakfast cheese
- ~ 6 eggs
- ~ 2 tbsp. steeped saffron
- ~ 14 cups water

oil, salt, pepper and turmeric

Instructions before starting

- Soak the rice in salted water 3 hours ahead.
- Mince the fresh dill thoroughly and keep in a bowl.
- Mash the cheese in a bowl.
- Remove the fava beans skins (if the fava beans are fresh, the skins are removed easily but if they are dry, you need to soak them overnight to remove the skins).

To prepare

Put the rice over the heat until it reaches to drain time (Abkesh method[1]). Stir-fry the peeled fava beans in another pot, then let them simmer with 2 cups of water and some salt for 30 minutes. When they get tender, turn off the heat and drain them in a colander and put them aside.

Choose a pot to cook the rice and pour some oil in the pot and cover the bottom of the pot with thin bread (bread is used as "Tah Dig[2]" to make crusty bread), then mix the boiled rice from the colander with fava beans and ½ dill and put them in the pot to steam. After 45 minutes the Po'low is ready.

Until cooking the rice, fry the remaining dill with some oil and ½ teaspoon of turmeric in a pan with low heat. Then add the mashed cheese and stir-fry. Now add the eggs to the ingredients and stir for 2 minutes until get tough as much as you like, then turn off the heat. Toasted cheese is ready.

[1] See pages 84 and 310
[2] See pages 256 and 371

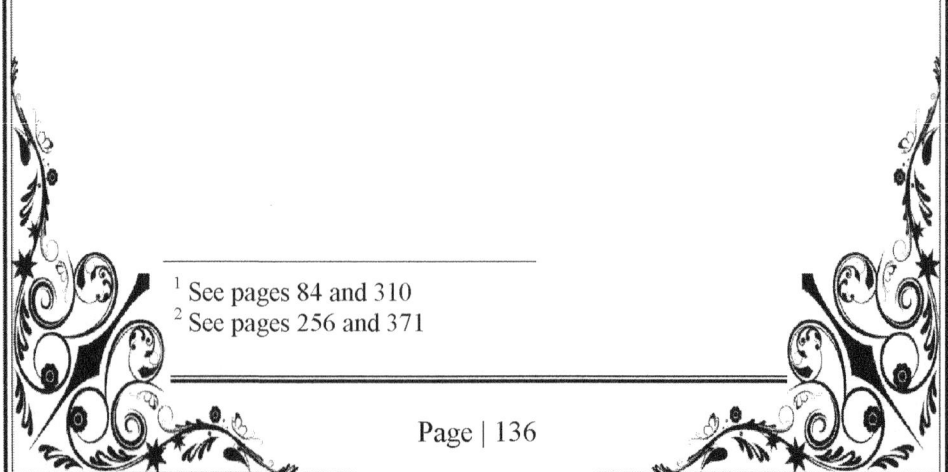

Tips for this food

1. Iranians serve this food with vegetables[1], pickles[2], olives and Sâ'lâ'd-e Fasl[3].

Bon Appétit

---

[1] See pages 256 and 353
[2] See pages 351 and 352
[3] See pages 212 and 340

VEGANS ASSISTANT

Kho'resh't-e Ka'du[1]

INFORMATION ABOUT THE MEAL

Basic Information:

Cuisine: *Gilanian*

Course: *Main Dish*

Formal meal (for guest): ~~*Yes*~~, *No*

Recommend for: ~~*Breakfast*~~, *Lunch, Dinner*

Yield: *5 servings*

Level (From Gilanian people viewpoint): *Medium, Time-consuming*

Calories:

The stew: *~ 45 calories per 1 tablespoon*

Timing Information:

To soak: —

To prep: *~ 45 minutes*

To cook: *~ 1 hour 45 minutes*

Total time: *~ 2 hours 30 minutes*

---

[1] Pumpkin Stew

Ingredients

herbs including:

~ ½ lb / 200g eryngium planum, ziziphora

~ 2 oz / 50g coriander and

~ 2 oz / 50g parsley and leek

and

~ 2½ lb / 1 kg pumpkin

~ 5 oz / 150g lima beans

~ 1 lb / 450g walnuts

~ 5 cups water

~ 4 garlic cloves

~ 1 small onion

salt and pepper

Instructions before starting

- Peel the pumpkin and chop it into 1-2 in / 3-5 cm cubes.
- If you use dried beans, soak them in water overnight.
- Grind the walnuts to crush thoroughly.
- Dice the onion.
- Grind the herbs and garlic.

To prepare

Drain the soaked beans and put them in a pot along with 5 cups of water, the diced onion, a little salt and pepper. Place the pot on the stove to boil, then reduce the heat to simmer the stew for 30 minutes and bake it partly. Now add the pumpkin cubes to the cooking beans. After about 20 minutes, add the ground walnuts and herbs to the ingredients in the pot and stir them a few times. Let it simmer for 30 minutes. During this time, it is necessary to stir the food regularly so that it does not stick at the bottom, and the pumpkin can be mashed thoroughly. The stew is ready.

Tips for this food

1. This food is served with bread (for dinner) or Po'low (for lunch).
2. Some people add butter at the time of baking.
3. While serving, you can also sprinkle the food with cinnamon.

Bon Appétit

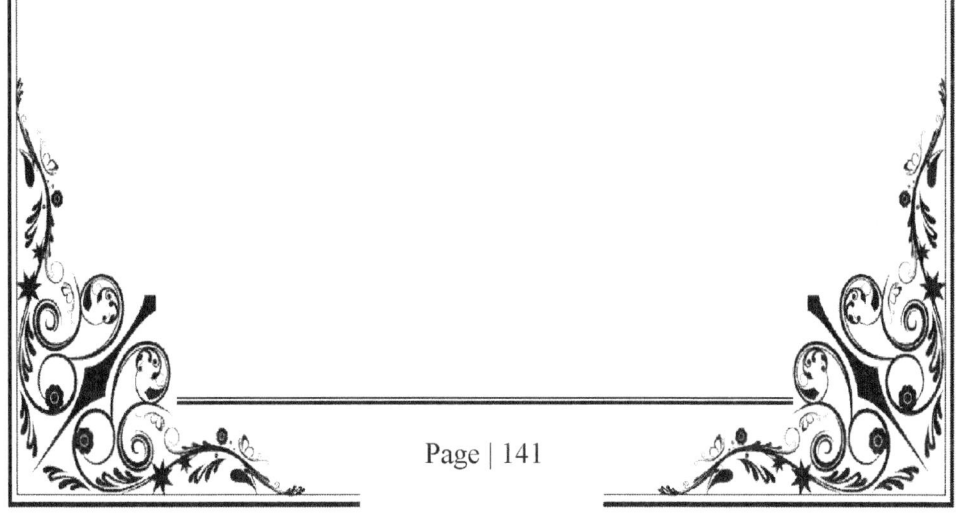

Khu'li Ou (Hâ'li Ou)[1]

INFORMATION ABOUT THE MEAL

Basic Information:

Cuisine: *Gilanian*

Course: *Main Dish*

Formal meal (for guest): ~~*Yes*~~*, No*

Recommend for: ~~*Breakfast*~~*, Lunch,* ~~*Dinner*~~

Yield: *4 servings*

Level (From Gilanian people viewpoint): *Easy*

Calories:

The meal: *unknown*

Timing Information:

To soak: —   **To prep:** *~ 20 minutes*

                              To cook: *~ 40 minutes*

_____

Total time: *~ 1 hour*

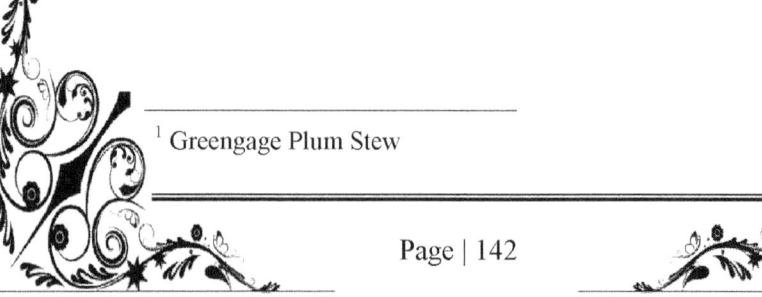

_____

[1] Greengage Plum Stew

Ingredients

~ 11 oz / 300g sour greengage plums

~ 11 oz / 300g sweet greengage plums

~ 4 tbsp. Da'lâr[1]

~ 3 eggs

~ 2 cup water

oil, salt and pepper

Instructions before starting

- Deseed the sour greengage plums.

---

[1] See pages 254 and 347

To prepare

Put the deseeded sour greengage plums with 2 cup of water in a pot to cook (watch out not to boil over). After cooking sour greengage plums (about 20 minutes), add 4 tablespoons of Da'lâr (It is more likely that the stew boils over after adding Da'lâr). Then add oil, too. As Da'lâr herbs are salted, taste the stew at this moment to check the salt amount). At the end, add the eggs to the pot ingredients and turn the heat off after 2 minutes. The food is ready.

Tips for this food

1. The food is served with Po'low.

2. You can also make this food without eggs.

3. This food is very thin and it is sour due to the sour greengage plums. Therefore, it is not recommended to people who have stomachaches.

4. Gilanian people usually serve this stew with Ku'ku She'vid[1] and Po'low[2] beside other side items like raw fava beans[3], garlic and cucumber.

Bon Appétit

---

[1] See pages 150 and 325
[2] See page 82
[3] See page 350

VEGANS ASSISTANT

Ku'ku Bâ'dem'jân[1]

INFORMATION ABOUT THE MEAL

Basic Information:

Cuisine: *Gilanian*

Course: *Main Dish*

Formal meal (for guest): ~~Yes~~, *No*

Recommend for: ~~Breakfast~~, ~~Lunch~~, *Dinner*

Yield: *5 servings*

Level (From Gilanian people viewpoint): *Easy, Time-consuming*

Calories:

The meal: *unknown*

Timing Information:

To soak: —

To prep: ~ *30 minutes*

To cook: ~ *30 minutes*

Total time: ~ *1 hour*

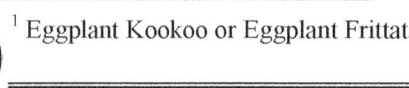

[1] Eggplant Kookoo or Eggplant Frittata

Ingredients

~ 4 medium eggplants

~ 1 medium onion

~ 4 eggs

~ 1 tbsp. rice flour

oil, salt and pepper

Instructions before starting

- Peel the eggplants and onion, then grate them.

To prepare

First, mix 4 eggs with grated eggplants and onion in a bowl, then add 1 tablespoon of flour to them and stir well. Now spread the mix into a hot frying pan with some oil and lower the heat. Put the lid on and wait until one side fries. Then flip it over to fry the other side. At the end, divide the food into the desired pieces.

Tips for this food

1. This food is served with bread (for dinner) or Po'low (for lunch).

2. As this food absorbs too much oil, use oil absorbent paper to soak up the excess oil after frying. So the food would be healthier.

3. This food can be served with sides such as Dough[1], "sliced onion, sliced tomato and parsely"[2] and pickles[3].

Bon Appétit

---

[1] See pages 200 and 255
[2] See page 350
[3] See pages 351 and 352

VEGANS ASSISTANT

Ku'ku She'vid[1]

INFORMATION ABOUT THE MEAL

Basic Information:

Cuisine: *Gilanian*

Course: *Main Dish*

Formal meal (for guest): ~~Yes~~, *No*

Recommend for: ~~Breakfast~~, ~~Lunch~~, *Dinner*

Yield: *4 servings*

Level (From Gilanian people viewpoint): *Easy, Time-consuming*

Calories:

The meal: ~ *306 calories per 100g / 3½oz*

Timing Information:

To soak: —   **To prep:** ~ *15 minutes*

                To cook: ~ *45 minutes*

────────────

Total time: ~ *1 hour*

────────────────────────

[1] Dill Kookoo

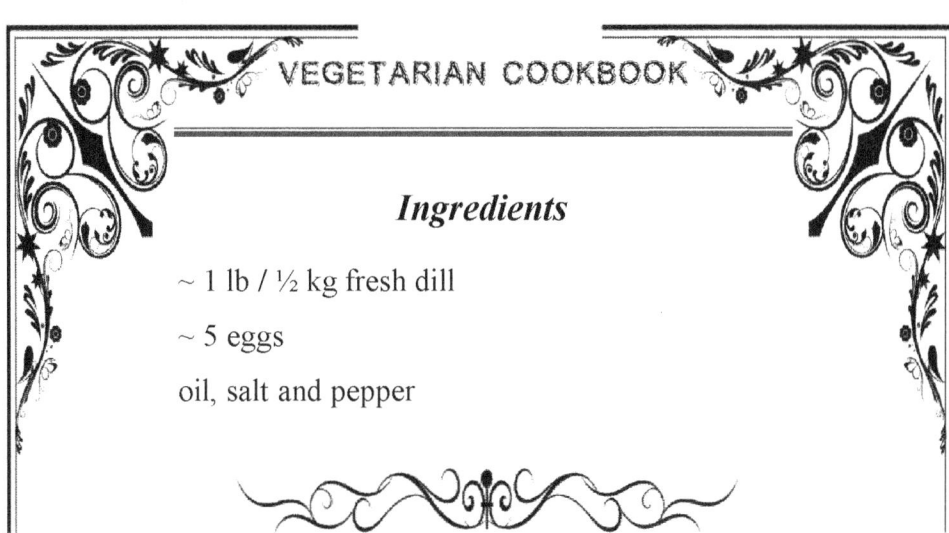

Ingredients

~ 1 lb / ½ kg fresh dill

~ 5 eggs

oil, salt and pepper

Instructions before starting

- Mince the dill.

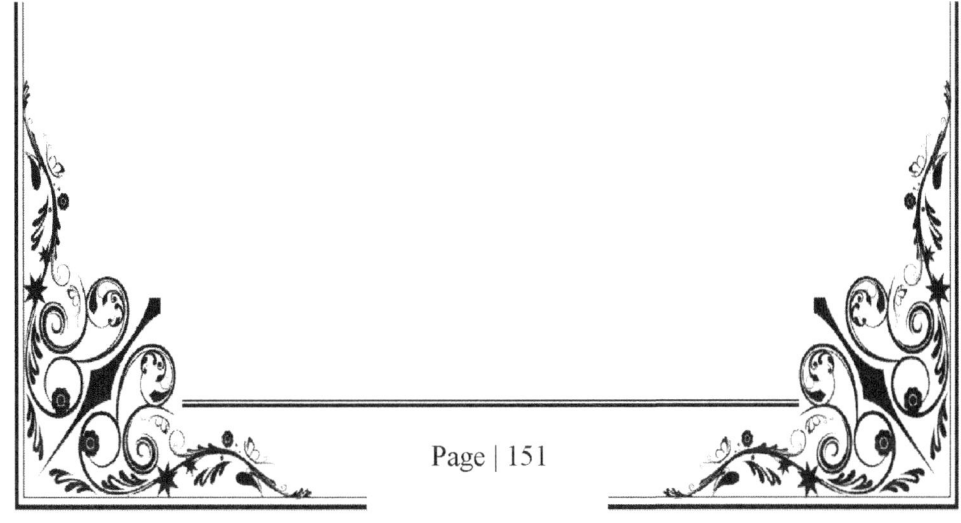

To prepare

Put the minced dill in a dish and then add the eggs, salt and pepper and stir well. If you feel your mixed ingredients are too watery, you can lightly add rice flour.

For frying

Place a large frying pan on the stove and pouring 5-6 tablespoons oil into that to heat. Then make small patties, flatten them in an oval or a round shape and carefully place them in the pan to fry. Where you see that the bottom and the edges are crispy, turn them over to fry the other sides. After frying all the mixed ingredients the food is ready.

Tips for this food

1. This food is served with bread.

2. As the food absorbs too much oil, use oil absorbent paper to soak up the excess oil after frying. So the food would be healthier.

3. This food can be served with side items like Dough[1] or "sliced onion, sliced tomato and parsley"[2].

Bon Appétit

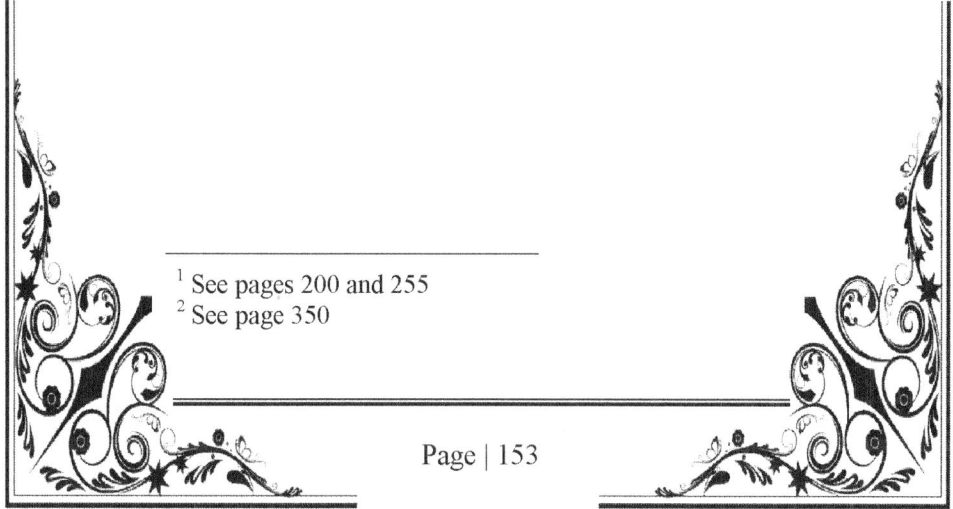

[1] See pages 200 and 255
[2] See page 350

Ku'ku Sir[1]

INFORMATION ABOUT THE MEAL

Basic Information:

Cuisine: *Gilanian*

Course: *Main Dish*

Formal meal (for guest): ~~Yes~~, *No*

Recommend for: ~~Breakfast~~, *Lunch, Dinner*

Yield: *4 servings*

Level (From Gilanian people viewpoint): *Easy, Time-consuming*

Calories:

The meal: *~ 306 calories per 100g / 3½oz*

Timing Information:

To soak: —

To prep: *~ 15 minutes*

To cook: *~ 45 minutes*

————————

Total time: *~ 1 hour*

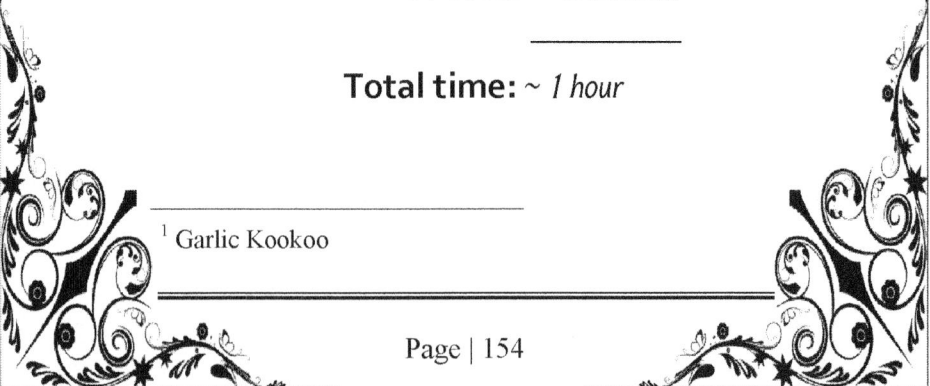

[1] Garlic Kookoo

Ingredients

~ 1 lb / 450g garlic leaves

~ 6 eggs

~ 1 tbsp. rice flour

oil, salt and pepper

Instructions before starting

- Mince the garlic leaves and grind them along with some salt by mortar and pestle until they become a little withered. Add pepper, rice flour and eggs, then mix them well.

To prepare

For frying

Place a large frying pan on the stove and pouring 5-6 tablespoons oil into that to heat. Then make small patties, flatten them in an oval or a round shape and carefully place them in the pan to fry. Where you see that the bottom and the edges are crispy, turn them over to fry the other sides. After frying all the mixed ingredients the food is ready.

Tips for this food

1. This food is served with bread (for dinner) or Po'low (for lunch).

2. As this food absorbs too much oil, use oil absorbent paper to soak up the excess oil after frying. So the food would be healthier.

3. This food can be served with sides such as "sliced onion, sliced tomato and parsely"[1], Dough[2] or pickles[3].

Bon Appétit

---

[1] See page 350
[2] See pages 200 and 255
[3] See pages 351 and 352

INFORMATION ABOUT THE MEAL

Basic Information:

Cuisine: *Gilanian*

Course: *Main Dish*

Formal meal (for guest): ~~Yes~~, *No*

Recommend for: ~~Breakfast~~, *Lunch*, ~~Dinner~~

Yield: *4 servings*

Level (From Gilanian people viewpoint): *Easy, Time-consuming*

Calories:

The meal: *unknown*

Timing Information:

To soak: *~ 1 hour*

To prep: *~ 30 minutes*

To cook: *~ 1 hour 30 minutes*

───────────────

Total time: *~ 2 hours*

───────────────

[1] Black-Eyed Bean Stew

Ingredients

~ ½ lb / 200g black-eyed beans (or lima beans)

~ 2 medium eggplants

~ 4 large tomatoes

~ 2 medium onions

~ 4 cups water

oil, salt, pepper and turmeric

Instructions before starting

- Peel the eggplants and dice them. Then soak them in salted water for 1 hour. After this time, drain and wash them with cold water to rinse the salt. Then let the diced eggplants dry.
- Dice the tomatoes.
- Dice the onions.

To prepare

First, put the beans in a pot along with water, a little salt, pepper and turmeric, and place the pot on the stove over medium heat to boil. Then add the diced onions. After 5 minutes, add the diced tomatoes and stir once, then put the lid on. Let the food boil over the medium heat for 30 minutes. After that, lower the heat and add the diced eggplants along with oil, a little salt and pepper to the ingredients inside the pot and mix them well. Stir the food frequently so as not to stick at the bottom. After 40 minutes, make sure that the beans are completely cooked. The food is ready.

Tips for this food

1. This food is served with Po'low.
2. Gilanian people serve this food with garlic and vegetables[1].

Bon Appétit

---

[1] See pages 256 and 353

VEGANS ASSISTANT

Mâ'kâ'ro'ni Bâ Ja'fa'ri Vâ'ram'bu[1]

INFORMATION ABOUT THE MEAL

Basic Information:
Cuisine: *Gilanian*
Course: *Main Dish*
Formal meal (for guest): ~~*Yes*~~, *No*
Recommend for: ~~*Breakfast*~~, ~~*Lunch*~~, *Dinner*
Yield: *4 servings*
Level (From Gilanian people viewpoint): *Easy, Time-consuming*

Calories:
The pasta: *~ 182 calories per cup 140g / 5 oz*

Timing Information:
To soak: —   **To prep:** *~ 30 minutes*
                        To cook: *~ 45 minutes*

Total time: *~ 1 hour 15 minutes*

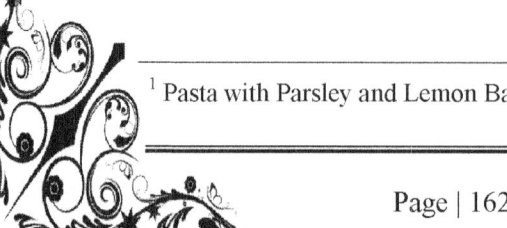

---
[1] Pasta with Parsley and Lemon Balm

Ingredients

~ 1 lb / 450g spaghetti

~ ½ lb / 200g parsley

~ 4 oz / 100g lemon balm[1]

~ 1 large onion

~ 4 medium tomatoes

oil, salt and pepper

Instructions before starting

- Mince the herbs.
- Dice the tomatoes.
- Dice the onion.

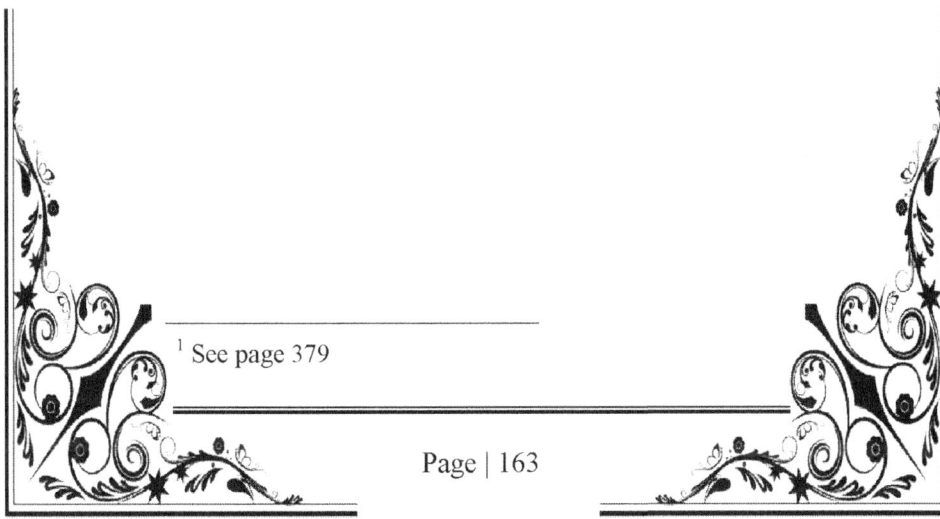

---

[1] See page 379

To prepare

Fry the diced onion along with salt and turmeric in oil. Then add the minced herbs to fry. Now, add the tomatoes with some salt, pepper and turmeric to the pan and mix them well. At this stage, put the lid on to cook the tomatoes for a while.

Drain the spaghetti while the tomatoes are cooking. After that, place a pot over low heat. Then, sprinkle oil and a little turmeric into the pot, and spread a thin layer of bread at the bottom. Mix the spaghetti and the pan ingredients thoroughly and put the mix in the pot. At the end, put the lid on and let the spaghetti steam for 10 minutes. After this time, the food is ready.

Tips for this food

1. Do not change the mentioned amounts of parsley and lemon balm because both herbs give perfect flavor to the food and decreasing or increasing each of them has a significant effect on taste and quality of food.

2. You can serve this food with onion, pickled garlic[1], olives, yogurt and Dough[2].

Bon Appétit

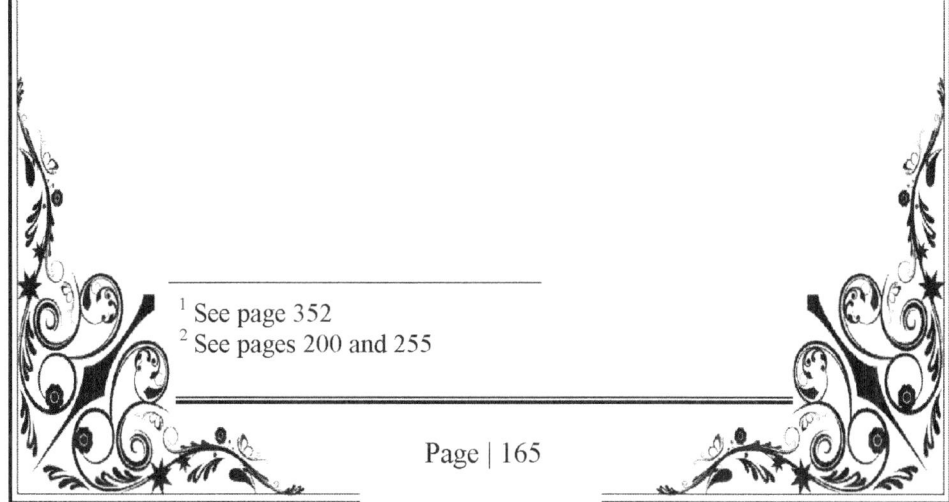

---

[1] See page 352
[2] See pages 200 and 255

Mir'zâ Ghâ'se'mi[1]

INFORMATION ABOUT THE MEAL

Basic Information:

Cuisine: *Gilanian*

Course: *Main Dish*

Formal meal (for guest): *Yes,* ~~No~~

Recommend for: ~~Breakfast~~, *Lunch, Dinner*

Yield: *4 servings*

Level (From Gilanian people viewpoint): *Medium, Time-consuming*

Calories:

The meal:

~ 50 calories per 1 tablespoon

~ 157 calories per 100g / 3½oz

Timing Information:

To soak: —   **To prep:** *~ 1 hour 15 minutes*

                        To cook: *~ 1 hour*

_____

Total time: *~ 2 hours 15 minutes*

_____

[1] Garlicky Eggplant with Tomato Spread

Ingredients

~ 5 medium eggplants

~ 1 lb / 450g tomatoes

~ 1 medium garlic head

~ 4 eggs

oil, salt, pepper and turmeric

Instructions before starting

- Grill the eggplants on the fire. Then remove their skins and mash them, and keep them in a bowl.
- Peel the tomatoes and chop them.
- Peel the garlic cloves and grate them.

To prepare

First, fry the grated garlic with some salt, pepper and turmeric in a frying pan. When the garlic fried golden, add the chopped tomatoes to fry for a while. Add the mashed eggplants when the tomatoes liquid dried out. After this stage, reduce the heat and stir the ingredients every few minutes because this food sticks at the bottom. Add the eggs after 20 minutes and stir a bit to mix them all. At this moment, be careful that the food doesn't burn. Turn off the heat 10 minutes after adding the eggs.

Tips for this food

1. This food is served with Po'low or Iranian breads like San'gak[1] or Bar'ba'ri[2].

2. The food usually sticks at the bottom and burns fast so you need to watch out.

3. Gilanian people serve the food with pickled garlic[3] and vegetables[4].

Bon Appétit

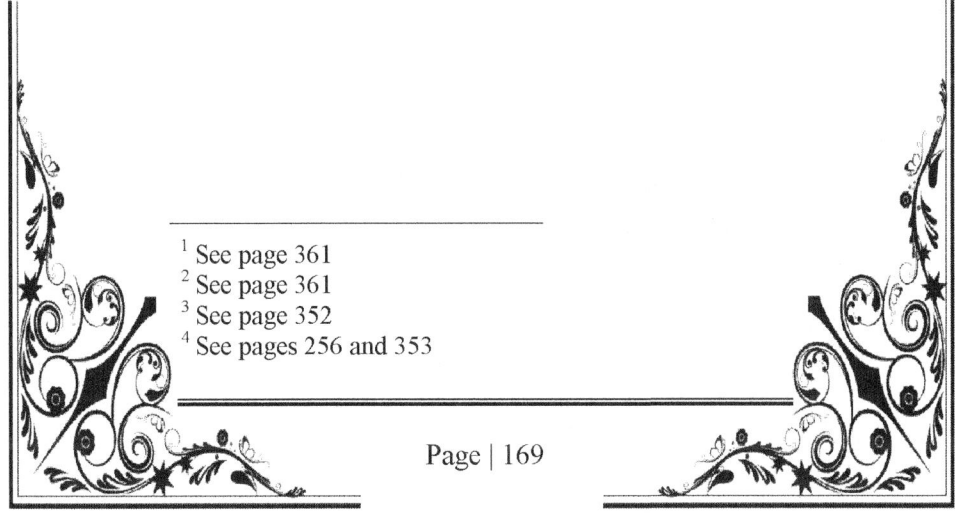

---

[1] See page 361
[2] See page 361
[3] See page 352
[4] See pages 256 and 353

VEGANS ASSISTANT

Mor'ju Vâ'vij[1]

INFORMATION ABOUT THE MEAL

Basic Information:

Cuisine: *Gilanian*

Course: *Main Dish*

Formal meal (for guest): ~~*Yes*~~, *No*

Recommend for: ~~*Breakfast*~~, *Lunch, Dinner*

Yield: *4 servings*

Level (From Gilanian people viewpoint): *Medium, Time-consuming*

Calories:

The meal: *unknown*

Timing Information:

To soak: —   **To prep:** —

To cook: ~ *2 hour 15 minutes*

Total time: ~ *2 hour 15 minutes*

[1] Crushed Bean Stew

Ingredients

~ 1⅔ lb / 800g fresh black-eyed beans

~ 4 garlic cloves

~ 4 cups water

oil, salt, pepper and turmeric

Instructions before starting

- If the fresh beans are not available, you can use dried beans but soak them in salted water overnight. Then rinse it with cold water in a colander.
- Peel the garlic cloves.

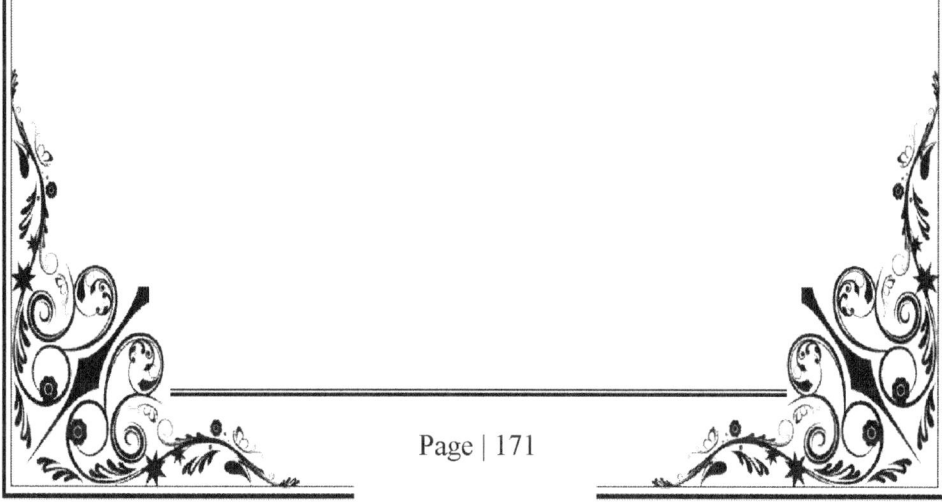

To prepare

Pour 4 cups of water and black-eyed beans along with garlic and a little salt in a pot and place it over medium heat to cook well. During the cooking time, put the lid in half way, because the food boils over soon. Baking the black-eyed beans takes about 2 hours, and by that time, ⅔ of the water will have disappeared.

When the time passed, take the pot from the stove and separate the water. Then mash the baked black-eyed beans with a masher. Now, mix the mashed ingredients with some oil, salt, pepper and turmeric, and add the removed water from the beans again to the ingredients and stir together to mix thoroughly. Then place the pot over the low heat for about 15 minutes. After this time, turn off the heat and the food is ready.

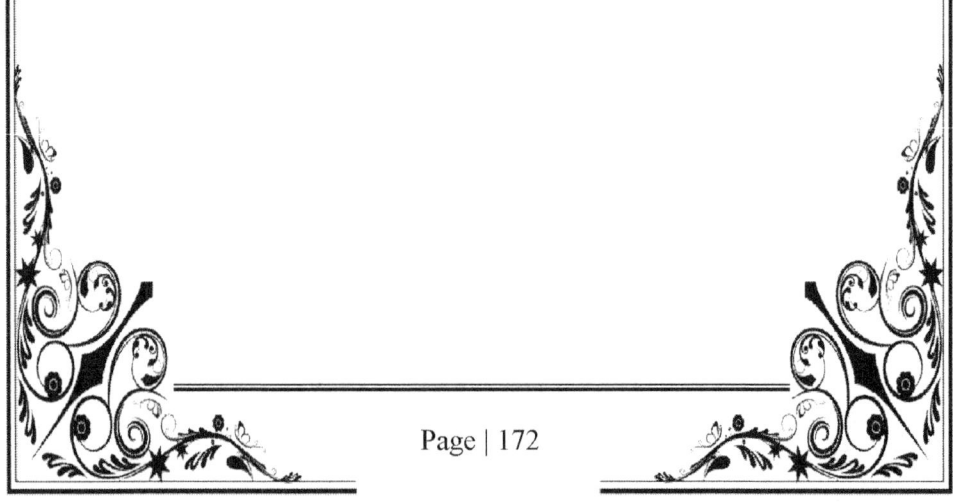

Tips for this food

1. This stew is served with Po'low.

2. The dish should be made with fresh black-eyed beans, because other beans or dried beans reduce considerably the quality of the food.

3. Common side items are garlic and Bu'râ'ni-e Bâ'dem'jân[1].

Bon Appétit

---

[1] See pages 218 and 341

Om'let Bâ Sir[1]

INFORMATION ABOUT THE MEAL

Basic Information:

Cuisine: *Gilanian*

Course: *Main Dish*

Formal meal (for guest): ~~Yes~~, *No*

Recommend for: ~~Breakfast~~, *Lunch, Dinner*

Yield: *4 servings*

Level (From Gilanian people viewpoint): *Easy, Time-consuming*

Calories:

The meal:

~ 45 calories per 1 tablespoon

Timing Information:

To soak: —

To prep: *~ 15 minutes*

To cook: *~ 30 minutes*

Total time: *~ 45 minutes*

[1] Omelet with Garlic and Tomato

Ingredients

~ 2½ lb / 1 kg tomatoes

~ 2 eggs

~ 4 garlic cloves

oil, salt, pepper and turmeric

Instructions before starting

- Peel the garlic cloves and grate them.
- Peel the tomatoes and slice them.

To prepare

Fry the garlic with a little oil, salt and turmeric in the pan, then add the tomatoes and stir them a few times to mix with the garlic thoroughly. Put the lid on the pan and let it boil and simmer for 3 minutes. Then reduce the heat and when ⅔ of the water disappeared, beat the eggs in a bowl and add to the ingredients in the pan, either stir the food with the eggs or spread the eggs over it. After 5 minutes, check the amounts of salt and pepper and then turn off the heat. Now the food is ready.

Tips for this food

1. This food is usually served with bread, but it can also be served with Po'low[1].

2. Onion can be used instead of garlic. In this way, dice only 2 medium-sized onions and fry them, then follow the other steps to the end.

3. Gilanian people use this stew with onion and white radish[2].

Bon Appétit

---

[1] See page 82
[2] See page 383

She'vid Po'low Bâ Pa'nir Be'resh'teh[1]

INFORMATION ABOUT THE MEAL

Basic Information:

Cuisine: *Gilanian*

Course: *Main Dish*

Formal meal (for guest): ~~*Yes*~~, *No*

Recommend for: ~~*Breakfast*~~, *Lunch*, ~~*Dinner*~~

Yield: *5 servings*

Level (From Gilanian people viewpoint): *Easy, Time-consuming*

Calories:

The meal (combination): *~ 600 calories per serving*

Timing Information:

To soak: *~ 3 hours*   **To prep:** *~ 15 minutes*

                                   To cook: *~ 1 hour 30 minutes*

                                   _____

                             Total time: *~ 1 hour 45 minutes*

[1] Dill Rice with Fried Cheese

Ingredients

- ~ 4 cups rice
- ~ 1 lb / ½ kg fresh dill
- ~ 2 tbsp. dried dill
- ~ ½ lb / 250g breakfast cheese
- ~ 5 eggs
- ~ ¼ cup steeped saffron
- ~ 12 cups water

oil, salt, pepper and turmeric

Instructions before starting

- Soak the rice in salted water 3 hours ahead.
- Mince the fresh dill and keep it in a dish.
- Mash the cheese.
- Heat 1 cup of the water.
- To make steeped saffron, dissolve a few threads in ¼ cup of warm water. See also "How to brew saffron?" on pages 255 and 365.

To prepare

Prepare the rice according to Âb'kesh method[1] up to draining step. Then put a pot on the stove with low heat and pour 4 tablespoons of water, 3 tablespoons of oil, 2 spatulas of Po'low and steeped saffron (or turmeric) in the pot and stir them. Remove the pot from the stove after 2 minutes and spread them at the bottom of the pot. Mix the drained Po'low with the chopped dill and put them into the pot. Then place the pot on the stove to steam Po'low, but before putting the lid on, mix 2 tablespoons of oil, ½ cup of warm water and a pinch of salt and sprinkle over Po'low. It takes 45 minutes to get ready.

Until steaming Po'low, fry the dried dill with ½ teaspoon of turmeric in some oil over low heat. Then add the cheese to stir-fry in the frying pan. Now it is the time for adding eggs. Stir all ingredients with the eggs for 2 minutes to get tough as much as you like. Then turn off the heat. The toasted cheese is ready. Dish up the food in a plate along with the prepared Po'low.

[1] See pages 84 and 310

Tips for this food

1. You can mix and cook the drained rice with dill in a rice cooker.

2. You can also use fresh dill to prepare the toasted cheese, but dried dill makes it tastier.

3. Gilanian people serve the food along with various kinds side items like Zey'tun Par'var'deh[1], yogurt, Dough[2], raw fava beans[3] and garlic.

Bon Appétit

---

[1] See pages 226 and 344
[2] See pages 200 and 255
[3] See page 350

Sir Vâ'vij[1]

INFORMATION ABOUT THE MEAL

Basic Information:
Cuisine: *Gilanian*
Course: *Main Dish*
Formal meal (for guest): ~~Yes~~, *No*
Recommend for: ~~Breakfast~~, *Lunch*, ~~Dinner~~
Yield: *4 servings*
Level (From Gilanian people viewpoint): *Easy, Time-consuming*

Calories:
The meal: *unknown*

Timing Information:
To soak: —   **To prep:** *~ 10 minutes*
                        To cook: *~ 30 minutes*

              Total time: *~ 40 minutes*

---

[1] Green Garlic and Eggs Dish

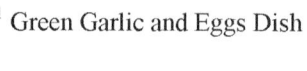

Ingredients

~ 1 lb / 450g garlic leaves

~ 4 eggs

~ ½ cup water

oil and salt

Instructions before starting

- Mince the garlic leaves.
- Heat the water.

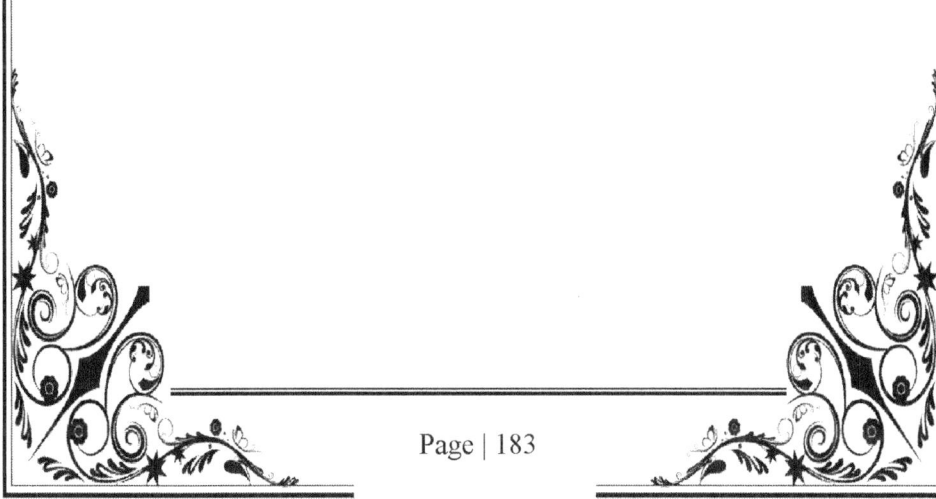

To prepare

First, fry the minced garlic leaves in oil along with some salt over the low heat. Then add the water and put the lid on to cook the ingredients well for 10 to 15 minutes. After this time, if the water inside the pan is halved, crack the eggs over the ingredients and stir them to mix with fried garlic leaves. Now put the lid on for 5 minutes to cook the eggs, then turn off the heat. The food is ready.

Tips for this food

1. This is usually served with Po'low (Ka'teh method[1]).

2. Gilanian people serve this food with Bu'râ'ni-e Bâ'dem'jân[2] and vegetables[3].

Bon Appétit

---

[1] See pages 88 and 311
[2] See pages 218 and 341
[3] See pages 256 and 353

VEGANS ASSISTANT

Tah Bur'yân[1]

INFORMATION ABOUT THE MEAL

Basic Information:

Cuisine: *Gilanian*

Course: *Main Dish*

Formal meal (for guest): ~~*Yes*~~, *No*

Recommend for: ~~*Breakfast*~~, *Lunch*, ~~*Dinner*~~

Yield: *4 servings*

Level (From Gilanian people viewpoint): *Easy, Time-consuming*

Calories:

The meal: *unknown*

Timing Information:

To soak: —

To prep: *~ 20 minutes*

To cook: *~ 1 hour*

Total time: *~ 1 hour 20 minutes*

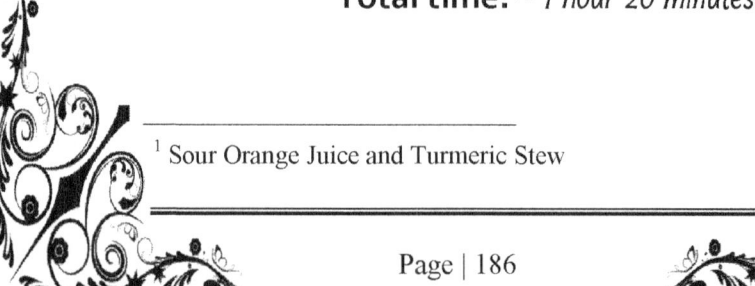

[1] Sour Orange Juice and Turmeric Stew

Ingredients

- ~ 2 medium potatoes
- ~ 1 small onion
- ~ 2 tbsp. rice flour
- ½ cup of sour orange juice
- ~ 2 eggs
- ~ 5 cups water
- oil, salt, pepper and turmeric

Instructions before starting

- Peel the potatoes and chop them into ~ ½ in / 1½ cm cubes.
- Dice the onions.
- Boil the water.

To prepare

Stir-fry the potatoes and onion with turmeric, salt, pepper and some oil in a pan (turmeric should be more than salt and pepper). Then add the boiled water to it. When the water boils again, reduce the heat and put the lid on to cook the potatoes for 40 minutes.

Now add 2 tablespoons of rice flour to the sour orange juice and mix them well, then add the mix to the stew. At this stage, you have to stir the ingredients constantly and gently in order not to clump together (after adding the flour, there is no need to put the lid on). After 5 minutes, beat 2 eggs in a bowl and add to the stew and after another 5 minutes, check the amounts of salt and sour, if necessary, add a little salt and sour orange juice and turn off the heat then the food is ready.

Tips for this food

1. Gilanian people serve the stew with Po'low.
2. You can balance the amount of sour orange juice according to your taste.
3. Gilanian people serve the stew with side items such as onion, vegetables[1], and olives.

Bon Appétit

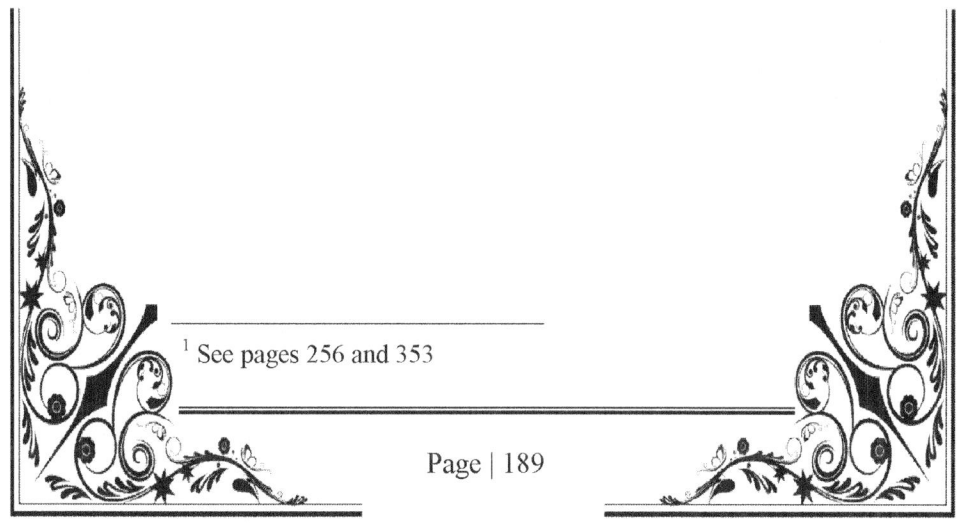

[1] See pages 256 and 353

VEGANS ASSISTANT

Tor'sh-e Ta'reh[1]

INFORMATION ABOUT THE MEAL

Basic Information:

Cuisine: *Gilanian*

Course: *Main Dish*

Formal meal (for guest): ~~Yes~~, *No*

Recommend for: ~~Breakfast~~, *Lunch, Dinner*

Yield: *4 servings*

Level (From Gilanian people viewpoint): *Easy*

Calories:

The meal:

~ 430 calories with bread

~ 680 calories with 12 tablespoons of Po'low (Low oil)

Timing Information:

To soak: —

To prep: *~ 10 minutes*

To cook: *~ 30 minutes*

Total time: *~ 40 minutes*

[1] Sour Herb Stew

Ingredients

herbs including:

~ ½ lb / 200g spinach

~ 5 oz / 150g eryngium planum, ziziphora and mint

~ 4 oz / 100g coriander

~ 4 oz / 100g dock

~ 4 oz / 100g garlic leaves

~ 2 oz / 50g green onion (scallion) and leek

~ 2 oz / 50g dill

and

~ 2 tbsp. rice flour

~ 2 eggs

~ ½ cup sour orange juice

~ 2 cups water

oil, salt and pepper

Instructions before starting

- Mince the herbs.
- Boil the water.

To prepare

Stir-fry the minced herbs with salt, pepper and some oil in a pan. Then add 2 cups of boiling water to simmer the herbs over medium heat for 20 minutes. After this, add 2 tablespoons of rice flour along with sour orange juice to the ingredients in the pan and stir slowly to mix them all. Reduce the heat immediately and beat the eggs in a bowl and spread them over the surface of the ingredients and put the lid on to cook for a little while. After 5 minutes, check the amounts of salt and sour, and if necessary, add a little salt and sour orange juice and turn off the heat. The food is ready.

Tips for this food

1. This food is usually served with bread, but it can also be served with Po'low.

2. It is possible to use 4 cloves of garlic instead of garlic leaves.

3. Gilanian people serve this stew with onion and white radish[1].

Bon Appétit

---

[1] See page 383

Iranian Side Items

Iranian side items names

Alphabetical order

38- Bu'râ'ni-e Es'fe'nâj   page 196

39- Dough   page 200

40- Mâs't-o Khi'yâr   page 204

41- Sâ'lâd Shi'ra'zi   page 208

42- Sâ'lâ'd-e Fasl   page 212

Bu'râ'ni-e Es'fe'nâj[1]

INFORMATION ABOUT THE SIDE ITEM

Basic Information:

Cuisine: *Iranian*

Course: *Side Item*

Formal side item (for guest): *Yes, ~~No~~*

Recommend for: *~~Breakfast~~, Lunch, Dinner*

Yield: *5 servings*

Level (From Iranian viewpoint): *Easy*

Calories:

Spinach: *~ 23 calories per 100g / 3½oz*

Yogurt (low fat): *~ 110 calories per glass*

The side item (combination): *~ 143 calories per serving*

Timing Information:

To soak: —   **To prep:** *~ 5 minutes*

                              To cook: *~ 20 minutes*

_____

Total time: *~ 25 minutes*

_____

[1] Spinach Bu'râ'ni

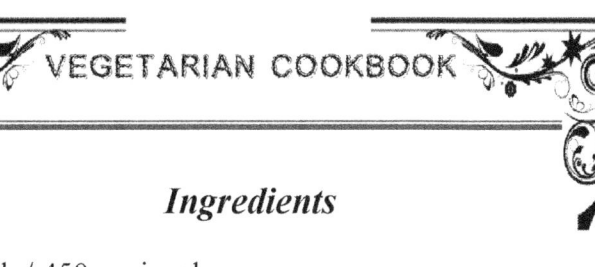
Ingredients

~ 1 lb / 450g spinach

~ 2 lb / 1 kg yogurt

salt

Instructions before starting

- Chop the herbs (~ ½ in / 1 cm).

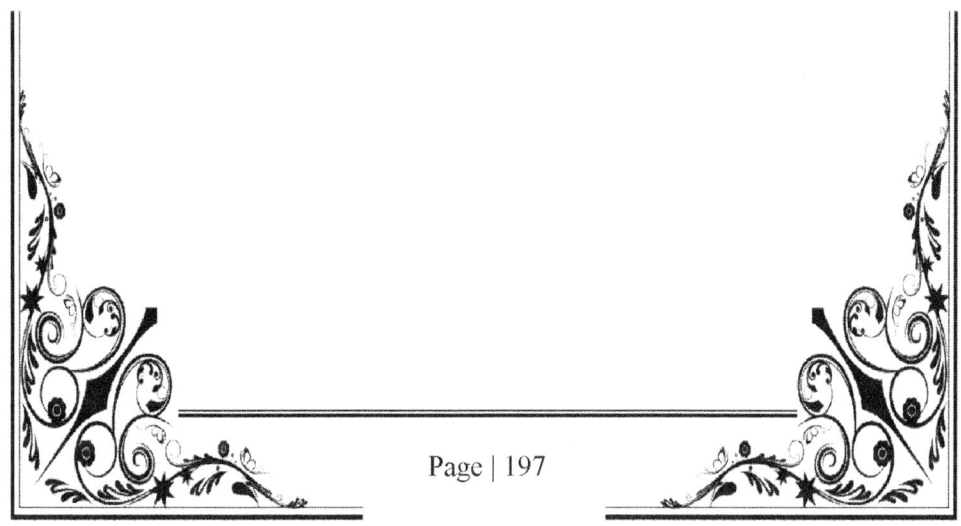

To prepare

First, put the spinach with ½ cup of water inside a pot and place the pot over the medium heat to cook for 15 to 20 minutes. When the spinach cooked, let it cool. Then mix it with yogurt and some salt in a dish and keep the dish in the refrigerator for 1 hour. After this time the Bu'râ'ni-e Es'fe'nâj is ready.

Tips for this side item

1. The thicker yogurt makes it more delicious.
2. This recipe is helpful for those who cannot use raw spinach due to an upset stomach or have difficulty with its taste.
3. This dessert is mostly served with dry foods in Iran like spaghetti or Ku'ku Sab'zi[1].

Bon Appétit

---

[1] See pages 66 and 306

VEGANS ASSISTANT

Dough[1]

INFORMATION ABOUT THE BEVERAGE

Basic Information:

Cuisine: *Iranian*

Course: *Side Item*

Formal beverage (for guest): *Yes, ~~No~~*

Recommend for: *~~Breakfast~~, Lunch, Dinner*

Yield: *5 servings*

Level (From Iranian viewpoint): *Easy*

Calories:

~ *77 calories per glass 200g / ~ ½lb*

Timing Information:

To soak: —   **To prep:** ~ *10 minutes*

                              To cook: —

                              _____

                              Total time: ~ *10 minutes*

[1] Yogurt Drink

Ingredients

~ 3 cups sour yogurt

~ 2 cups water

~ 2 tbsp. Da'lâr[1]

~ ½ tsp. salt

Instructions before starting

- Stir the sour yogurt 3-5 minutes.

[1] See pages 254 and 347

To prepare

Mix yogurt with water and Da'lâr in a pitcher and stir them well, then check the amount of salt and add more if necessary. Keep Dough in the refrigerator for an hour to make it tastier. After this time, the beverage is ready.

Tips for this beverage

1. As Da'lâr contains a lot of salt, you must add Da'lâr at first step and then check the amount of salt.

2. This beverage is commonly served with different kinds of dry foods such as spaghetti or Ku'ku Sab'zi[1].

Bon Appétit

---

[1] See pages 66 and 306

Mâs't-o Khi'yâr[1]

INFORMATION ABOUT THE SIDE ITEM

Basic Information:

Cuisine: *Iranian*

Course: *Side Item*

Formal side item (for guest): *Yes, ~~No~~*

Recommend for: *~~Breakfast~~, Lunch, Dinner*

Yield: *5 servings*

Level (From Iranian viewpoint): *Easy*

Calories:

~ 140 calories per small bowl

Timing Information:

To soak: —

To prep: *~ 30 minutes*

To cook: —

Total time: *~ 30 minutes*

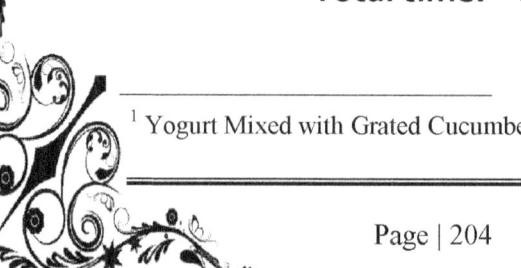

[1] Yogurt Mixed with Grated Cucumber

Ingredients

~ 5 medium cucumbers

~ 2 lb / 1 kg yogurt

~ 1 tbsp. Da'lâr[1]

~ 1 garlic clove

~ 2 oz / 50g raisins

~ 2 oz / 50g walnuts

salt and pepper

Instructions before starting

- Peel the cucumbers and dice them.
- Grate the garlic or mince it.
- Chop the walnuts.

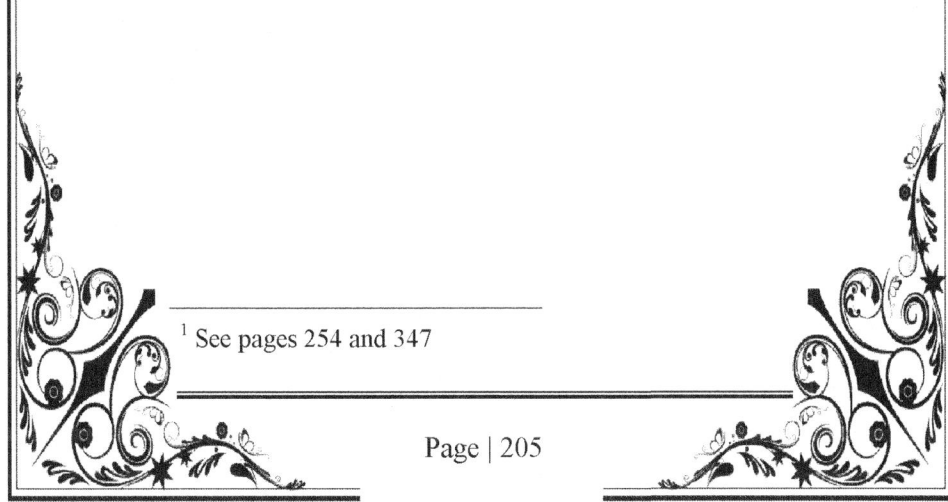

---

[1] See pages 254 and 347

To prepare

Mix the cucumbers and garlic with 1 tablespoons of Da'lâr in a special bowl and then after adding the walnuts, raisins, and a little salt and pepper, stir them well to mix the ingredients thoroughly. Then keep the bowl in the refrigerator for 1 hour to make it tastier.

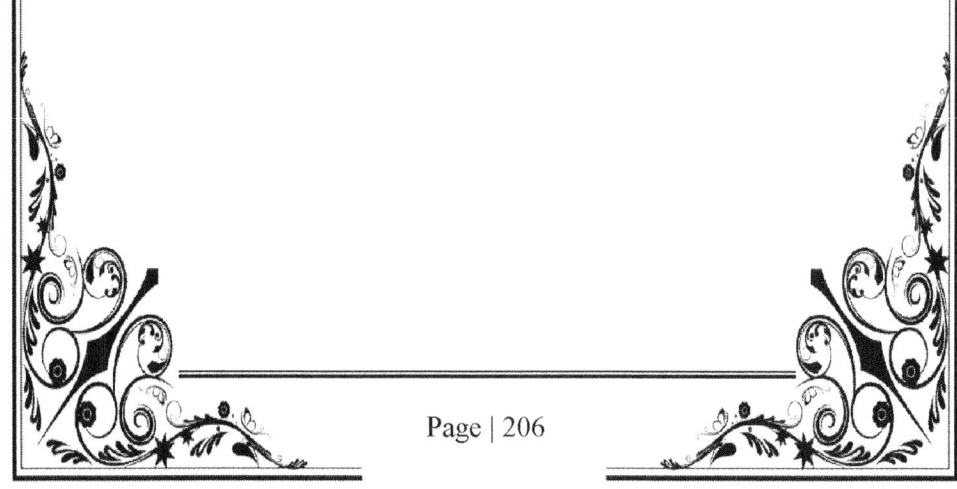

Tips for this side item

1. Iranians serve this salad with dry foods such as Ku'ku Sab'zi[1] or Ku'ku She'vid[2].

2. Da'lâr is used for making this salad more delicious and if it is not available, ½ tablespoon of dried mint can be used instead.

Bon Appétit

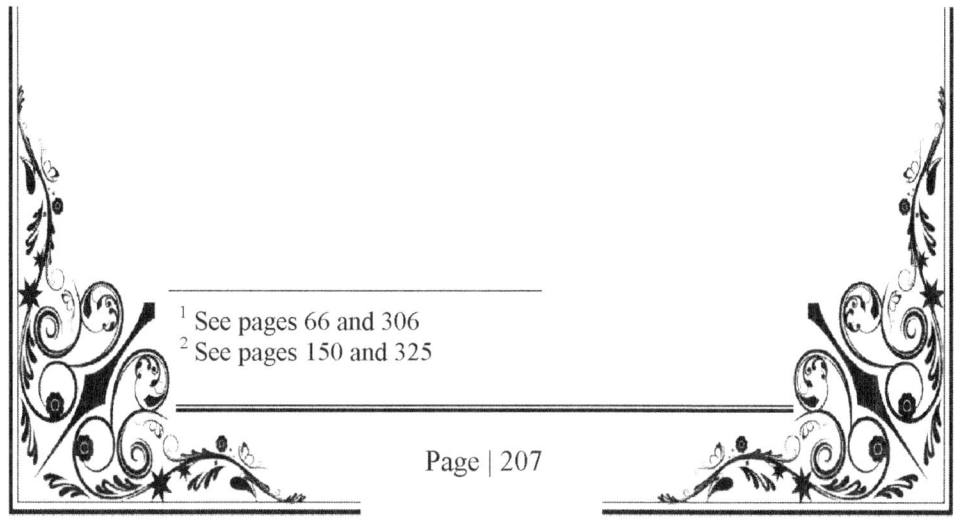

---
[1] See pages 66 and 306
[2] See pages 150 and 325

VEGANS ASSISTANT

Sâ'lâd Shi'râ'zi[1]

INFORMATION ABOUT THE SIDE ITEM

Basic Information:

Cuisine: *Iranian*

Course: *Side Item*

Formal side item (for guest): *Yes, ~~No~~*

Recommend for: *~~Breakfast,~~ Lunch, Dinner*

Yield: *4 servings*

Level (From Iranian viewpoint): *Easy*

Calories:

~ *5 calories per 1 dessertspoon*

~ *50 calories per small bowl*

~ *80 calories per glass*

Timing Information:

To soak: —

To prep: ~ *30 minutes*

To cook: —

Total time: ~ *30 minutes*

---

[1] Shi'râ'zi Salad

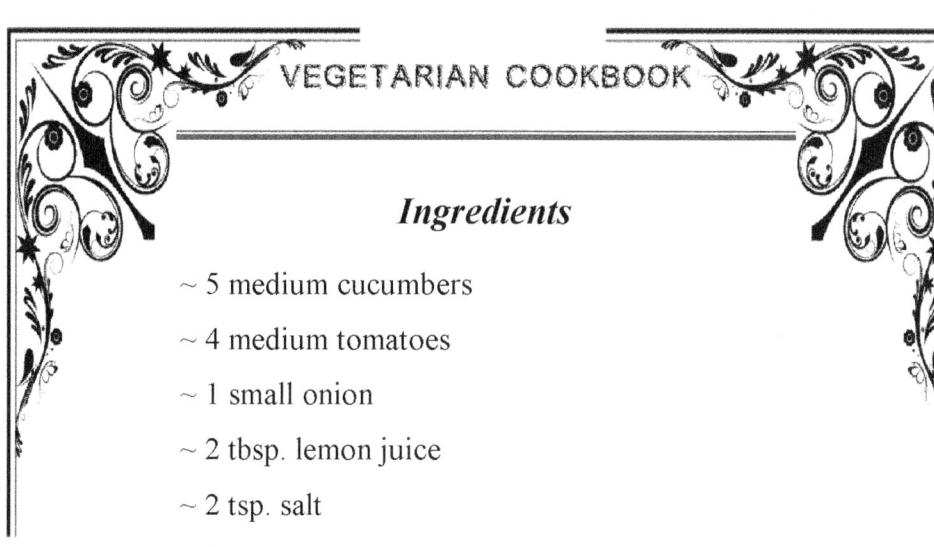

Ingredients

- ~ 5 medium cucumbers
- ~ 4 medium tomatoes
- ~ 1 small onion
- ~ 2 tbsp. lemon juice
- ~ 2 tsp. salt
- ~ 1 tsp. pepper

Instructions before starting

- Peel the cucumbers, tomatoes and onion. Then dice them.

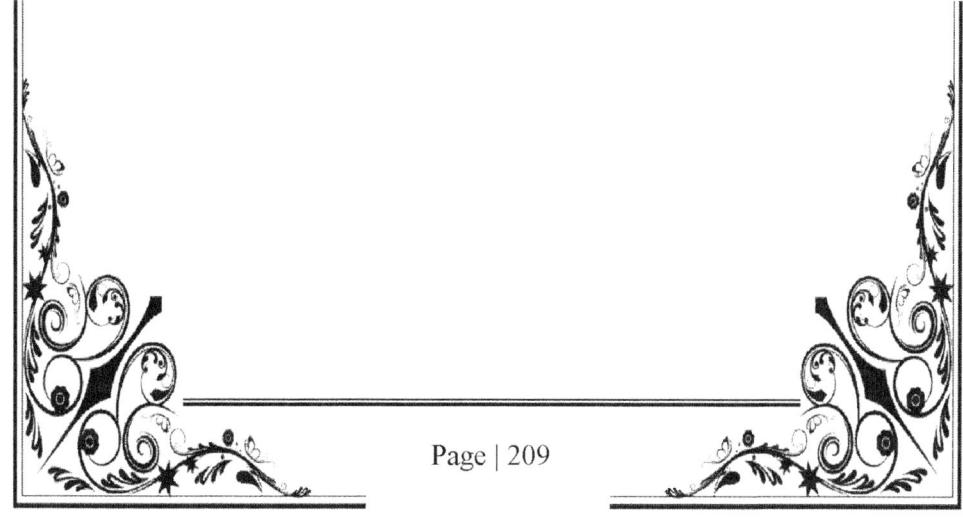

To prepare

Mix all diced ingredients with salt, pepper and lemon juice in a large bowl. Keep the bowl in the refrigerator for an hour to make it tastier. After this time, salad is ready.

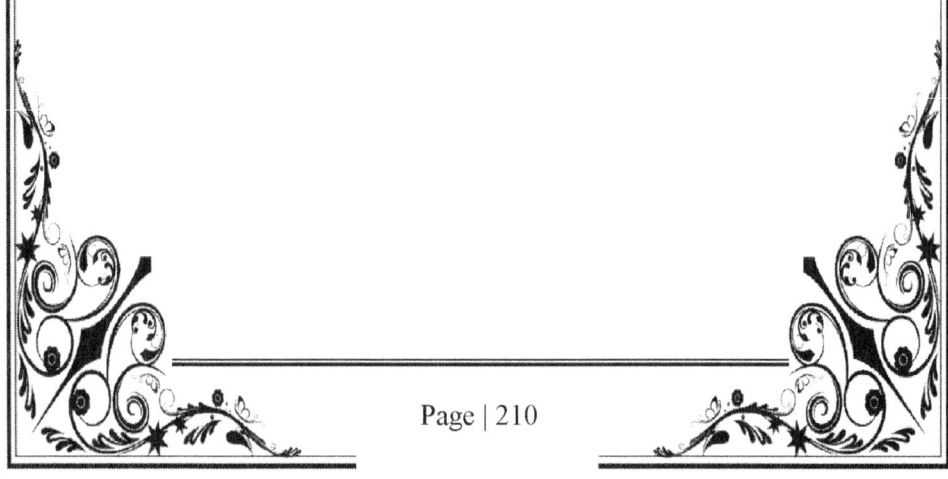

Tip for this salad

1. Sâ'lâd Shi'ra'zi is one of the popular salads in Iran, which is recommended with Es'tân'bo'li Po'low[1], and kinds of Ku'ku, etc. because it makes the taste of this Iranian dish more favorable.

Bon Appétit

---

[1] See pages 42 and 300

Sâ'lâ'd-e Fasl[1]

INFORMATION ABOUT THE SIDE ITEM

Basic Information:

Cuisine: *Iranian*

Course: *Side Item*

Formal side item (for guest): *Yes,* ~~*No*~~

Recommend for: ~~*Breakfast,*~~ *Lunch, Dinner*

Yield: *4 servings*

Level (From Iranian viewpoint): *Easy*

Calories:

~ 30 calories per small bowl (without mayonnaise)

~ 50 calories per serving

~ 400 calories per small bowl (with mayonnaise)

Timing Information:

To soak: —	**To prep:** *~ 40 minutes*
	To cook: —

Total time: *~ 40 minutes*

[1] Season Salad

Ingredients

- ~ ½ lb / 200g lettuces
- ~ 4 oz / 100g red cabbage
- ~ 4 oz / 100g white cabbage
- ~ 3 small cucumbers
- ~ 3 small tomatoes
- ~ 2 small carrots
- ~ 1 cup mayonnaise
- ~ 1 tbsp. lemon juice

salt

Instructions before starting

- Chop the lettuce, red cabbage and white cabbage separately into very small thin pieces.
- Cut the cucumbers into thin slices.
- Cut the tomatoes into thin slices.
- Grate the carrots.

To prepare

At first, choose a flat dish and put each of chopped lettuce, white cabbage and red cabbage on one side of the dish and then cover them with the tomatoes and cucumbers. At the end, put the grated carrots on the center. Mix the mayonnaise with lemon juice and keep the mix into a sauce boat. Salad is ready. Now you can serve some salad and coat it with some sauce.

Tips for this salad

1. This salad is served with all kinds of Ku'ku.

2. You can also serve this salad with different kinds of sauces, but most Iranian people prefer it with mayonnaise.

3. If you are limited to use mayonnaise, it is possible to mix the mayonnaise with 1 cup of yogurt and 1 tablespoon lemon juice and serve with this salad. In this mix the sauce flavor does not change.

Bon Appétit

Gilanian Side Items

Gilanian side items names
Alphabetical order

43- Bu'râ'ni-e Bâ'dem'jân   page 218

44- Kâl Ka'bâb   page 222

45- Zey'tun Par'var'deh   page 226

VEGANS ASSISTANT

Bu'râ'ni-e Bâ'dem'jân[1]

INFORMATION ABOUT THE SIDE ITEM

Basic Information:

Cuisine: *Gilanian*

Course: *Side Item*

Formal side item (for guest): *Yes, ~~No~~*

Recommend for: *~~Breakfast~~, Lunch, Dinner*

Yield: *5 servings*

Level (From Gilanian people viewpoint): *Easy*

Calories:

Eggplant: *~ 25 calories per 100g / 3½oz*

Yogurt (low fat): *~ 110 calories per glass*

The side item (combination): *~ 150 calories per serving*

Timing Information:

To soak: —

To prep: —

To cook: *~ 40 minutes*

Total time: *~ 40 minutes*

---

[1] Eggplant Bu'râ'ni or Yogurt Bu'râ'ni

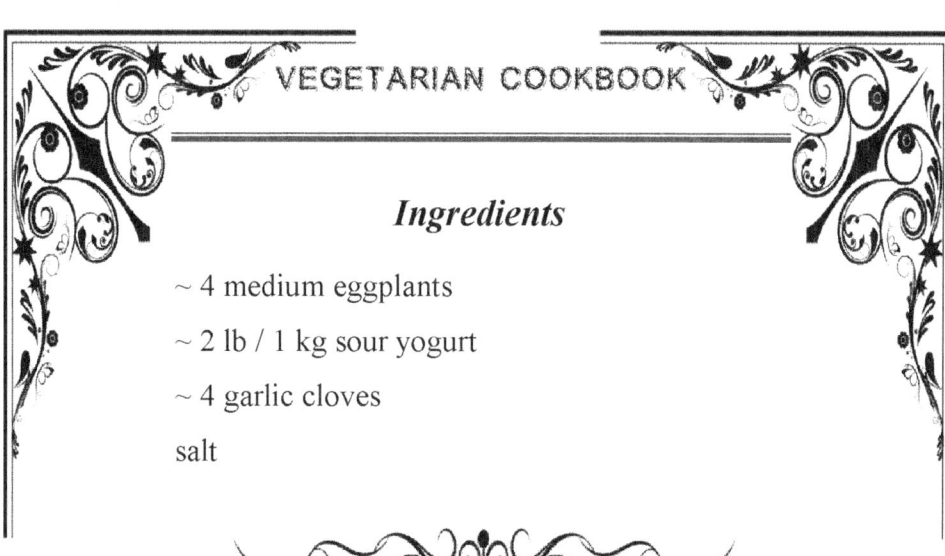

Ingredients

~ 4 medium eggplants

~ 2 lb / 1 kg sour yogurt

~ 4 garlic cloves

salt

Instructions before starting

* Peel the garlic cloves and grate them.

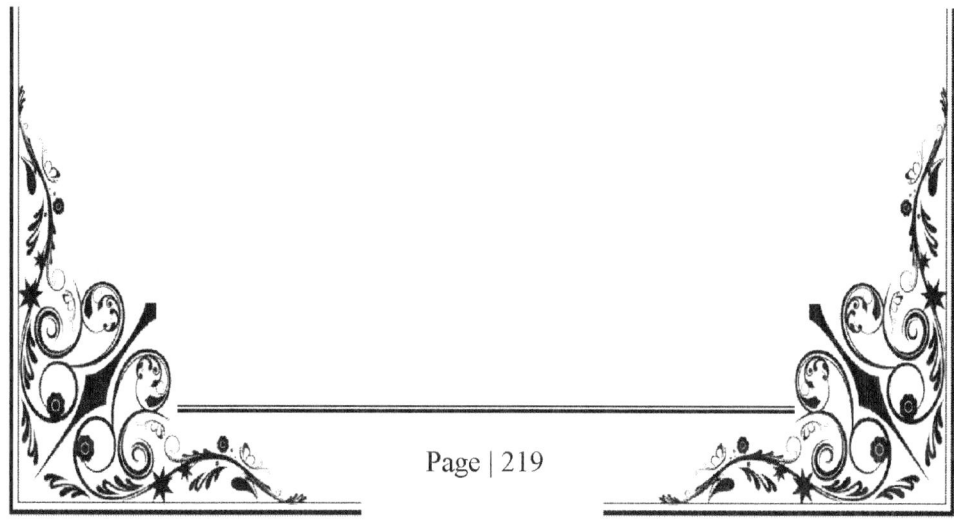

To prepare

Grill the eggplants with skin to cook them directly on the fire and after baking, peel the skins, then chop the eggplants. In this step, add the garlic and yogurt to the eggplants and stir them to mix well. Bu'râ'ni-e Bâ'dem'jân is ready.

Tips for this side item

1. It is better to keep the dessert in the refrigerator for an hour to make it more delicious.

2. This food item is usually served with dry foods such as Es'tân'bo'li Po'low[1] or A'das Po'low[2].

Bon Appétit

---

[1] See pages 42 and 300
[2] See pages 38 and 299

Kâl Ka'bâb[1]

INFORMATION ABOUT THE SIDE ITEM

Basic Information:

Cuisine: *Gilanian*

Course: *Side Item*

Formal side item (for guest): *Yes, ~~No~~*

Recommend for: *~~Breakfast~~, Lunch, Dinner*

Yield: *5 servings*

Level (From Gilanian people viewpoint): *Medium, Time-consuming*

Calories:

The side item: *unknown*

Timing Information:

To soak: —

To prep: *~ 10 minutes*

To cook: *~ 1 hour*

Total time: *~ 1 hour 10 minutes*

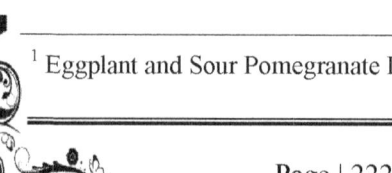

-----

[1] Eggplant and Sour Pomegranate Dish

Ingredients

~ 1⅓ lb / 600g eggplants

~ 12 oz / 350g walnuts

~ 12 oz / 350g sour pomegranate seeds

~ 4 garlic cloves

salt, pepper and ground angelica[1]

Instructions before starting

- Peel the garlic cloves and grate them.
- Grind the sour pomegranate seeds and walnuts separately.

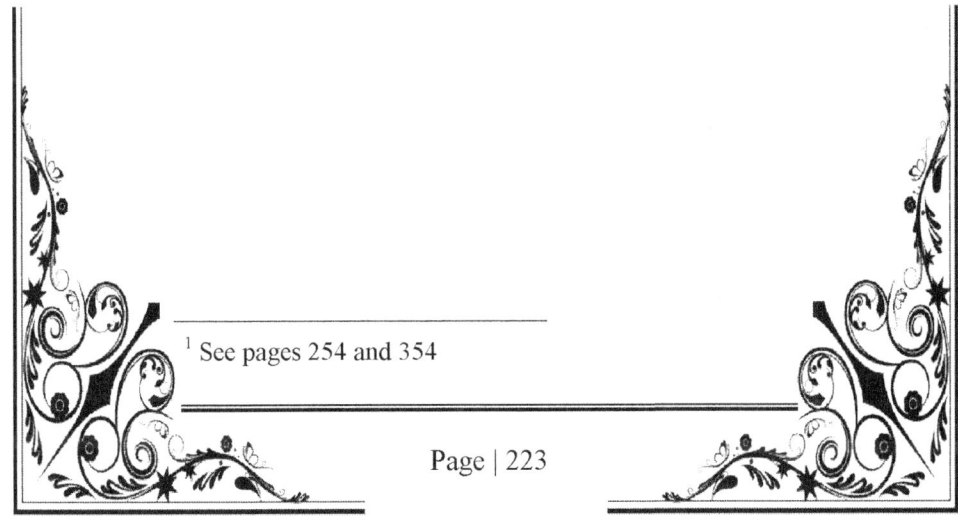

---

[1] See pages 254 and 354

To prepare

Grill the eggplants with skin or cook directly on the fire and after baking, peel the skins and then chop the eggplants. Now mix the eggplants with other ingredients that have already been crushed and ground, then add salt, pepper and ground angelica to them and stir well. At this time, Kâl Ka'bâb is ready to eat but keep it in the refrigerator for 1 hour to make it tastier.

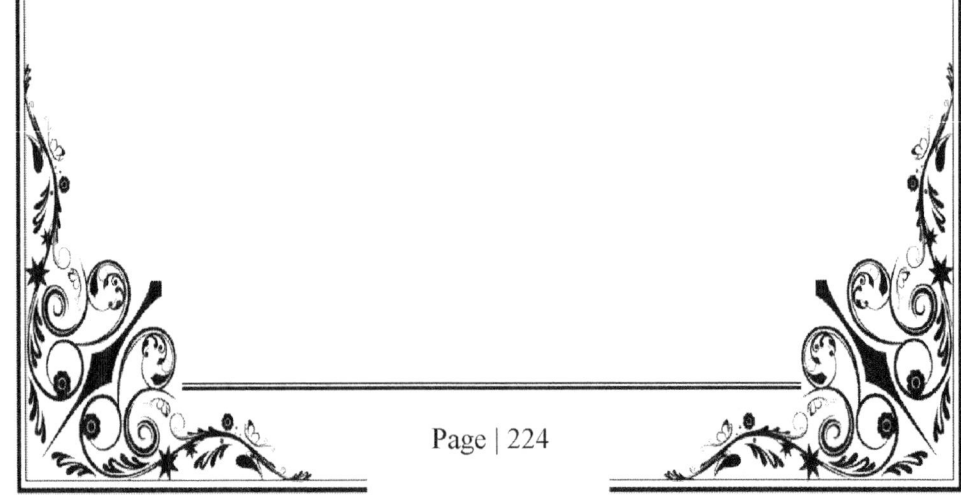

Tips for this side item

1. Ground angelica is the main part of this food item, so if it is not available, do not make the item.

2. The flavor is strongly related to the proportions of the ingredients.

3. The best way for grinding the pomegranate seeds is through using Nam'kâr[1].

4. This food item is served as a meal in the Northern villages of Iran.

5. Kâl Ka'bâb can be served with many foods like Ku'ku Sab'zi[2], Ku'ku Sib Za'mi'ni[3], Spaghetti, Es'tân'bo'li Po'low[4], etc.

Bon Appétit

---

[1] See page 367
[2] See pages 66 and 306
[3] See pages 70, 74, 307 and 308
[4] See pages 42 and 300

Zey'tun Par'var'deh[1]

INFORMATION ABOUT THE SIDE ITEM

Basic Information:

Cuisine: *Gilanian*

Course: *Side Item*

Formal side item (for guest): *Yes, ~~No~~*

Recommend for: *~~Breakfast~~, Lunch, Dinner*

Yield: *4 servings*

Level (From Gilanian people viewpoint): *Easy*

Calories:

~ *45 calories per 1 tablespoon*

~ *134 calories per 100g / 3½ oz*

Timing Information:

To soak: —

To prep: ~ *15 minutes*

To cook: —

Total time: *15 minutes*

---

[1] Olives with Walnut Dip or Olives with Walnut Sauce

Ingredients

~ 4 oz / 100g herbs including coriander, parsley, eryngium planum, ziziphora, mint and leek

and

~ 1 lb / ½ kg pitted olives

~ ½ lb / 200g walnuts

~ 1 tbsp. pomegranate paste

~ 2 garlic cloves

Instructions before starting

- Grind the herbs, walnuts and garlic cloves.

To prepare

Put all ingredients in a dish and stir them well until the olives absorb them. This dessert is ready to serve now, but keep it in the refrigerator for 1 hour to make it tastier.

Tip for this dessert

1. Zey'tun Par'var'deh can be served with many foods like Ku'ku Sab'zi[1], A'das Po'low[2], Spaghetti, etc.

Bon Appétit

---

[1] See pages 66 and 306
[2] See pages 38 and 299

Pickles

Pickles names
Alphabetical order

46- *Tor'shi-e Bâ'dem'jân Chu'châgh*   *page 232*
47- *Tor'shi-e Li'teh*   *page 236*

Tor'shi-e Bâ'dem'jân Chu'châgh[1]

INFORMATION ABOUT THE PICKLE

Basic Information:

Cuisine: *Gilanian*

Course: *Side Item*

Formal side item (for guest): *Yes, ~~No~~*

Recommend for: *~~Breakfast~~, Lunch, Dinner*

Yield: —

Level (From Gilanian people viewpoint): *Easy, Time-consuming*

Calories:

~ 100 calories per small bowl

Timing Information:

To soak: —

To prep: *~ 20 minutes*

To cook: *~ 10 minutes*

Total time: *~ 30 minutes*

---

[1] Pickled Eggplant with Eryngium Planum

Ingredients

- ~ 2 lb / 1 kg eggplants
- ~ ½ lb / 250g eryngium planum
- ~ 2 garlic heads
- ~ 8 cups vinegar
- ~ 1 tbsp. ground angelica[1]
- ~ 1 tsp. pepper
- ~ 1 tbsp. salt

Instructions before starting

- Mince the herbs.
- Grate the garlic cloves.
- Chop the eggplants (skin-in).

---

[1] See pages 254 and 354

To prepare

Put the chopped eggplants with 1 cup of water and a little salt into a pot. Place the pot over the heat to cook, and stir a few times. When the eggplants cooked partly, remove the excess water through a colander and wait for them to cool. At this stage, move the eggplants into a bowl and add the minced herbs and grated garlic to the eggplants and after adding salt, pepper and ground angelica, move all the ingredients into a jar and pour the vinegar into the jar as it covers the surface of the eggplants. Then, cover the jar with a lid firmly so that air does not penetrate into it. It takes a week to prepare the pickle.

Tips for the pickle

1. Pickles need more salt than other foods do.

2. There is no alternative to eryngium planum in this pickle, so if this local herb is not available, avoid making the pickle.

3. Iranians serve the pickle with food like Khu'râ'k-e Na'khod (Âb Na'khod)[1], Âsh Resh'teh[2], Bâ'ghe'lâ Po'low Bâ Pa'nir Be'resh'teh[3].

Bon Appétit

---

[1] See pages 62 and 305
[2] See pages 34 and 298
[3] See pages 134 and 321

Tor'shi-e Li'teh[1]

INFORMATION ABOUT THE PICKLE

Basic Information:
Cuisine: *Iranian*
Course: *Side Item*
Formal meal (for guest): *Yes, No*
Recommend for: *Breakfast, Lunch, Dinner*
Yield: —
Level (From Iranian viewpoint): *Medium, Time-consuming*

Calories:
~ 100 calories per small bowl

Timing Information:
To soak: —   **To prep:** *~ 1 hour 30 minutes*
                              To cook: —

                              Total time: *~ 1 hour 30 minutes*

[1] Pickled Eggplant and Vegetables

Ingredients

~ 1 lb / 450g herbs including mint, sweet basil, tarragon, savory and coriander

~ 3⅓ lb / 1½ kg eggplants

~ 10 garlic cloves

~ 8 cups vinegar

~ 2 spicy green peppers

~ 2 tbsp. salt

~ 1½ tbsp. ground angelica[1]

~ 1 tsp. pepper

Instructions before starting

- Grill the eggplants with skin or cook directly on the fire and then peel the skins and mash the eggplants.

- Mince the garlic cloves.

- Mince the green peppers.

- Mince the herbs.

---

[1] See pages 254 and 354

To prepare

Mix the garlic, salt, pepper (both green and black), herbs and mashed eggplants, and move all the ingredients into a jar. Then add the vinegar as it covers the surface of the ingredients. At this stage, cover the jar with a lid firmly and keep it in the refrigerator or in a cold place for 4 or 5 days so that the vinegar can penetrate into the ingredients and pickle gets ready.

Tips for the pickle

1. Pickles need more salt than other foods do.

2. If vinegar goes below the surface of the ingredients, add more vinegar to cover them thoroughly.

3. Iranians serve the pickle with food like Khu'râk-e Na'khod[1] (Âb Na'khod), Âsh Resh'teh[2], Bâ'ghe'lâ Po'low Bâ Pa'nir Be'resh'teh[3].

Bon Appétit

---

[1] See pages 62 and 305
[2] See pages 34 and 298
[3] See pages 134 and 321

Others

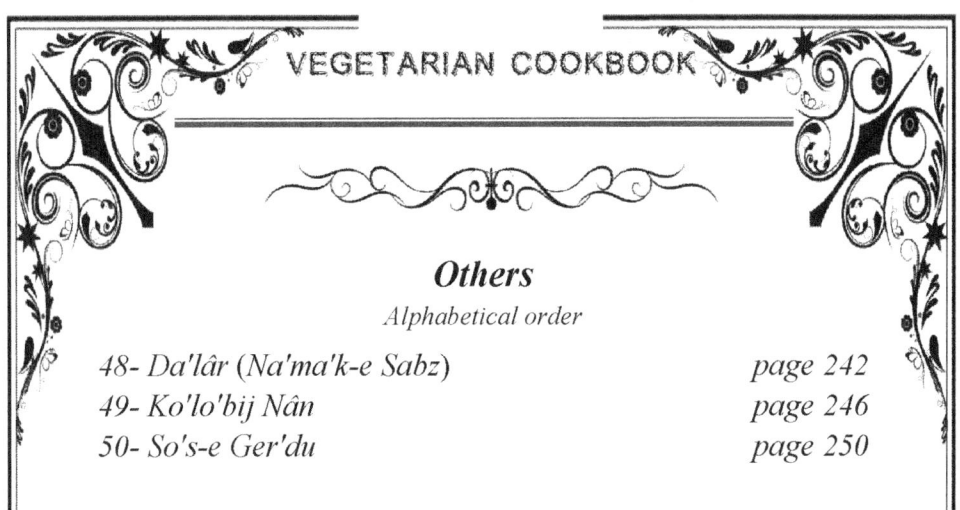

Others

Alphabetical order

48- Da'lâr (*Na'ma'k-e Sabz*)   page 242
49- Ko'lo'bij Nân   page 246
50- So's-e Ger'du   page 250

Da'lâr[1] (*Na'ma'k-e Sabz*)

INFORMATION ABOUT DA'LÂR

Basic Information:

Cuisine: —

Course: —

Formal meal (for guest): *Yes, ~~No~~*

Recommend for: *~~Breakfast, Lunch, Dinner~~*

Yield: —

Level (From Iranian viewpoint): *Easy*

Calories:

unknown

Timing Information:

To soak: —   **To prep:** *~ 15 minutes*

To cook: —

—————

Total time: *~ 15 minutes*

[1] Green Salt

Ingredients

herbs including:

~ 1⅓ lb / 600g coriander

~ ½ lb / 200g mint

~ ½ lb / 200g ziziphora

~ 20 sticks eryngium planum

and

~ 2 tbsp. salt

Instructions before starting

- Wash the herbs and let them dry (if they do not dry completely, Da'lâr spoils soon and molds).

To prepare

Grind the herbs twice, then mix them with 2 tablespoons of salt. Da'lâr is ready.

Tips for Da'lâr

1. In the North of Iran, a clay dish called Nam'kâr[1] is used to make Da'lâr. It has a special stone for grinding herbs.

2. Eating fruits such as cucumber, sour orange and sour greengage plum along with Da'lâr or mixing it with yogurt, Dough[2] and verjuice will give you an incredible flavor. This additive is also used in "Khu'li Ou (Hâ'li Ou)[3]" stew.

3. Be careful about the amounts of herbs, because the mentioned amounts have significant effects on the taste of Da'lâr.

4. Da'lâr is known as Na'ma'k-e Sabz (Green salt) in the North of Iran.

Bon Appétit

---

[1] See page 367
[2] See pages 200 and 255
[3] See pages 142 and 323

Ko'lo'bij Nân[1]

INFORMATION ABOUT THE MEAL

Basic Information:

Cuisine: *Gilanian*

Course: —

Formal meal (for guest): ~~Yes~~, No

Recommend for: ~~Breakfast~~, ~~Lunch~~, Supper, ~~Dinner~~

Yield: *4 servings*

Level (From Iranian viewpoint): *Easy, Time-consuming*

Calories:

The snack: *unknown*

Timing Information:

To soak: —

To prep: ~ *15 minutes*

To cook: ~ *1 hour 15 minutes*

_____

Total time: ~ *1 hour 30 minutes*

[1] Pumpkin Snack

Ingredients

~ 1 cup pumpkin

~ 2 cups wheat flour

~ 2 egg

~ ½ cup sugar

~ ½ cup yogurt or milk

~ ½ cup walnuts

~ ½ cup raisins

oil and salt

Instructions before starting

- Crush the walnuts.
- Peel the pumpkin and chop it into 1-2 in / 3-5 cm cubes.

To prepare

Bake the chopped pumpkin for 20 minutes and mash them thoroughly. Then mix all ingredients in a dish and stir well. Now leave it for 30 minutes.

For frying

Place a large frying pan on the stove and pouring 5-6 tablespoons oil into that to heat. Then make small patties, flatten them in an oval or a round shape and carefully place them in the pan to fry. Where you see that the bottom and the edges are crispy, turn them over to fry the other sides. After frying all the mixed ingredients the snack food is ready. You can garnish them with pistachio or almond slices.

Tips for this snack

1. Ko'lo'bij Nân can be made without walnuts and raisins, although the taste gets less delicious.

2. Ko'lo'bij Nân is usually served as a snack, so it is not a good alternative to lunch or dinner.

3. It should be noted that Ko'lo'bij Nân paste gets tender and soft with milk but crispy and dry with yogurt. So, according to your taste, you can choose one of these two ingredients.

Bon Appétit

So's-e Ger'du[1]

INFORMATION ABOUT THE SAUCE

Basic Information:

Cuisine: *Gilanian*

Course: —

Formal meal (for guest): —

Recommend for: —

Yield: *4 servings*

Level (From Gilanian people viewpoint): *Easy*

Calories:

The walnut dip: ~ *173 calories per serving*

Timing Information:

To soak: —   **To prep:** ~ *15 minutes*

                        To cook: —

                        _____

                        Total time: ~ *15 minutes*

[1] Walnut Dip or Walnut Sauce

Ingredients

herbs including:

~ ½ lb / 200g mint, ziziphora, parsley and coriander

~ 3 sticks leek

and

~ 12 oz / 350g walnuts

~ 2 garlic cloves

~ 2 tbsp. sour pomegranate paste

~ ¾ cup water

salt and pepper

Instructions before starting

- Grind the walnuts.
- Grind the herbs and garlic cloves to crush thoroughly.

To prepare

To make this simple food item, mix all ingredients thoroughly. The sauce is ready.

Tip for this item

1. This special sauce can be served with different kinds of dry foods such as Ku'ku She'vid[1], Ku'ku Sab'zi[2], Ku'ku Sib Za'mi'ni[3], etc.

Bon Appétit

---

[1] See pages 150 and 325
[2] See pages 66 and 306
[3] See pages 70, 74, 307 and 308

Words you might not know
Alphabetical order

Angelica (See page 354)

Golpar in Persian language, (pronounced /Gol'par/) (botanical name: Heracleum persicum) angelica or Persian Hogweed, commonly known as Persian hogweed or simply hogweed, is a polycarpic perennial herbaceous flowering plant in the carrot family Apiaceas, native to Iran that is a flowering spice plant, growing wild in its mountainous regions. Gol'par seedpods contain seeds that are ground into a powder form and used as a spice.

Be'renj (See pages 310, 311 and 368)

Be'renj is a generic term for grains; Che'low means cooked plain rice, but it doesn't refer to any particular variety.

Curd

curd (also curds [plural]) a thick soft substance that is formed when milk turns sour. (Oxford Dictionary)

Da'lâr (See page 347)

Da'lâr is an exact mixture of local plants in the North of Iran. In Gilan, Da'lâr is an alternative to salt for eating fruits like sour orange or cucumber which makes the fruit to taste savory. Da'lâr is used with some stews like Kholi Ou (See pages 142 and 323).

Dam'ko'ni

Dam'koni, a cloth to cover the lid of the pot. Iranians generally cover the rice pot-lid with the Dam'koni when steaming it to prevent the vapor from escaping. It causes steam drops to be absorbed by the fitted fabric pot-lid cover and not to return to Po'low, then the rice grains are distinct and apart from each other.

Dough (See page 200)

Dough is one of the most valuable Iranian beverages that is made by diluting yogurt and adding aromatic herbs and flavorings such as dried mint and sweet basil. This healthy drink is drunk as a beverage with most dry foods in Iran. In addition, Dough is the best alternative to sparkling soft drinks.

How to brew saffron? (Related to cooking rice) (See page 365)

One of the methods of brewing saffron is to grind a few threads finely and then mix the ground saffron with ½ cup of warm water in a small bowl to dissolve saffron completely. Then, in the step that you put Po'low into a pot to steam, place the small bowl in the pot over Po'low. This method both helps saffron release its aroma, and Po'low take a delicate flavor after merging with saffron aroma.

Saffron (See pages 364 and 365)

An autumn-flowering crocus with reddish-purple flowers, native to warmer regions of Eurasia. Enormous numbers of flowers are required to produce a small quantity of the large

red stigmas used for the spice. (Longman Dictionary)

Tah Dig (See page 371)

Tah Dig also known as crunchy rice, is a crispy crust at the bottom of the rice, that can be a layer of thin La'vâsh bread (and sometimes is a mixture of thinly sliced potatoes, egg, yogurt and saffron). Tah Dig is produced during the cooking of rice and it's the best part of several dishes Iranians cook.

Vegetables (See page 353)

"Vegetables" are served as side dishes on the Iranian tables. The side dish consists of some known vegetables including leek, radish, green onion (scallion), parsley, coriander, mint, sweet basil and cress. To serve, you need to cut them into small pieces and use them in combination along with the meal in small dishes on the table. These combination of vegetables give more flavor to the Iranian foods like Kash'k-e Bâ'dem'jân (See pages 54 and 303), and Mir'zâ Ghâ'se'mi (See pages 166, 329 and 330).

Foods ingredients at a glance
Iranian cuisines
Alphabetical order

Âsh Resh'teh
herbs (including spinach, mint, leek, coriander and parsley), pasteurized curd, thin noodle, lentil, chickpea, lima bean, pinto bean, red bean, mung bean, peeled wheat, onion, garlic, dried mint, oil, pepper, turmeric and salt. (See pages 34 and 298)

A'das Po'low
rice, lentil, raisin, walnut, onion, tomato paste, saffron, oil, pepper, turmeric and salt. (See pages 38 and 299)

Es'tân'bo'li Po'low
rice, soy protein, green bean, onion, tomato paste, milk, steeped saffron, oil, pepper, turmeric and salt. (See pages 42 and 300)

Fe're'ni
milk, rice flour, sugar, rose water, cinnamon, ground cardamom and salt. (See pages 46 and 301)

Ha'lim
peeled wheat, peeled sesame, walnut, pistachio, sugar, sesame oil, ground cinnamon and salt. (See pages 50 and 302)

Kash'k-e Bâ'dem'jân
eggplant, pasteurized curd, garlic, onion, dried mint, oil,

pepper and salt. (See pages 54 and 303)

Khu'râ'k-e A'da'si
lentils, onion, tomato paste, oil, pepper, turmeric and salt. (See pages 58 and 304)

Khu'râ'k-e Na'khod (*Âb Na'khod*)
chickpea, onion, potato, turmeric, pepper and salt. (See pages 62 and 305)

Ku'ku Sab'zi
herbs (including coriander, fenugreek, parsley and leek), egg, rice flour, oil, pepper and salt. (See pages 66 and 306)

Ku'ku Sib Za'mi'ni (*with baked potato*)
potato, egg, onion, steeped saffron, thick yogurt, oil, pepper and salt. (See pages 70 and 307)

Ku'ku Sib Za'mi'ni (*with raw potato*)
potato, onion, egg, oil, turmeric, pepper and salt. (See pages 74 and 308)

Mâ'kâ'ro'ni-e Sab'zi'jât
herbs (including coriander, parsley, leek, lemon balm and spinach), spaghetti, onion, sour pomegranate seeds, oil, pepper, turmeric and salt. (See pages 78 and 309)

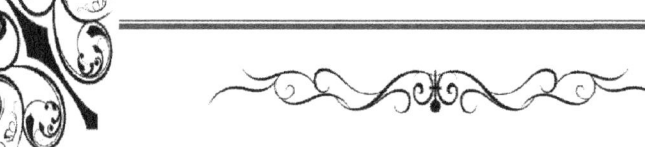

Po'low: Âb'kesh method
rice, steeped saffron, oil and salt. (See pages 84 and 310)

Po'low: Ka'teh method
rice and salt. (See pages 88 and 311)

Shir Be'renj
milk, rice, sugar and salt. (See pages 92 and 312)

Sho'leh Zard
rice, sugar, steeped saffron, almond and salt. (See pages 96 and 313)

Gilanian cuisines
Alphabetical order

Â'sh-e Ka'du
pumpkin, rice, milk, sugar and salt. (See pages 102 and 314)

Â'sh-e Se'fid (Â'sh-e A'nâr)
rice, Da'lâr, sour pomegranates, sour plum paste, ground angelica and salt. (See page 106)

Â'sh-e Torsh
rice, herbs (including leek, parsley, beet green, coriander, mint, ziziphora, creeping wood sorrel, and eryngium planum), fava bean, sour greengage plum, onion, garlic, oil, pepper and salt. (See pages 110 and 315)

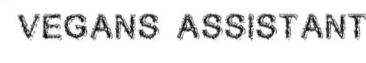

Ash'ke'neh Ta'reh

herbs (including Ash'ke'neh, coriander, leek, parsley, scallion, ziziphora and mint) fava bean, garlic, greengage plum, oil, pepper and salt. (See pages 114 and 316)

Bâdem'jân Kabâb

herbs (including coriander, pennyroyal, leek, parsley, eryngium planum and ziziphora), eggplant, tomato, walnut, garlic, pomegranate paste, oil, pepper and salt. (See pages 118 and 317)

Bâ'dem'jân Ta'reh

eggplant, tomato, egg, onion, oil, pepper, turmeric and salt. (See pages 122 and 318)

Bâ'dem'jân Va'ra'gheh Bâ Gou'jeh

eggplant, tomato, egg, oil, pepper, turmeric and salt. (See pages 126 and 319)

Bâ'ghe'lâ Ghâ'togh

lima bean, dill, egg, garlic, oil, pepper, turmeric and salt. (See pages 130 and 320)

Bâ'ghe'lâ Po'low Bâ Pa'nir Be'resh'teh

rice, fava bean, dried dill (or fresh dill), breakfast cheese, eggs, steeped saffron, oil, pepper, turmeric and salt. (See pages 134 and 321)

Kho'resh't-e Ka'du

herbs (including eryngium planum, ziziphora, coriander, parsley and leek), pumpkin, lima bean, walnut, garlic, onion, pepper and salt. (See pages 138 and 322)

Khu'li Ou (*Hâ'li Ou*)

sour greengage plum, sweet greengage plum, Da'lâr, egg, oil, pepper and salt. (See pages 142 and 323)

Ku'ku Bâ'dem'jân

eggplant, onion, egg, rice flour, oil, pepper and salt. (See pages 146 and 324)

Ku'ku She'vid

dill, egg, oil, pepper and salt. (See pages 150 and 325)

Ku'ku Sir

garlic leaf, egg, rice flour, oil, pepper and salt. (See pages 154 and 326)

La'gad Da'mo'jey

black-eyed bean, eggplant, tomato, onion, oil, pepper, turmeric and salt. (See pages 158 and 327)

Mâ'kâ'ro'ni Bâ Ja'fa'ri Vâ'ram'bu

herbs (including parsley and lemon balm), spaghetti, onion, tomato, oil, pepper and salt. (See pages 162 and 328)

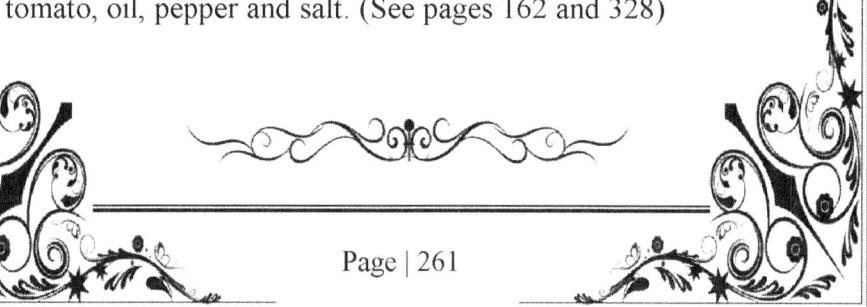

Mir'zâ Ghâ'se'mi

eggplant, tomato, garlic, egg, oil, pepper, turmeric and salt. (See pages 166, 329 and 330)

Mor'ju Vâ'vij

fresh black-eyed bean, garlic, oil, pepper, turmeric and salt. (See pages 170 and 331)

Om'let Bâ Sir

tomato, egg, garlic, oil, pepper, turmeric and salt. (See pages 174 and 332)

She'vid Po'low Bâ Pa'nir Be'resh'teh

rice, fresh dill, dried dill, breakfast cheese, egg, steeped saffron, oil, pepper, turmeric and salt. (See pages 178 and 333)

Sir Vâ'vij

garlic leaf, egg, oil and salt. (See pages 182 and 334)

Tah Bur'yân

potato, sour orange juice, rice flour, egg, onion, oil, pepper, turmeric and salt. (See pages 186 and 335)

Tor'sh-e Ta'reh

herbs (including spinach, coriander, dock, garlic leaf, scallion, leek, dill, mint, eryngium planum and ziziphora), rice

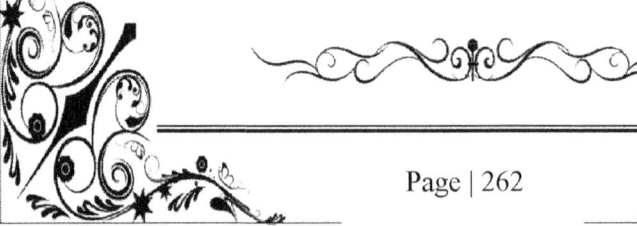

flour, egg, sour orange juice, oil pepper and salt. (See pages 190 and 336)

Iranian Side Items
Alphabetical order

Bu'râ'ni-e Es'fe'nâj
spinach, yogurt and salt. (See pages 196 and 337)

Dough
sour yogurt, Da'lâr and salt. (See pages 200 and 255)

Mâs't-o Khi'yâr
cucumber, yogurt, Da'lâr, garlic, raisin, walnut, pepper and salt. (See pages 204 and 338)

Sâ'lâd Shi'ra'zi
cucumber, tomato, onion, lemon juice, pepper, salt. (See pages 208 and 339)

Sâ'lâ'd-e Fasl
lettuce, red cabbage, white cabbage, cucumber, tomato, carrot, mayonnaise, lemon juice and salt. (See pages 212 and 340)

Gilanian Side Items
Alphabetical order

Bu'râ'ni-e Bâ'dem'jân
eggplant, sour yogurt, garlic and salt. (See pages 218 and

341)

Kâl Ka'bâb

eggplant, walnut, sour pomegranate seed, garlic, ground angelica, pepper and salt. (See pages 222, 342 and 343)

Zey'tun Par'var'deh

herbs (including coriander, parsley, eryngium planum, ziziphora, mint and leek), olive, walnut, pomegranate paste and garlic. (See pages 226 and 344)

Pickles

Alphabetical order

Tor'shi-e Bâ'dem'jân Chu'châgh

herb (eryngium planum), eggplant, garlic, vinegar, ground angelica, pepper and salt. (See pages 232, 345 and 346)

Tor'shi-e Li'teh

herbs (including mint, sweet basil, tarragon, savory and coriander), eggplant, garlic, vinegar, spicy green pepper, ground angelica, pepper and salt. (See page 236)

Others

Alphabetical order

Da'lâr (*Na'ma'k-e Sabz*)

herbs (including coriander, mint, ziziphora and eryngium planum), salt. (See pages 242 and 347)

Ko'lo'bij Nân

pumpkin, wheat flour, egg, sugar, yogurt (or milk), walnut, raisin, oil and salt. (See pages 242 and 348)

So's-e Ger'du

herbs (including mint, leek, ziziphora, parsley and coriander), walnut, garlic, sour pomegranate paste, pepper and salt. (See pages 250 and 349)

Table 1: Cooking Ingredients List
Alphabetical order

No.	Ingredients	In Farsi	Phonetics
1	almond	بادام	bâ'dâm
2	animal oil	روغن حیوانی	roug'han hey'vâ'ni
3	ashkeneh / eshkeneh	اشکنه	ash'ke'neh / esh'ke'neh
4	barberry	زرشک	ze'reshk
5	bean	لوبیا	lu'bi'yâ
6	beet green	برگ چغندر	bar'g-e cho'ghan'dar
7	bell pepper	فلفل دلمه ای	fel'fel dol'me'i
8	black beauty eggplant	بادمجان دلمه ای	bâ'dem'jân dol'me'i
9	black-eyed bean	لوبیا چشم بلبلی	lu'bi'yâ cheshm bol'bo'li
10	bread	نان	nân
11	breakfast cheese	پنیر صبحانه	pa'ni'r-e sob'hâ'neh
12	brew saffron	دم کردن زعفران	dam kar'da'n-e zaˆ'fa'rân
13	butter	کره	ka'reh
14	carrot	هویج	ha'vij
15	chickpea	نخود	no'khod
16	chopped almond	بادام خُرد شده	bâ'dâ'm-e khord sho'deh
17	cinnamon	دارچین	dâr'chin
18	coriander	گشنیز	gesh'niz
19	creeping wood sorrel	تُرش واش	tor'sh-e wâsh
20	cress	شاهی	shâ'hi
21	crunchy rice	ته دیگ	tah dig
22	cucumber	خیار	khi'yâr
23	dalar	دلار	da'lâr
24	dock	نرشک	tor'shak
25	dough	دوغ	dugh
26	drained rice	برنج آبکش شده	be'ren'j-e âb'kesh sho'deh

No.	Ingredients	In Farsi	Phonetics
27	dried apricot	زردآلوی خشک شده	zard'â'lu'y-e khoshk sho'deh
28	dried dill	شوید خشک شده	she'vi'd-e khoshk sho'deh
29	dried lime	لیمو امانی	li'mu a'mâ'ni
30	dried mint	نعنای خشک شده	na^'nâ'y-e khoshk sho'deh
31	egg	تخم مرغ	tokh'm-e morgh
32	eggplant	بادمجان	bâ'dem'jân
33	eryngium planum	چوچاق	chu'châgh
34	fava bean	باقلا (باقالی)	bâ'ghe'lâ (bâ'ghâ'li)
35	fenugreek	شنبلیله	shan'be'li'leh
36	fresh dill	شوید تازه	she'vi'd-e tâ'zeh
37	garlic clove	(۱) حبه سیر	(1) hab'be sir
38	garlic head	(۱) بوته سیر	(1) bu'teh sir
39	garlic leaf	برگ سیر	bar'ge sir
40	golden prune	آلو بخارا (آلو مشهد)	â'lu bo'khâ'râ (â'lu mash'had)
41	grain	حبوبات	ho'bu'bât
42	gram flour	آرد نخودچی	âr'd-e no'khod'chi
43	grated cucumber	خیار رنده شده	khi'yâ'r-e ran'deh sho'deh
44	green bean	لوبیا استانبلی	lu'bi'yâ s'tân'bo'li
45	green onion	پیازچه	pi'yâz'cheh
46	ground angelica	گلپر سابیده شده	gol'pa'r-e sâ'bi'deh sho'deh
47	ground cardamom	هل سابیده شده	he'l-e sâ'bi'deh sho'deh
48	ground cinnamon	دارچین سابیده شده	dâr'chi'n-e sâ'bi'deh sho'deh
49	herb	سبزی	sab'zi
50	hot ketchup	سس قرمز تند	so's-e gher'me'ze tond
51	kidney bean	لوبیا قرمز	lu'bi'yâ gher'mez
52	leek	تره	ta'reh
53	lemon balm	وارمبو	vâ'ram'bu
54	lemon juice	آبلیمو	âb'li'mu
55	lentil	عدس	a'das

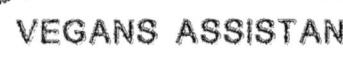

No.	Ingredients	In Farsi	Phonetics
56	lettuce	کاهو	kâ'hu
57	lima bean	لوبیا کشاورزی	lu'bi'yâ ke'shâ'var'zi
58	mayonnaise	سس مایونز	so's-e mâ'yo'nez
59	milk	شیر	shir
60	mint	نعنا	naˆ'nâˆ
61	mung bean	ماش	mâsh
62	oil	روغن	rou'ghan
63	olive oil	روغن زیتون	rou'ghan zey'tun
64	olive	زیتون	zey'tun
65	onion	پیاز	pi'yâz
66	parsley	جعفری	jaˆ'fe'ri
67	pasteurized	کشک	kashk
68	pasteurized curd	کشک پاستوریزه	kash'k-e pâs'to'ri'zeh
69	pea	نخود فرنگی	no'khod fa'ran'gi
70	peeled sesame	کنجد بدون پوست	kon'je'de be'du'ne pust
71	peeled wheat	گندم بدون پوست	gan'do'me be'du'ne pust
72	pennyroyal	پونه	pu'neh
73	pepper	فلفل	fel'fel
74	pickled garlic	ترشی سیر	tor'shi'y-e sir
75	pickle	ترشی	tor'shi
76	pinto bean	لوبیا چیتی	lu'bi'yâ chi'ti
77	pistachio	پسته	pes'teh
78	pomegranate	انار	a'nâr
79	potato	سیب زمینی	sib za'mi'ni
80	prune	آلوی خشک شده	â'lu'ye khoshk
81	pumpkin	کدو	ka'du
82	radish	تربچه	to'rob'cheh
83	raisin	کشمش	kesh'mesh
84	raw fava bean	باقلای خام (باقالی خام)	bâ'ghe'lâ'ye khâm

VEGETARIAN COOKBOOK

No.	Ingredients	In Farsi	Phonetics
85	red bean	لوبیا قرمز	lu'bi'yâ gher'mez
86	red cabbage	کلم قرمز	ka'lam gher'mez
87	rice	برنج	be'renj
88	rice	پلو	Po'low
89	rice flour	آرد برنج	âr'd-e be'renj
90	rose water	گلاب	go'lâb
91	saffron	زعفران	zaˆ'fa'rân
92	salt	نمک	na'mak
93	savory	مرزه	mar'zeh
94	scallion	پیازچه	pi'yâz'cheh
95	sesame oil	روغن کنجد	rou'gha'n-e kon'jed
96	shallot yogurt	ماست موسیر	mâst-e mu'sir
97	sour	ترش	torsh
98	sour greengage plum	گوجه سبز ترش	gou'jeh sab'z-e torsh
99	sour orange juice	آب نارنج ترش	âb nâ'renj-e torsh
100	sour plum paste	رب آلوچه ترش	ro'b-e â'lu'che'y-e torsh
101	sour pomegranate paste	رب انار ترش	ro'b-e a'nâ'r-e torsh
102	sour pomegranate seed	دانه انار ترش	dâ'ne'ye a'nâ'r-e torsh
103	sour yogurt	ماست ترش	mâs't-e torsh
104	spaghetti	ماکارونی	mâ'kâ'ro'ni
105	sparkling soft drinks	نوشابه های گازدار	nu'shâ'be'hâ'y-e gâz'dâr
106	spicy green pepper	فلفل سبز تند	fel'fel sab'z-e tond
107	spinach	اسفناج	es'fe'nâj
108	split pea	لپه	lap'pe
109	stalk of celery	کرفس	ka'rafs
110	steeped saffron	زعفران آب شده	zaˆ'fa'râ'n-e dam kar'deh
111	sugar	شکر	she'kâr
112	sweet basil	ریحان	rey'hân
113	tarragon	ترخون	tar'khum

No.	Ingredients	In Farsi	Phonetics
114	thick yogurt	ماست چکیده	mâs't-e che'ki'deh
115	thin noodle	رشته ی آش	resh'te'y-e âsh
116	thyme	آویشن	â'vi'shan
117	tomato	گوجه	gou'jeh
118	tomato paste	رب گوجه فرنگی	ro'b-e gou'jeh fa'ran'gi
119	turmeric	زردچوبه	zard'chu'beh
120	unripe grape	غوره عسگری	ghu'reh as'ga'ri
121	vegetable	سبزی خوردن	sab'zi khor'dan
122	verjuice	آبغوره	âb'ghu'reh
123	vinegar	سرکه	ser'keh
124	walnut	گردو	ger'du
125	walnut dip	سس گردو	so's-e ger'du
126	water	آب	âb
127	wheat flour	آرد گندم	âr'd-e gan'dom
128	white bean	لوبیا سفید	lu'bi'yâ se'fid
129	white cabbage	کلم سفید	ka'lam se'fid
130	white radish	تُرب سفید	to'rob se'fid
131	yogurt	ماست	mâst
132	ziziphora	کاکوتی	kâ'ku'ti

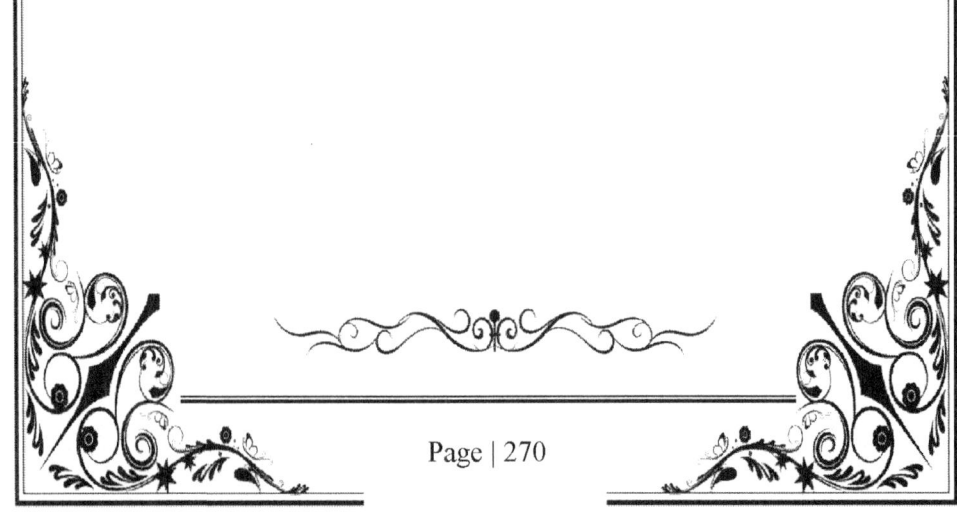

VEGETARIAN COOKBOOK

Nutrition facts

Percent Daily Values are based on a 2,000 calorie diet. Your daily values may be higher or lower depending on your calorie needs.

Sources include for tables 1, 2 and 3:

USDA Food Composition Databases.
United States
Department of Agriculture Agricultural Research Service.
website address: ndb.nal.usda.gov

and

nutritionix app
website address: nutritionix.com

Table 2: Nutrition facts (Calories, Total fat, Protein and Sugar)
Percent Daily Values are based on a 2,000-calorie diet.
Alphabetical order

No.	Ingredients	Calories	Total Fat	Protein	Sugar
1	almond (100g / 3½oz)	598	53g	21g	4.9g
		Daily value%	82%		
2	barberry (5 tbsp)	98	0.1g	4g	13g
			0%		
3	bean (1 cup)	239	0.9g	12g	20g
			1%		
4	beet green (100g / 3½oz)	19	0.2g	1.8g	1.1g
			0%	3%	
5	bell pepper (1 small / 74g)	15	0.1g	0.6g	1.8g
			0%	1%	

VEGANS ASSISTANT

No.	Ingredients	Calories	Total Fat	Protein	Sugar
6	black-eyed bean (100g / 3½oz)	116	0.5g 1%	7.7g	3.3g
7	butter (100g / 3½oz)	717	81g 124%	0.9g 1%	0.1g
8	carrot (100g / 3½oz)	35	0.2g 0%	0.8g	3.5g
9	chickpea (100g / 3½oz)	364	6g 9%	19g 38%	11g
10	chopped almond (100g / 3½oz)	576	49g 75%	21g 42%	3.9g
11	cinnamon (1 tbsp / 7.8g)	19	0.1g 0%	0.3g	0.2g
12	coriander (100g / 3½oz)	23	0.5g 0%	2.1g 4%	0.9g
13	cress (100g / 3½oz)	32	0.7g 1%	2.6g 5%	4.4g
14	cucumber (1 medium)	30	0.2g 0%	1.3g	3.4g
15	dough (100g / 3½oz)	445	25g 38%	3g	0g
16	dried apricot (100g / 3½oz)	241	0.5g 1%	3.4g	53g
17	dried dill (1 tbsp)	7.8	0.1g 0%	0.6g	0g
18	dried mint (1 tbsp)	4.6	0.1g 0%	0.3g	0g
19	egg (1 medium)	63	4.2g 6%	5.5g	0.2g
20	eggplant (1 medium)	198	1.3g 2%	4.7g	18g
21	fava bean (1 cup)	187	0.7g 1%	13g	3.1g
22	fenugreek (100g / 3½oz)	323	6g 9%	23g 46%	—
23	fresh dill (100g / 3½oz)	43	1.1g 2%	3.5g	0g

No.	Ingredients	Calories	Total Fat	Protein	Sugar
24	garlic clove (1 clove)	4.5	0g 0%	0.2g	0g
25	garlic head (1 head)	45	0.1g 0%	1.9g	0.3g
26	golden prune (100g / 3½oz)	240	0.4g 0%	2.2g 4%	38g
27	gram flour (1 cup)	356	6.2g 10%	21g	10g
28	green bean (4oz)	40	0.3g 0%	2.1g	4.1g
29	green onion (100g / 3½oz)	32	0.2g 0%	1.8g	2.3g
30	ground cinnamon (1 tbsp)	19	0.1g 0%	0.3g	0.2g
31	herb (100g / 3½oz)	23	0.6g 1%	3.1g	0.3g
32	hot ketchup (100g / 3½oz)	112	0.2g 0%	1.3g 2%	22g
33	kidney bean (1 cup / 184g)	613	1.5g 2%	43g 86%	4.1g
34	leek (1 cup)	54	0.3g 0%	1.3g 2%	3.5g
35	lemon juice (1 cup / 244g)	53	0.6g 0%	0.9g 1%	6g
36	lentil (100g / 3½oz)	116	0.4g 0%	9g 18%	1.8g
37	lima bean (100g / 3½oz)	115	0.4g 0%	8g 16%	2.9g
38	mayonnaise (1 tbsp / 13.8g)	94	10g 15%	0.1g 0%	0.1g
39	milk (1 cup / 244g)	103	2.4g 3%	8g 16%	13g
40	mint (100g / 3½oz)	44	0.7g 1%	3.3g	0g
41	mung bean (1 cup / 207g)	718	2.4g 3%	49g 98%	14g

VEGANS ASSISTANT

No.	Ingredients	Calories	Total Fat	Protein	Sugar
42	oil (1 tbsp / 13.6g)	120	14g 21%	0g 0%	0g
43	olive oil (1 tbsp / 13.5g)	119	14g 21%	0g 0%	0g
44	olive (100g / 3½oz)	115	11g 17%	0.8g	0g
45	onion (1 medium / 110g)	44	0.1g 0%	1.2g 2%	4.7g
46	parsley (100g / 3½oz)	36	0.8g 1%	3g 6%	0.9g
47	pasteurized curd (4oz / 113g)	111	4.9g 7%	13g 26%	3g
48	pea (100g / 3½oz)	81	0.4g 0%	5g 10%	6g
49	peeled sesame (100g / 3½oz)	573	50g 76%	18g 36%	0.3g
50	pepper (1 tsp, ground / 2.3g)	6	0.1g 0%	0.2g 0%	0g
51	pinto bean (100g / 3½oz)	347	1.2g 1%	21g 42%	2.1g
52	pistachio (100g / 3½oz)	562	45g 69%	20g 40%	8g
53	potato (1 medium / 213g)	77	0.1g 0%	2g 4%	0.8g
54	pumpkin (100g / 3½oz)	21	0.1g 0%	1g 2%	2.8g
55	radish (100g / 3½oz)	16	0.1g 0%	0.7g 1%	1.9g
56	raisin (100g / 3½oz)	299	0.5g 0%	3.1g 6g	59g
57	raw fava bean (100g / 3½oz)	110	0.4g 1%	7.6g	1.8g
58	red bean (1 cup)	225	0.9g 1%	15g	0.6g
59	red cabbage (100g / 3½oz)	29	0.1g 0%	1.5g	3.3g

No.	Ingredients	Calories	Total Fat	Protein	Sugar
60	rice (Basmati rice / 1 cup)	205	0.4g 1%	4.3g	0.1g
61	rice flour (1 cup / 158g)	578	2.2g 3%	9g 18%	0.2g
62	saffron (1 tsp / 0.7g)	2	0g 0%	0.1g 0%	
63	salt (1 tsp / 6g)	0	0g 0%	0g 0%	0g
64	savory (100g / 3½oz)	272	5.9g 9%	6.7g	0g
65	scallion (100g / 3½oz)	32	0.2g 0%	1.8g 3%	2.3g
66	spaghetti (100g / 3½oz)	150	0.6g 1%	5.3g	1.1g
67	spinach (100g / 3½oz)	23	0.3g 0%	3g	0.4g
68	split pea (1 cup / 197g)	671	2.3g 3%	48g 96%	16g
69	stalk of celery (1 stalk)	6.8	0.1g 0%	0.3g	0.9g
70	sugar (1 tsp / 4.2g)	16	0g 0%	0g	4.2g
71	sweet basil (100g / 3½oz)	22	0.6g 0%	3.2g 6%	0.3g
72	tarragon (100g / 3½oz)	295	7.2g 11%	23g	0g
73	thyme (1 tsp / 0.8g)	1	0mg 0%	0g 0%	
74	tomato (1 medium whole)	22	0.3g 0%	1.1g	3.2g
75	tomato paste (1 tbsp)	13	0.1g 0%	0.7g	1.9g
76	turmeric (1 tbsp)	24	0.7g 1%	0.5g 1%	0.2g
77	verjuice (1 tbsp / 20ml)	11	1g 1%	1g 1%	2g

No.	Ingredients	Calories	Total Fat	Protein	Sugar
78	vinegar (1 cup)	43	0g 0%	0g	0.1g
79	walnut (1 cup, ground / 80g)	523	52g 80%	12g 24%	2.1g
80	water (1 cup / 237g)	0	0g 0%	0g 0%	
81	wheat (1 cup)	632	3.7g 6%	30g	0.8g
82	white bean (100g / 3½oz)	67	0.7g 1%	6g 12%	
83	white cabbage (100g / 3½oz)	23	0.1g 0%	1.3g	2.8g
84	white radish (1 radish / 338g)	61	0.3g 0%	2g 4%	8g
85	yogurt (Greek, nonfat)	59	0.4g 0%	10g 20%	3.2g

Table 3: Nutrition facts (Cholesterol, Sodium, Potassium and Carbs)
Percent Daily Values are based on a 2,000-calorie diet.
Alphabetical order

No.	Ingredients	Cholesterol	Sodium	Potassium	Carbs
1	almond (100g / 3½oz)	0mg	498mg	713.0mg	21g
		Daily value = 0%	21%		7%
2	barberry (5 tbsp)	0mg	83mg		22g
		0%	3%		7%
3	bean (1 cup)	0mg	871mg	569mg	54g
		0%	36%		18%
4	beet green (100g / 3½oz)	0mg	213mg	379mg	3.7g
		0%	8%	10%	1%
5	bell pepper (1 small / 74g)	0mg	2.2mg	129.5mg	3.4g
		0%	0%	3%	1%
6	black-eyed bean (100g / 3½oz)	0mg	4mg	278mg	21g
		0%	0%		7%
7	butter (100g / 3½oz)	215mg	11mg	24mg	0.1g
		71%	0%	0%	0%
8	carrot (100g / 3½oz)	0mg	58mg	235.0mg	8.2g
		0%	2%		3%
9	chickpea (100g / 3½oz)	0mg	24mg	875mg	61g
		0%	1%	25%	20%
10	chopped almond (100g / 3½oz)	0mg	1mg	705mg	22g
		0%	0%	20%	7%
11	cinnamon (1 tbsp / 7.8g)	0mg	0.8mg	33.6mg	6g
		0%	0%	0%	2%
12	coriander (100g / 3½oz)	0mg	46mg	521mg	3.7g
		0%	1%	14%	1%
13	cress (100g / 3½oz)	0mg	14mg	606mg	6g
		0%	0%	17%	2%
14	cucumber (1 medium)	0mg	4mg	295.5mg	7.3g
		0%	0%		2%

No.	Ingredients	Cholesterol	Sodium	Potassium	Carbs
15	dough (100g / 3½oz)	0mg	409mg	73.0mg	51g
		0%	17%		17%
16	dried apricots (100g / 3½oz)	0mg	10mg	1162.5mg	63g
		0%	0%		21%
17	dried dill (1 tbsp)	0mg	6.4mg	102.5mg	1.7g
		0%	0%		1%
18	dried mint (1 tbsp)	0mg	5.5mg	30.8mg	0.8g
		0%	0%		0%
19	egg (1 medium)	164mg	62mg	60.7mg	0.3g
		55%	3%		
20	eggplant (1 medium)	0mg	5.7mg	696.2mg	49g
		1%	0%		16%
21	fava bean (1 cup)	0mg	410mg	455.6mg	33g
		0%	17%		11%
22	fenugreek (100g / 3½oz)	0mg	67mg	770mg	58g
		0%	2%	22%	19%
23	fresh dill (100g / 3½oz)	0mg	61mg	738.0mg	7g
		0%	3%		2%
24	garlic clove (1 clove)	0mg	0.5mg	12.0mg	1g
		0%	0%		0%
25	garlic head (1 head)	0mg	5.1mg	120.3mg	9.9g
		0%	0%		3%
26	golden prune (100g / 3½oz)	0mg	2mg	732mg	64g
		0%	0%		21%
27	gram flour (1 cup)	0mg	59mg	778.3mg	53g
		0%	2%		18%
28	green bean (4oz)	0mg	1.1mg	165.6mg	8.9g
		0%	0%		3%
29	green onion (100g / 3½oz)	0mg	16mg	276.0mg	7.3g
		0%	1%		2%
30	ground cinnamon (1 tbsp)	0mg	0.8mg	33.6mg	6.3g
		0%	0%		2%

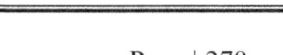

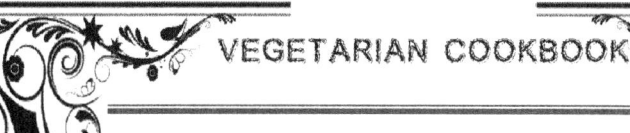

No.	Ingredients	Cholesterol	Sodium	Potassium	Carbs
31	herb (100g / 3½oz)	0mg	4mg	295.0mg	2.7g
		0%	0%		1%
32	hot ketchup (100g / 3½oz)	0mg	907mg	315mg	26g
		0%	37%	9%	
33	kidney bean (1 cup / 184g)	0mg	44.2mg	2587mg	110g
		0%	1%	73%	36%
34	leek (1 cup)	0mg	17.8mg	160.2mg	13g
		0%	0%	4%	4%
35	lemon juice (1 cup / 244g)	0mg	2.4mg	251.3mg	17g
		0%	0%	7%	5%
36	lentil (100g / 3½oz)	0mg	2mg	369mg	20g
		0%	0%	10%	6%
37	lima bean (100g / 3½oz)	0mg	2mg	5.8mg	21g
		0%	0%	14%	7%
38	mayonnaise (1 tbsp / 13.8g)	5.8mg	87.6mg	2.8mg	0.1g
		1%	3%	0%	0%
39	milk (1 cup / 244g)	12.2mg	107.4mg	366mg	12g
		4%	4%	10%	4%
40	mint (100g / 3½oz)	0mg	30mg	458.0mg	8.4g
		0%	1%		3%
41	mung bean (1 cup / 207g)	0mg	31.1mg	2579.2mg	130g
		0%	1%	73%	43%
42	oil (1 tbsp / 13.6g)	0mg	0mg		0g
		0%	0%		0%
43	olive oil (1 tbsp / 13.5g)	0mg	0.3mg	0.1mg	0g
		0%	0%	0%	0%
44	olive (100g / 3½oz)	0mg	735mg	8.0mg	6.3g
		0%	31%		2%
45	onion (1 medium / 110g)	0mg	4.4mg	160.6mg	10g
		0%	0%	4%	3%
46	parsley (100g / 3½oz)	0mg	56mg	554mg	6g
		0%	2%	15%	2%

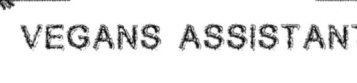

No.	Ingredients	Cholesterol	Sodium	Potassium	Carbs
47	pasteurized curd (4oz / 113g)	19.2mg	411.3mg	117.5mg	3.8g
		6%	17%	3%	1%
48	pea (100g / 3½oz)	0mg	5mg	244mg	14g
		0%	0%	6%	4%
49	peeled sesame (100g / 3½oz)	0mg	11mg	468mg	23g
		0%	0%	13%	7%
50	pepper (1 tsp, ground / 2.3g)	0mg	0.5mg	30.6mg	1.5g
		0%	0%	0%	0%
51	pinto bean (100g / 3½oz)	0mg	12mg	1393mg	63g
		0%	0%	39%	21%
52	pistachio (100g / 3½oz)	0mg	1mg	1025mg	28g
		0%	0%	29%	9%
53	potato (1 medium / 213g)	0mg	6mg	421mg	17g
		0%	0%	12%	5%
54	pumpkin (100g / 3½oz)	0mg	1mg	340mg	7g
		0%	0%	9%	2%
55	radish (100g / 3½oz)	0mg	39mg	233mg	3.4g
		0%	1%	6%	1%
56	raisin (100g / 3½oz)	0mg	11mg	749mg	79g
		0%	0%	21%	26%
57	raw fava bean (100g / 3½oz)	0mg	241mg	268.0mg	20g
		0%	10%		7%
58	red bean (1 cup)	0mg	1.8mg	716.9mg	40g
		0%	0%		13%
59	red cabbage (100g / 3½oz)	0mg	28mg	262.0	6.9g
		0%	1%		2%
60	rice (Basmati rice / 1 cup)	0mg	1.6mg	55.3mg	45g
		0%	0%		15%
61	rice flour (1 cup / 158g)	0mg	0mg	120.1mg	127g
		0%	0%	3%	42%
62	saffron (1 tsp / 0.7g)	0mg	1mg	12.1mg	0.5g
		0%	0%	0%	0%

No.	Ingredients	Cholesterol	Sodium	Potassium	Carbs
63	salt (1 tsp / 6g)	0mg	2325.5mg	0.5mg	0g
		0%	96%	0%	0%
64	savory (100g / 3½oz)	0mg	24mg	1051mg	69g
		0%	1%		23%
65	scallion (100g / 3½oz)	0mg	16mg	276mg	7g
		0%	0%	7%	2%
66	spaghetti (100g / 3½oz)	0mg	4.8mg	90.3mg	30g
		0%	0%		10%
67	spinach (100g / 3½oz)	0mg	70mg	466.0mg	3.8g
		0%	3%		1%
68	split pea (1 cup / 197g)	0mg	29.6mg	1932.6mg	119g
		0%	1%	55%	39%
69	stalk of celery (1 stalk)	0mg	34mg	106.5mg	1.5g
		0%	1%		1%
70	sugar (1 tsp / 4.2g)	0mg	0mg	0.1mg	4.2g
		0%	0%	0%	1%
71	sweet basil (100g / 3½oz)	0mg	4mg	295mg	2.7g
		0%	0%	8%	0%
72	tarragon (100g / 3½oz)	0mg	62mg	3020mg	50g
		0%	3%		17%
73	thyme (1 tsp / 0.8g)	0mg	0.1mg	4.9mg	0.2g
		0%	0%	0%	0%
74	tomato (1 medium whole)	0mg	6.2mg	291.5mg	4.8g
		0%	0%		2%
75	tomato paste (1 tbsp)	0mg	9.4mg	162.2mg	3g
		0%	0%		1%
76	turmeric (1 tbsp)	0mg	2.6mg	171.7mg	4.4g
		0%	0%	4%	1%
77	verjuice (1 tbsp / 20ml)		1mg		3g
			0%		1%
78	vinegar (1 cup)	0mg	4.8mg	4.8mg	0.1g
		0%	0%	0%	0%

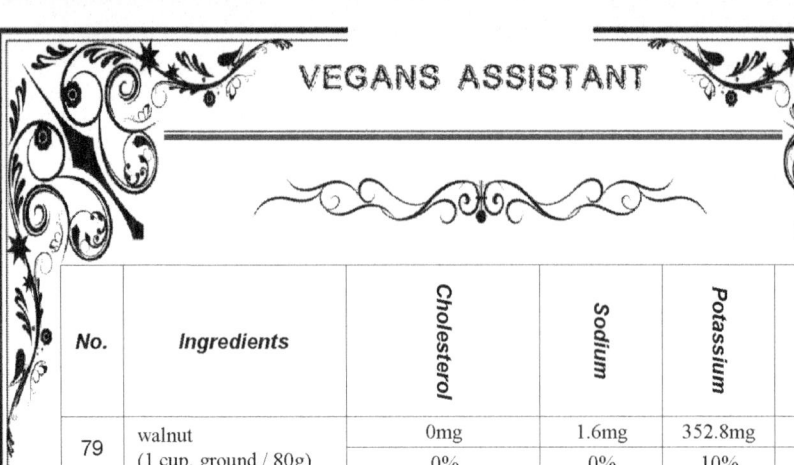

No.	Ingredients	Cholesterol	Sodium	Potassium	Carbs
79	walnut (1 cup, ground / 80g)	0mg	1.6mg	352.8mg	11g
		0%	0%	10%	3%
80	water (1 cup / 237g)		11.9mg		0g
			0%		0%
81	wheat (1 cup)	0mg	3.8mg	652.8mg	131g
		0%	0%		44%
82	white bean (100g / 3½oz)	0mg	13mg	307mg	13g
		0%	0%	8%	4%
83	white cabbage (100g / 3½oz)	0mg	8mg	196mg	5.5g
		0%	0%		2%
84	white radish (1 radish / 338g)	0mg	71mg	767.3mg	14g
		0%	2%	21%	4%
85	yogurt (Greek, nonfat)	5mg	36mg	141mg	3.6g
		1%	1%	4%	1%

Table 4: Nutrition facts (*Vitamins*)
Percent Daily Values are based on a 2,000-calorie diet.
Alphabetical order

No.	Ingredients	% Daily Value						
		Vitamin A	Vitamin C	Vitamin D	Vitamin B-6	Vitamin B-12	Calcium	Iron
1	almond (100g / 3½oz)	0%	0%				27%	21%
2	barberries (5 tbsp)	150%	23%				5.3%	11%
3	beans (1 cup)	5.5%	0%				8.6%	17%
4	beet greens (100g / 3½oz)	122%	50%	0%	5%	0%	5%	9%
5	bell pepper (1 small / 74g)	5%	99%	0%	10%	0%	0%	1%
6	black-eyed beans (100g / 3½oz)	0.3%	0.7%				2.4%	14%
7	butter (100g / 3½oz)	49%	0%	15%	0%	3%	2%	0%
8	carrot (100g / 3½oz)	341%	6%				3%	1.9%
9	chickpea (100g / 3½oz)	1%	6%	0%	25%	0%	10%	34%
10	chopped almonds (100g / 3½oz)	0%	0%	0%	5%	0%	26%	20%
11	cinnamon (1 tbsp / 7.8g)	0%	0%	0%	0%	0%	7%	3%
12	coriander (100g / 3½oz)	134%	45%	0%	5%	0%	6%	9%
13	cress (100g / 3½oz)	138%	115%	0%	10%	0%	8%	7%
14	cucumber (1 medium)	4.2%	9.4%				3.2%	3.1%

| No. | Ingredients | % Daily Value | | | | | | |
		Vitamin A	Vitamin C	Vitamin D	Vitamin B-6	Vitamin B-12	Calcium	Iron
15	dough (100g / 3½oz)	0%	0%				1%	5.7%
16	dried apricots (100g / 3½oz)	72%	1.7%				5.5%	15%
17	dried dill (1 tbsp)	3.6%	2.6%				5.5%	8.4%
18	dried mint (1 tbsp)	3.4%	0%				2.4%	7.8%
19	egg (1 medium)	4.8%	0%				2.5%	4.3%
20	eggplants (1 medium)	4.2%	12%				3.4%	7.9%
21	fava beans (1 cup)	0.5%	0.8%				6.1%	14%
22	fenugreek (100g / 3½oz)	1%	5%	0%	30%	0%	17%	186%
23	fresh dill (100g / 3½oz)	154%	142%				21%	37%
24	garlic clove (1 clove)	0%	1.6%				0.5%	0.3%
25	garlic head (1 head)	0.1%	16%				5.4%	2.8%
26	golden prunes (100g / 3½oz)	15%	1%	0%	10%	0%	4%	4%
27	gram flour (1 cup)	0.8%	0%				4.1%	25%
28	green beans (4oz)	14%	18%				5%	4.1%
29	green onion (100g / 3½oz)	20%	31%				7.2%	8.2%
30	ground cinnamon (1 tbsp)	0.5%	0.5%				7.8%	3.6%

No.	Ingredients	% Daily Value						
		Vitamin A	Vitamin C	Vitamin D	Vitamin B-6	Vitamin B-12	Calcium	Iron
31	herb (100g / 3½oz)	106%	30%				18%	18%
32	hot ketchup (100g / 3½oz)	10%	6%	0%	10%	0%	1%	2%
33	kidney bean (1 cup / 184g)	0%	13%	0%	35%	0%	26%	83%
34	leek (1 cup)	29%	17%	0%	10%	0%	5%	10%
35	lemon juice (1 cup / 244g)	0%	157%	0%	5%	0%	1%	1%
36	lentils (100g / 3½oz)	0%	2%	0%	10%	0%	1%	18%
37	lima beans	0%	0%	0%	10%	0%	1%	13%
38	mayonnaise (1 tbsp / 13.8g)	0%	0%	0%	0%	0%	0%	0%
39	milk (1 cup / 244g)	2%	0%	0%	5%	18%	30%	0%
40	mint (100g / 3½oz)	81%	22%				20%	66%
41	mung beans (1 cup / 207g)	4%	16%	0%	40%	0%	27%	77%
42	oil (1 tbsp / 13.6g)	0%	0%	0%	0%	0%	0%	0%
43	olive oil (1 tbsp / 13.5g)	0%	0%	0%	0%	0%	0%	0%
44	olive (100g / 3½oz)	8.1%	1.5%				8.8%	18%
45	onion (1 medium / 110g)	0%	13%	0%	5%	0%	2%	1%
46	parsley (100g / 3½oz)	168%	221%	0%	5%	0%	13%	34%

No.	Ingredients	% Daily Value						
		Vitamin A	Vitamin C	Vitamin D	Vitamin B-6	Vitamin B-12	Calcium	Iron
47	pasteurized curd (4oz / 113g)	3%	0%	0%	5%	8%	9%	0%
48	pea (100g / 3½oz)	15%	66%	0%	10%	0%	2%	8%
49	peeled sesame (100g / 3½oz)	0%	0%	0%	40%	0%	97%	81%
50	pepper (1 tsp, ground / 2.3g)	0%	0%	0%	0%	0%	1%	1%
51	pinto bean (100g / 3½oz)	0%	10%	0%	25%	0%	11%	28%
52	pistachio (100g / 3½oz)	8%	9%	0%	85%	0%	10%	21%
53	potato (1 medium / 213g)	0%	32%	0%	15%	0%	1%	4%
54	pumpkin (100g / 3½oz)	170%	15%	0%	5%	0%	2%	4%
55	radish (100g / 3½oz)	0%	24%	0%	5%	0%	2%	1%
56	raisins (100g / 3½oz)	0%	3%	0%	10%	0%	5%	10%
57	raw fava bean (100g / 3½oz)	0.3%	0.5%				3.6%	8.3%
58	red beans (1 cup)	0%	3.5%				6.2%	22%
59	red cabbage (100g / 3½oz)	0.7%	57%				4.2%	3.7%
60	rice (Basmati rice / 1 cup)	0%	0%				1.6%	11%
61	rice flour (1 cup / 158g)	0%	0%	0%	35%	0%	1%	3%
62	saffron (1 tsp / 0.7g)	0%	1%	0%	0%	0%	0%	0%

No.	Ingredients	% Daily Value						
		Vitamin A	Vitamin C	Vitamin D	Vitamin B-6	Vitamin B-12	Calcium	Iron
63	salt (1 tsp / 6g)	0%	0%	0%	0%	0%	0%	0%
64	savory (100g / 3½oz)	103%	83%				213%	210%
65	scallion (100g / 3½oz)	19%	31%	0%	5%	0%	7%	8%
66	spaghetti (100g / 3½oz)	0%	0%				1%	7.4%
67	spinach (100g / 3½oz)	210%	16%				14%	20%
68	split peas (1 cup / 197g)	5%	5%	0%	15%	0%	10%	48%
69	stalk of celery (1 stalk)	3.9%	3.8%				1.6%	0.9%
70	sugar (1 tsp / 4.2g)	0%	0%	0%	0%	0%	0%	0%
71	sweet basil (100g / 3½oz)	105%	30%	0%	10%	0%	17%	17%
72	tarragon (100g / 3½oz)	84%	83%				114%	179%
73	thyme (1 tsp / 0.8g)	0%	2%	0%	0%	0%	0%	0%
74	tomato (1 medium whole)	20%	28%				1.2%	1.8%
75	tomato paste (1 tbsp)	4.9%	5.8%				0.6%	2.6%
76	turmeric (1 tbsp)	0%	3%	0%	5%	0%	1%	15%
77	verjuice (8 fl. oz)	0%	48%				0%	0%
78	vinegar (1 cup)	0%	0%				1.4%	0.4%

VEGANS ASSISTANT

No.	Ingredients	% Daily Value						
		Vitamin A	Vitamin C	Vitamin D	Vitamin B-6	Vitamin B-12	Calcium	Iron
79	walnut (1 cup, ground / 80g)	0%	1%	0%	20%	0%	7%	12%
80	water (1 cup / 237g)						0%	0%
81	wheat (1 cup)	0.3%	0%				4.8%	38%
82	white beans (100g / 3½oz)	0%	31%	0%	10%	0%	1%	10%
83	white cabbage (100g / 3½oz)	1.6%	63%				4.8%	0.9%
84	white radish (1 radish / 338g)	0%	124%	0%	10%	0%	9%	7%
85	yogurt (Greek, nonfat)	0%	0%	0%	5%	13%	11%	0%

VEGETARIAN COOKBOOK

Table 5: Basic features (Timing Information)

No.	Name	Servings	To soak	To prep	To cook	Page
Iranian Cuisines						
1	Âsh Resh'teh	6	12 hr	40 min	6 hr	34
2	A'das Po'low	5	3 hr	30 min	2 hr	38
3	Es'tân'bo'li Po'low	6	3 hr	45 min	2 hr	42
4	Fe're'ni	5	-	-	20 min	46
5	Ha'lim	4	12 hr	-	2 hr	50
6	Kash'k-e Bâ'dem'jân	5	1 hr	1¼ hr	1¾ hr	54
7	Khu'râ'k-e A'da'si	5	2 hr	15 min	1½ hr	58
8	Khu'râ'k-e Na'khod (Âb Na'khod)	5	2 hr	15 min	7 hr	62
9	Ku'ku Sab'zi	4	-	20 min	40 min	66
10-1	Ku'ku Sib'za'mi'ni (with baked potato)	4	-	10 min	1¾ hr	70
10-2	Ku'ku Sib'za'mi'ni (with raw potato)	5	-	30 min	45 min	74
11	Mâ'kâ'ro'ni-e Sab'zi'jât	4	-	30 min	1 hr	78
12-1	Po'low: Âb'kesh method	5	3 hr	-	1 hr	84
12-2	Po'low: Ka'teh method	5	3 hr	-	50 min	88
13	Shir Be'renj	5	3 hr	-	50 min	92
14	Sho'leh Zard	4	12 hr	-	4 hr	96
Gilanian Cuisines						
15	Â'sh-e Ka'du	5	12 hr	20 min	3 hr	102
16	Â'sh-e Se'fid (Â'sh-e A'nâr)	5	3 hr	45 min	1 hr	106
17	Â'sh-e Torsh	5	3 hr	40 min	3 hr	110
18	Ash'ke'neh Ta'reh	6	-	15 min	1¼ hr	114
19	Bâdem'jân Kabâb	5	1 hr	15 min	1½ hr	118
20	Bâ'dem'jân Ta'reh	4	1 hr	30 min	45 min	122
21	Bâ'dem'jân Va'ra'gheh Bâ Gou'jeh	4	1 hr	15 min	1 hr	126
22	Bâ'ghe'lâ Ghâ'togh	4	-	1 hr	1 hr	130
23	Bâ'ghe'lâ Po'low Bâ Pa'nir Be'resh'teh	5	3 hr	30 min	1½ hr	134
24	Kho'resh't-e Ka'du	5	-	45 min	1¾ hr	138
25	Khu'li Ou (Hâ'li Ou)	4	-	20 min	40 min	142

VEGANS ASSISTANT

No.	Name	Servings	To soak	To prep	To cook	Page
26	Ku'ku Bâ'dem'jân	5	-	30 min	30 min	146
27	Ku'ku She'vid	4	-	15 min	45 min	150
28	Ku'ku Sir	4	-	15 min	45 min	154
29	La'gad Da'mo'jey	4	1 hr	30 min	1½ hr	158
30	Mâ'kâ'ro'ni Bâ Ja'fa'ri Vâ'ram'bu	4	-	20 min	45 min	162
31	Mir'zâ Ghâ'se'mi	4	-	1¼ hr	1 hr	166
32	Mor'ju Vâ'vij	4	-	-	2¼ hr	170
33	Om'let Bâ Sir	4	-	15 min	30 min	174
34	She'vid Po'low Bâ Pa'nir Be'resh'teh	5	3 hr	15 min	1½ hr	178
35	Sir Vâ'vij	4	-	10 min	30 min	182
36	Tah Bur'yân	4	-	20 min	1 hr	186
37	Tor'sh-e Ta'reh	4	-	10 min	30 min	190
Iranian Side Items						
38	Bu'râ'ni-e Es'fe'nâj	5	-	5 min	20 min	196
39	Dough	5	-	10 min	-	200
40	Mâs't-o Khi'yâr	5	-	30 min	-	204
41	Sâ'lâd Shi'ra'zi	4	-	30 min	-	208
42	Sâ'lâ'd-e Fasl	4	-	40 min	-	212
Gilanian Side Items						
43	Bu'râ'ni-e Bâ'dem'jân	5	-	-	40 min	218
44	Kâl Ka'bâb	5	-	10 min	1 hr	222
45	Zey'tun Par'var'deh	4	-	15 min	-	226
Pickles						
46	Tor'shi-e Bâ'dem'jân Chu'châgh	-	-	20 min	10 min	232
47	Tor'shi-e Li'teh	-	-	1½ hr	-	236
Others						
48	Da'lâr (Na'ma'k-e Sabz)	-	-	15 min	-	242
49	Ko'lo'bij Nân	5	-	15 min	1¼ hr	246
50	So's-e Ger'du	4	-	15 min	-	250

Table 6: Basic features (Difficulty)

No.	Name	Easy	Medium	Hard	Time Consuming	Page
			Difficulty			
Iranian Cuisines						
1	Âsh Resh'teh			✓	✓	34
2	A'das Po'low		✓		✓	38
3	Es'tân'bo'li Po'low		✓		✓	42
4	Fe're'ni	✓				46
5	Ha'lim			✓	✓	50
6	Kash'k-e Bâ'dem'jân		✓		✓	54
7	Khu'râ'k-e A'da'si	✓			✓	58
8	Khu'râ'k-e Na'khod (Âb Na'khod)	✓			✓	62
9	Ku'ku Sab'zi	✓			✓	66
10-1	Ku'ku Sib'za'mi'ni (with baked potato)	✓			✓	70
10-2	Ku'ku Sib'za'mi'ni (with raw potato)	✓			✓	74
11	Mâ'kâ'ro'ni-e Sab'zi'jât	✓			✓	78
12-1	Po'low: Âb'kesh method	✓			✓	84
12-2	Po'low: Ka'teh method	✓			✓	88
13	Shir Be'renj	✓				92
14	Sho'leh Zard			✓	✓	96
Gilanian Cuisines						
15	Â'sh-e Ka'du		✓		✓	102
16	Â'sh-e Se'fid (Â'sh-e A'nâr)		✓		✓	106
17	Â'sh-e Torsh		✓		✓	110
18	Ash'ke'neh Ta'reh	✓			✓	114
19	Bâdem'jân Kabâb		✓		✓	118
20	Bâ'dem'jân Ta'reh	✓			✓	122
21	Bâ'dem'jân Va'ra'gheh Bâ Gou'jeh	✓			✓	126
22	Bâ'ghe'lâ Ghâ'togh	✓			✓	130
23	Bâ'ghe'lâ Po'low Bâ Pa'nir Be'resh'teh	✓			✓	134
24	Kho'resh't-e Ka'du		✓		✓	138
25	Khu'li Ou (Hâ'li Ou)	✓				142

No.	Name	Difficulty			Time Consuming	Page
		Easy	Medium	Hard		
26	Ku'ku Bâ'dem'jân	✓			✓	146
27	Ku'ku She'vid	✓			✓	150
28	Ku'ku Sir	✓			✓	154
29	La'gad Da'mo'jey	✓			✓	158
30	Mâ'kâ'ro'ni Bâ Ja'fa'ri Vâ'ram'bu	✓				162
31	Mir'zâ Ghâ'se'mi		✓		✓	166
32	Mor'ju Vâ'vij		✓		✓	170
33	Om'let Bâ Sir	✓				174
34	She'vid Po'low Bâ Pa'nir Be'resh'teh	✓			✓	178
35	Sir Vâ'vij	✓				182
36	Tah Bur'yân	✓			✓	186
37	Tor'sh-e Ta'reh	✓				190
Iranian Side Items						
38	Bu'râ'ni-e Es'fe'nâj	✓				196
39	Dough	✓				200
40	Mâs't-o Khi'yâr	✓				204
41	Sâ'lâd Shi'ra'zi	✓				208
42	Sâ'lâ'd-e Fasl	✓				212
Gilanian Side Items						
43	Bu'râ'ni-e Bâ'dem'jân	✓				218
44	Kâl Ka'bâb		✓		✓	222
45	Zey'tun Par'var'deh	✓				226
Pickles						
46	Tor'shi-e Bâ'dem'jân Chu'châgh	✓			✓	232
47	Tor'shi-e Li'teh		✓		✓	236
Others						
48	Da'lâr (Na'ma'k-e Sabz)	✓				242
49	Ko'lo'bij Nân	✓			✓	246
50	So's-e Ger'du	✓				250

Table 7: Basic features (When should you eat the meals?)

No.	Name	Breakfast	Lunch	Dinner	Formal meal	Page
Iranian Cuisines						
1	Âsh Resh'teh			✓	✓	34
2	A'das Po'low		✓		✓	38
3	Es'tân'bo'li Po'low		✓		✓	42
4	Fe're'ni (as a first course)			✓	✓	46
4	Fe're'ni (as a main course)	✓		✓		46
5	Ha'lim	✓			✓	50
6	Kash'k-e Bâ'dem'jân			✓	✓	54
7	Khu'râ'k-e A'da'si			✓		58
8	Khu'râ'k-e Na'khod (Âb Na'khod)			✓		62
9	Ku'ku Sab'zi			✓		66
10-1	Ku'ku Sib'za'mi'ni (with baked potato)			✓		70
10-2	Ku'ku Sib'za'mi'ni (with raw potato)			✓		74
11	Mâ'kâ'ro'ni-e Sab'zi'jât			✓		78
12-1	Po'low: Âb'kesh method		✓	✓	✓	84
12-2	Po'low: Ka'teh method		✓	✓		88
13	Shir Be'renj	✓		✓		92
14	Sho'leh Zard (as a first course)			✓	✓	96
14	Sho'leh Zard (as a main course)			✓		96
Gilanian Cuisines						
15	Â'sh-e Ka'du			✓		102
16	Â'sh-e Se'fid (Â'sh-e A'nâr)			✓		106
17	Â'sh-e Torsh			✓		110
18	Ash'ke'neh Ta'reh		✓	✓		114
19	Bâdem'jân Kabâb		✓		✓	118
20	Bâ'dem'jân Ta'reh		✓	✓		122
21	Bâ'dem'jân Va'ra'gheh Bâ Gou'jeh		✓			126
22	Bâ'ghe'lâ Ghâ'togh		✓		✓	130
23	Bâ'ghe'lâ Po'low Bâ Pa'nir Be'resh'teh		✓			134

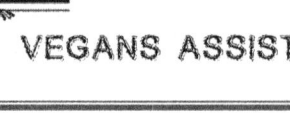

VEGANS ASSISTANT

No.	Name	Breakfast	Lunch	Dinner	Formal meal	Page
24	Kho'resh't-e Ka'du		✓	✓		138
25	Khu'li Ou (Hâ'li Ou)		✓			142
26	Ku'ku Bâ'dem'jân			✓		146
27	Ku'ku She'vid			✓		150
28	Ku'ku Sir		✓	✓		154
29	La'gad Da'mo'jey		✓			158
30	Mâ'kâ'ro'ni Bâ Ja'fa'ri Vâ'ram'bu			✓		162
31	Mir'zâ Ghâ'se'mi		✓	✓	✓	166
32	Mor'ju Vâ'vij		✓			170
33	Om'let Bâ Sir		✓	✓		174
34	She'vid Po'low Bâ Pa'nir Be'resh'teh		✓			178
35	Sir Vâ'vij		✓			182
36	Tah Bur'yân		✓			186
37	Tor'sh-e Ta'reh		✓	✓		190
	Iranian Side Items					
38	Bu'râ'ni-e Es'fe'nâj		✓	✓	✓	196
39	Dough		✓	✓	✓	200
40	Mâs't-o Khi'yâr		✓	✓	✓	204
41	Sâ'lâd Shi'ra'zi		✓	✓	✓	208
42	Sâ'lâ'd-e Fasl		✓	✓	✓	212
	Gilanian Side Items					
43	Bu'râ'ni-e Bâ'dem'jân		✓	✓	✓	218
44	Kâl Ka'bâb		✓	✓	✓	222
45	Zey'tun Par'var'deh		✓	✓	✓	226
	Pickles					
46	Tor'shi-e Bâ'dem'jân Chu'châgh		✓	✓	✓	232
47	Tor'shi-e Li'teh		✓	✓	✓	236
	Others					
48	Da'lâr (Na'ma'k-e Sabz)	-	-	-	-	242
49	Ko'lo'bij Nân	-	-	-	-	246
50	So's-e Ger'du	-	-	-	-	250

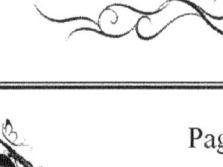

Table 8: Common abbreviations

Length	
millimeter	mm
centimeter	cm
inch	in
Volume	
teaspoon	tsp.
tablespoon	tbsp.
milliliter	ml
Weight	
ounce	oz
pound	lb
gram	g
kilogram	kg

Table 9: Equivalent measures (Length)

Inch	Millimeter	Centimeter
¼ in	~ 6 mm	-
½ in	~ 13 mm	-
1 in	-	~ 2.5 cm
2 in	-	~ 5 cm
3 in	-	~ 7.5 cm
6 in	-	~ 15 cm

Table 10: Equivalent measures (Volume)

U.S. tsp.	U.S. tbsp.	Milliliter (cc)
1 tsp.	⅓ tbsp.	~ 5 ml
2 tsp.	⅔ tbsp.	~ 10 ml
3 tsp.	1 tbsp.	~ 15 ml
4 tsp.	1⅓ tbsp.	~ 20 ml
5 tsp.	1⅔ tbsp.	~ 25 ml
6 tsp.	2 tbsp.	~ 30 ml

U.S. cup	U.S. tbsp.	Milliliter (cc)
¼ cup	4 tbsp.	~ 59 ml
½ cup	8 tbsp.	~ 118 ml
⅔ cup	11 tbsp.	~ 163 ml
1 cup	16 tbsp.	~ 237 ml
1½ cups	-	~ 355 ml
2 cups	-	~ 473 ml
3 cups	-	~ 710 ml
4 cups	-	~ 946 ml
5 cups	-	~ 1183 ml
6 cups	-	~ 1420 ml
7 cups	-	~ 1656 ml
8 cups	-	~ 1893 ml
9 cups	-	~ 2129 ml
10 cups	-	~ 2365 ml
15 cups	-	~ 3549 ml
20 cups	-	~ 4732 ml

Table 11: Equivalent measures (*Weight*)

Ounce	Pound	Gram
1 oz	-	~ 28g
2 oz	-	~ 57g
3 oz	-	~ 85g
3½ oz		~ 100g
4 oz	¼ lb	~ 113g
5 oz	-	~ 142g
6 oz	-	~ 170g
7 oz	-	~ 198g
8 oz	½ lb	~ 227g
9 oz	-	~ 255g
10 oz	-	~ 283g
11 oz	-	~ 311g
12 oz	¾ lb	~ 340g
13 oz	-	~ 369g
14 oz	-	~ 397g
15 oz	-	~ 425g
16 oz	1 lb	~ 454g
-	1¼ lb	~ 567g
-	1½ lb	~ 680g
-	1¾ lb	~ 794g
-	2 lb	~ 907g
-	2.2 lb	~ 1000g = ~ 1 kg

Iranian main course images
Âsh Resh'teh

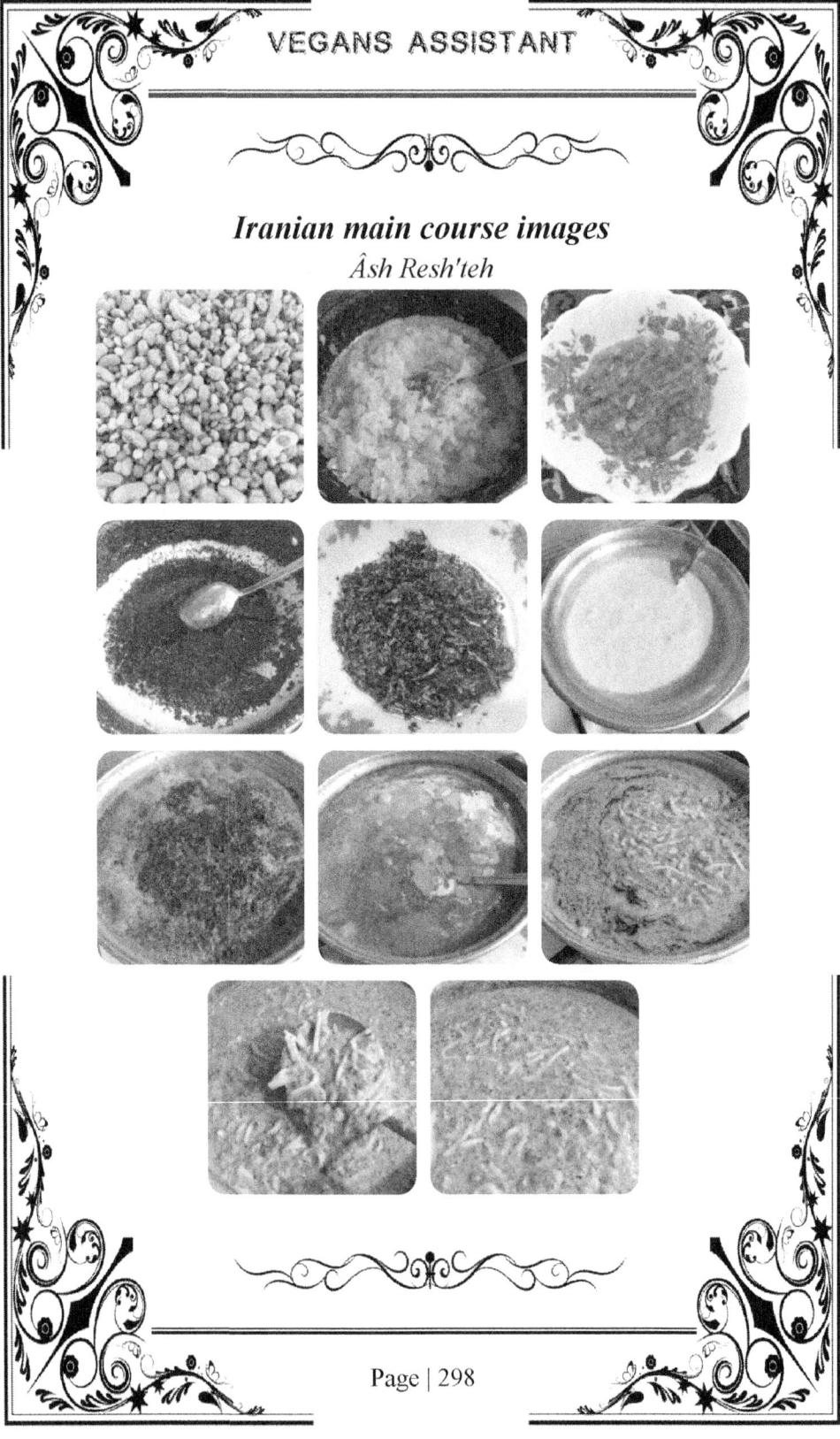

A'das Po'low

Es'tân'bo'li Po'low

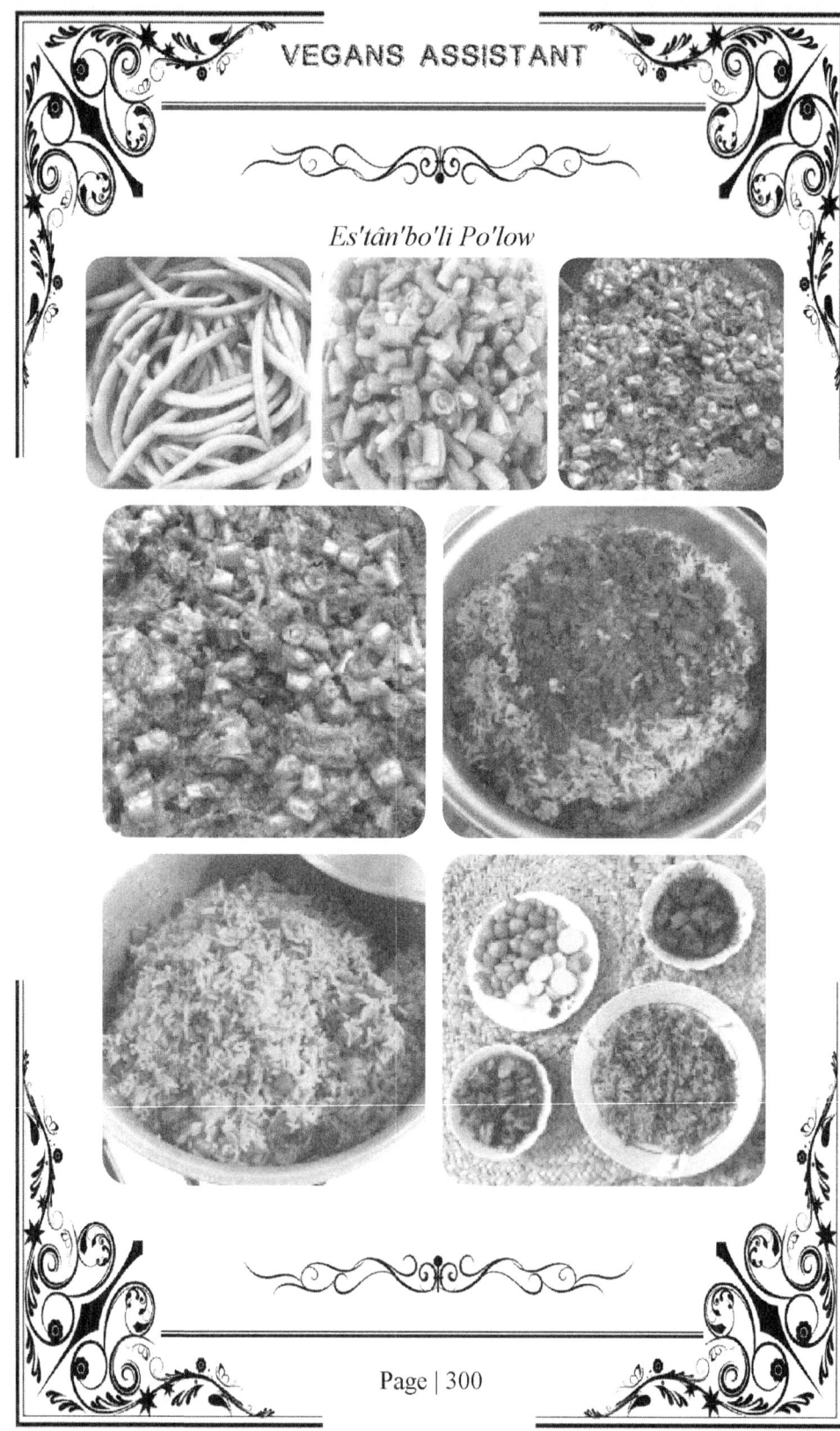

Fe're'ni

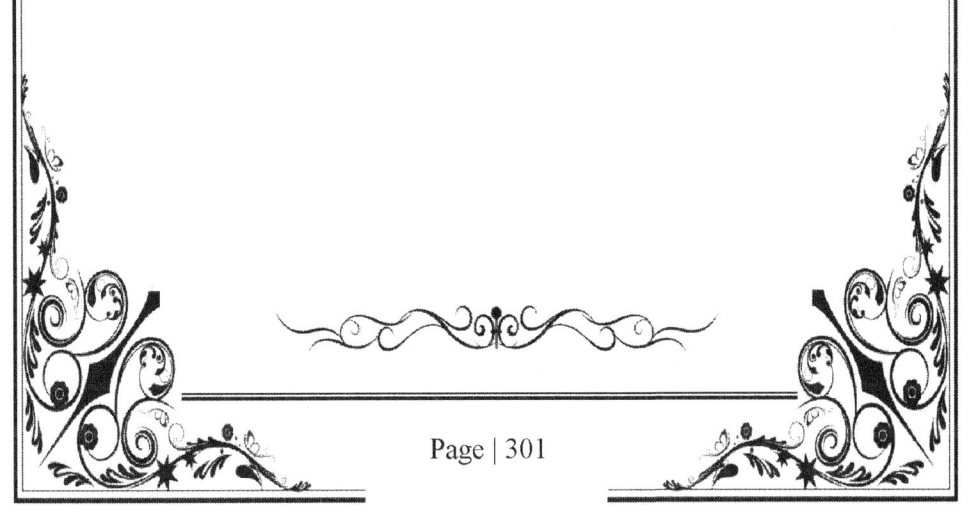

Ha'lim

Kash'k-e Bâ'dem'jân

Khu'râ'k-e A'da'si

Khu'râ'k-e Na'khod (Âb Na'khod)

Ku'ku Sab'zi

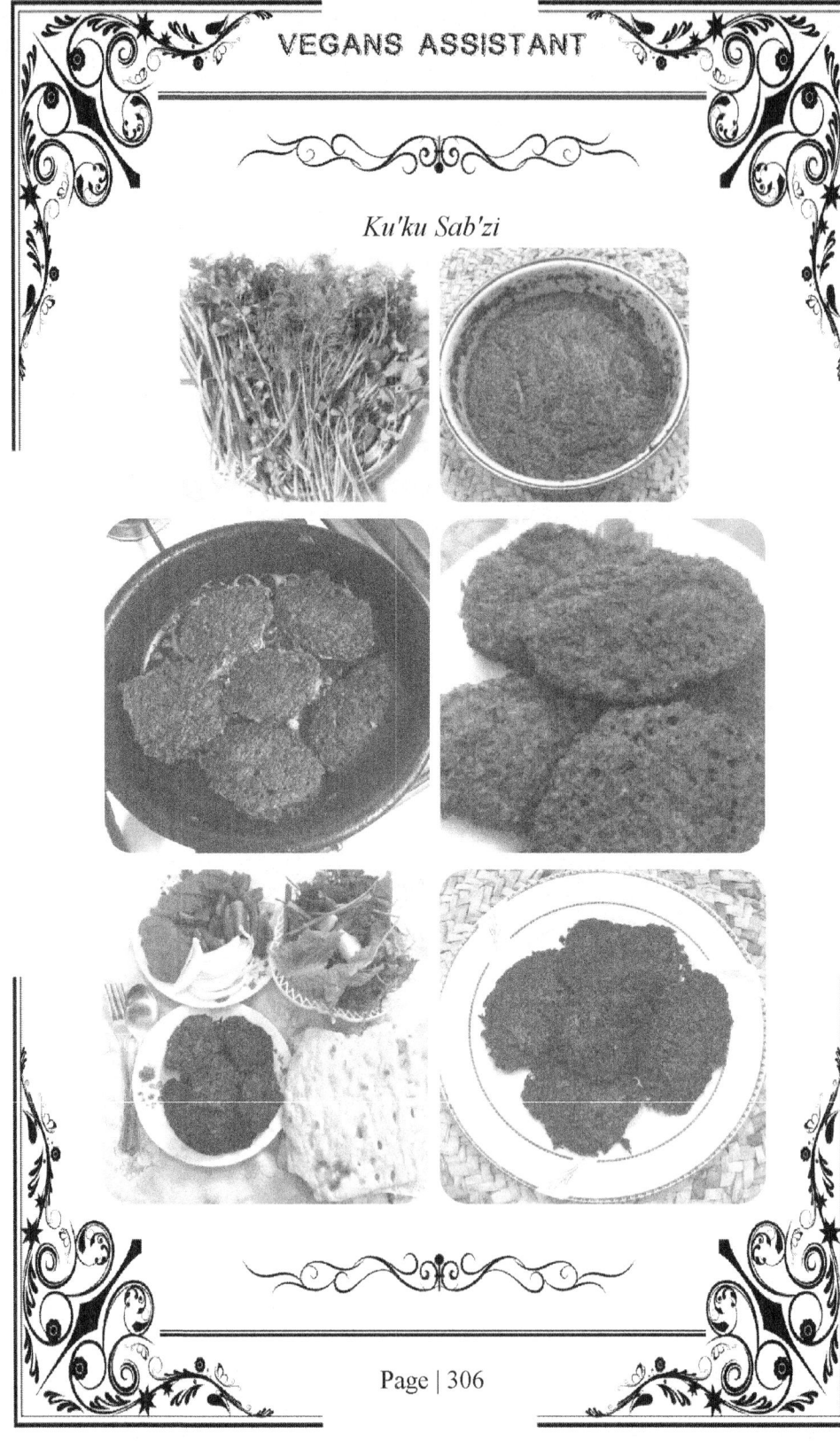

Ku'ku Sib Za'mi'ni (with baked potato)

Ku'ku Sib Za'mi'ni (with raw potato)

Mâ'kâ'ro'ni-e Sab'zi'jât

Po'low: Âb'kesh Method

Po'low: Ka'teh method

Shir Be'renj

Sho'leh Zard

Gilanian main course images

Â'sh-e Ka'du

Â'sh-e Torsh

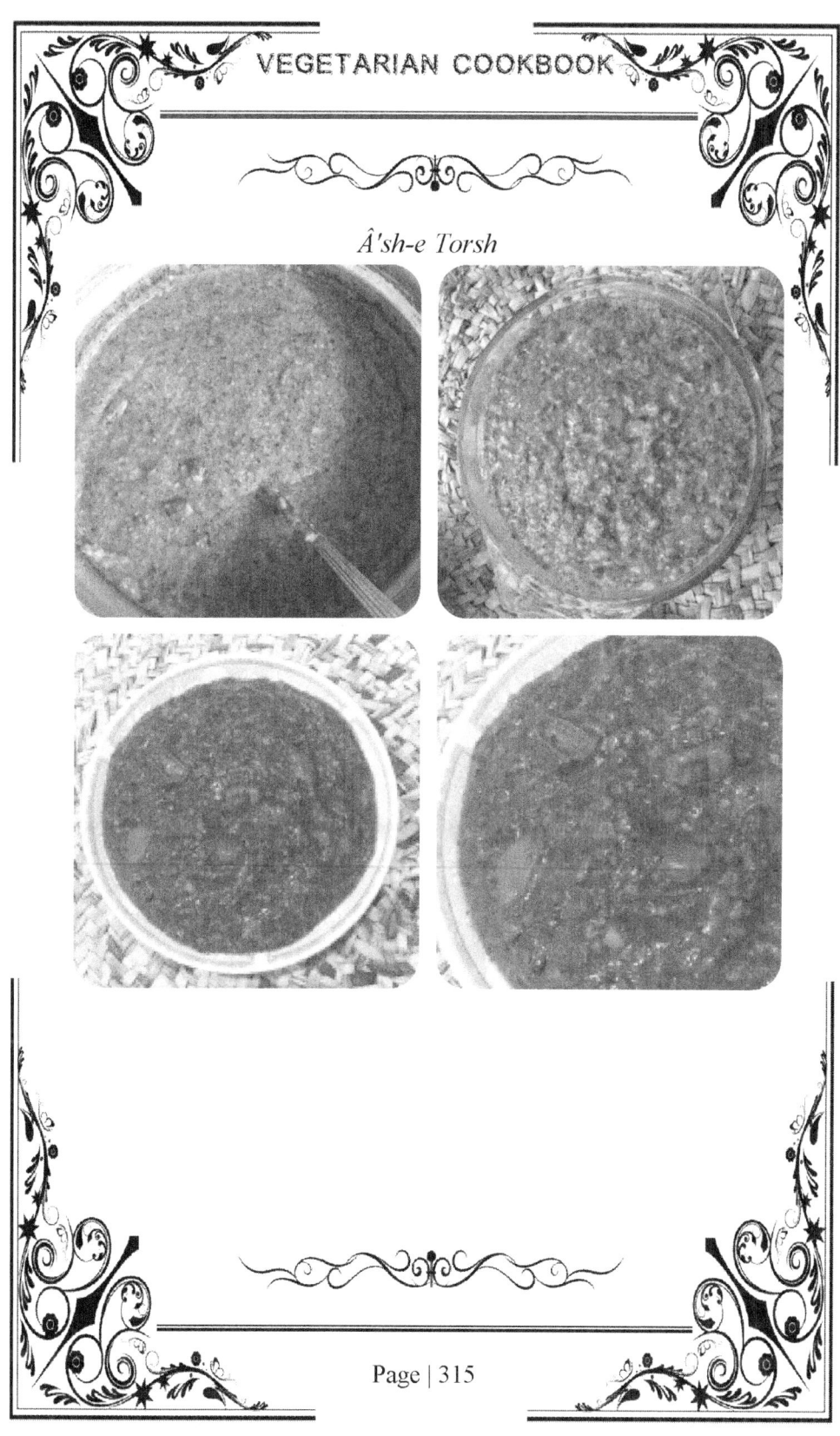

Ash'ke'neh Ta'reh

Bâ'dem'jân Ka'bâb

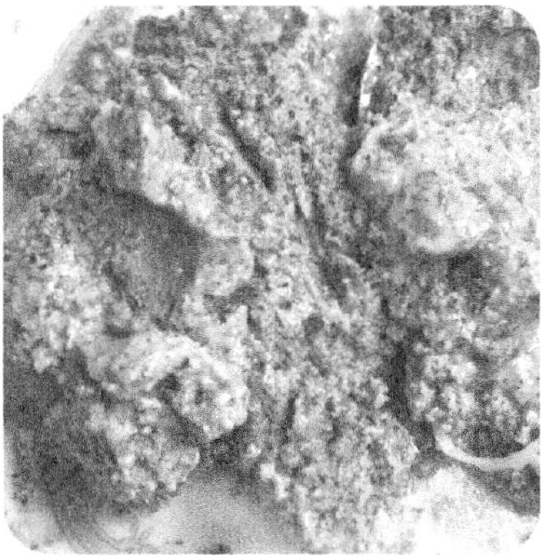

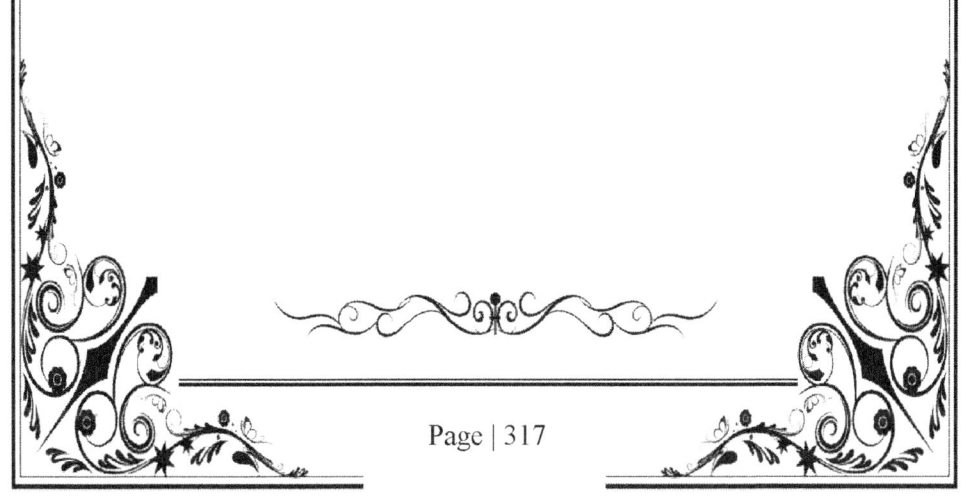

Bâ'dem'jân Ta'reh

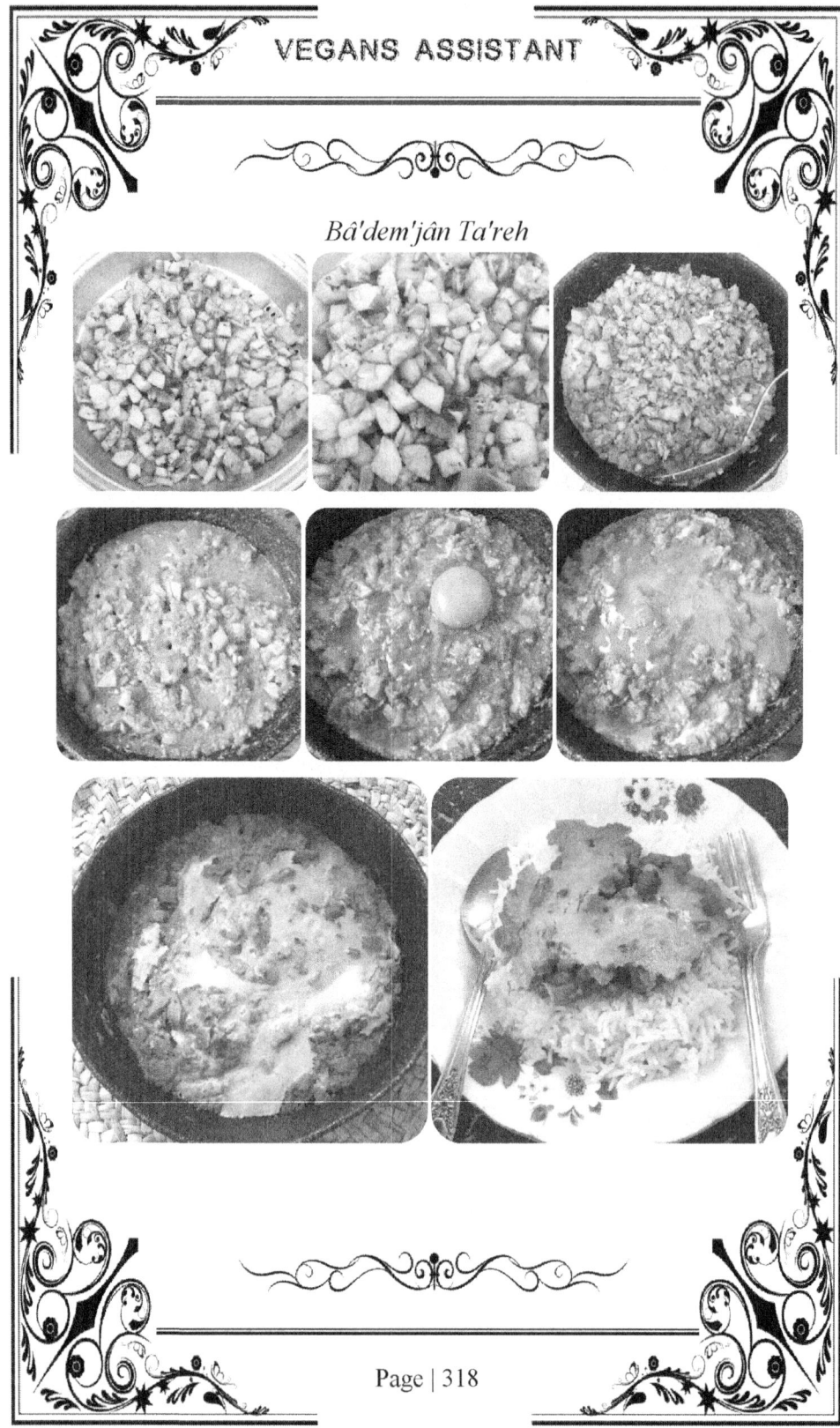

Bâ'dem'jân Va'ra'gheh Bâ Gou'jeh

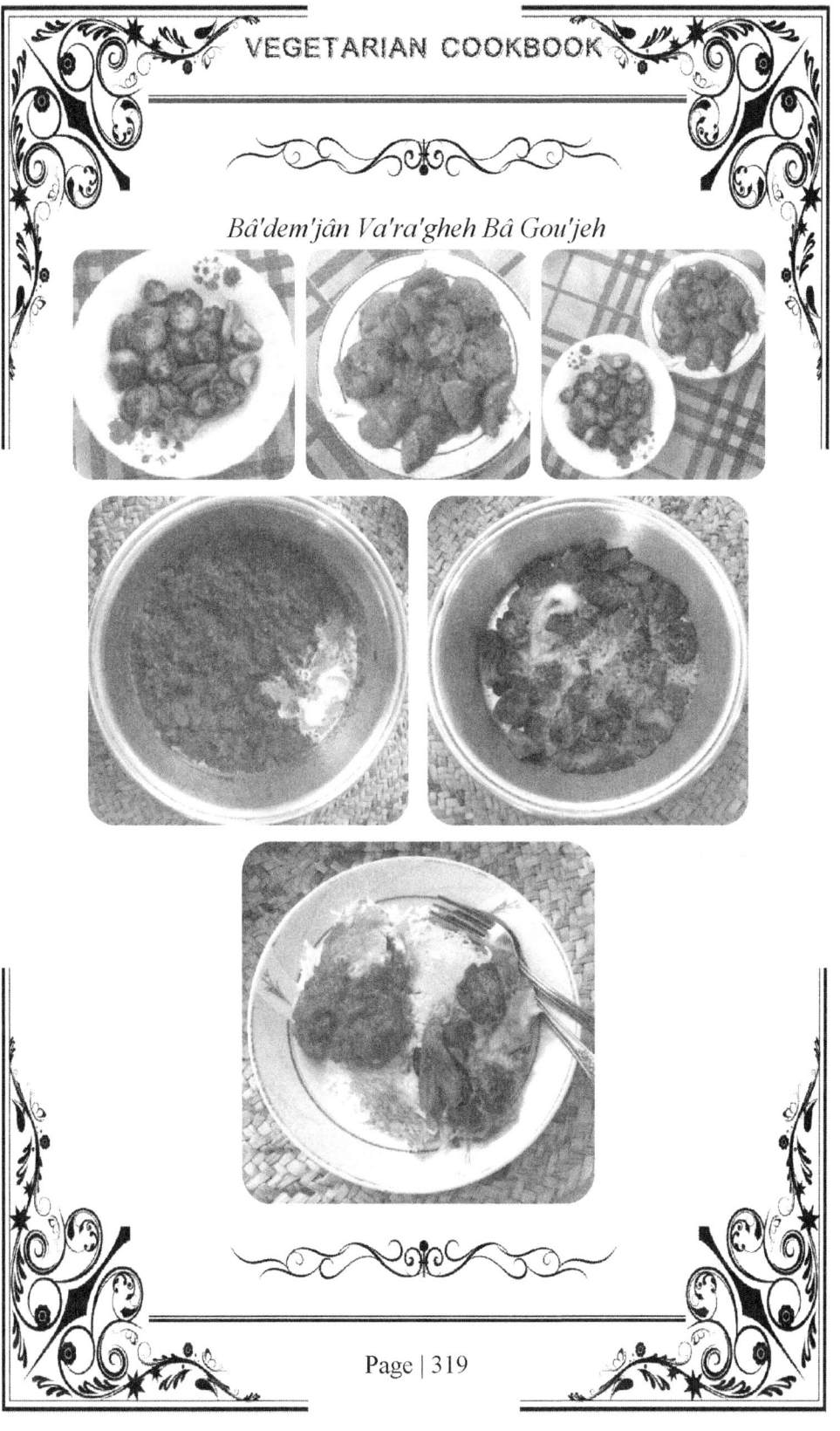

Bâ'ghe'lâ Ghâ'togh

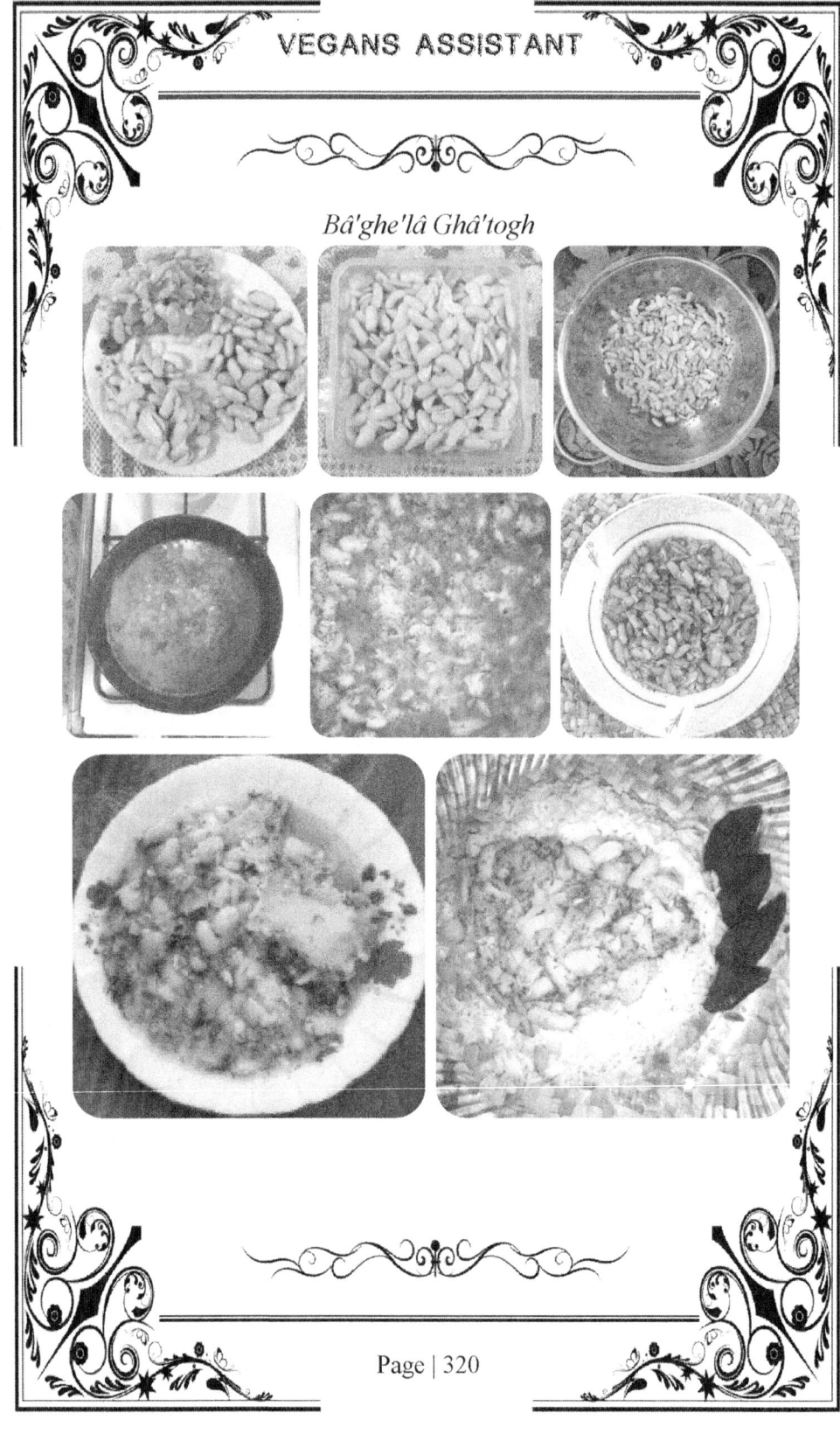

Bâ'ghe'lâ Po'low Bâ Pa'nir Be'resh'teh

Kho'resh't-e Ka'du

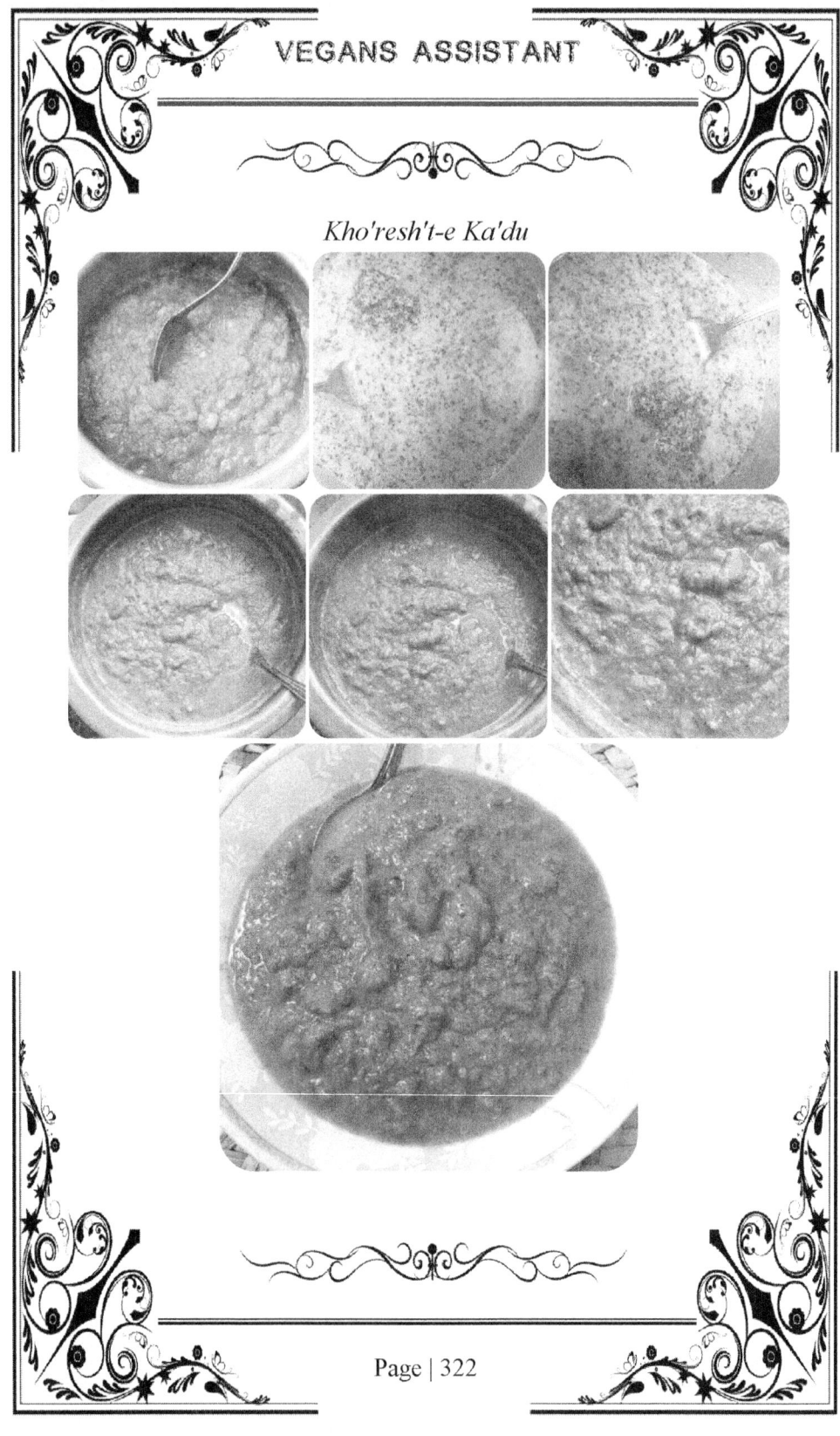

Khu'li Ou (Hâ'li Ou)

Ku'ku Bâ'dem'jân

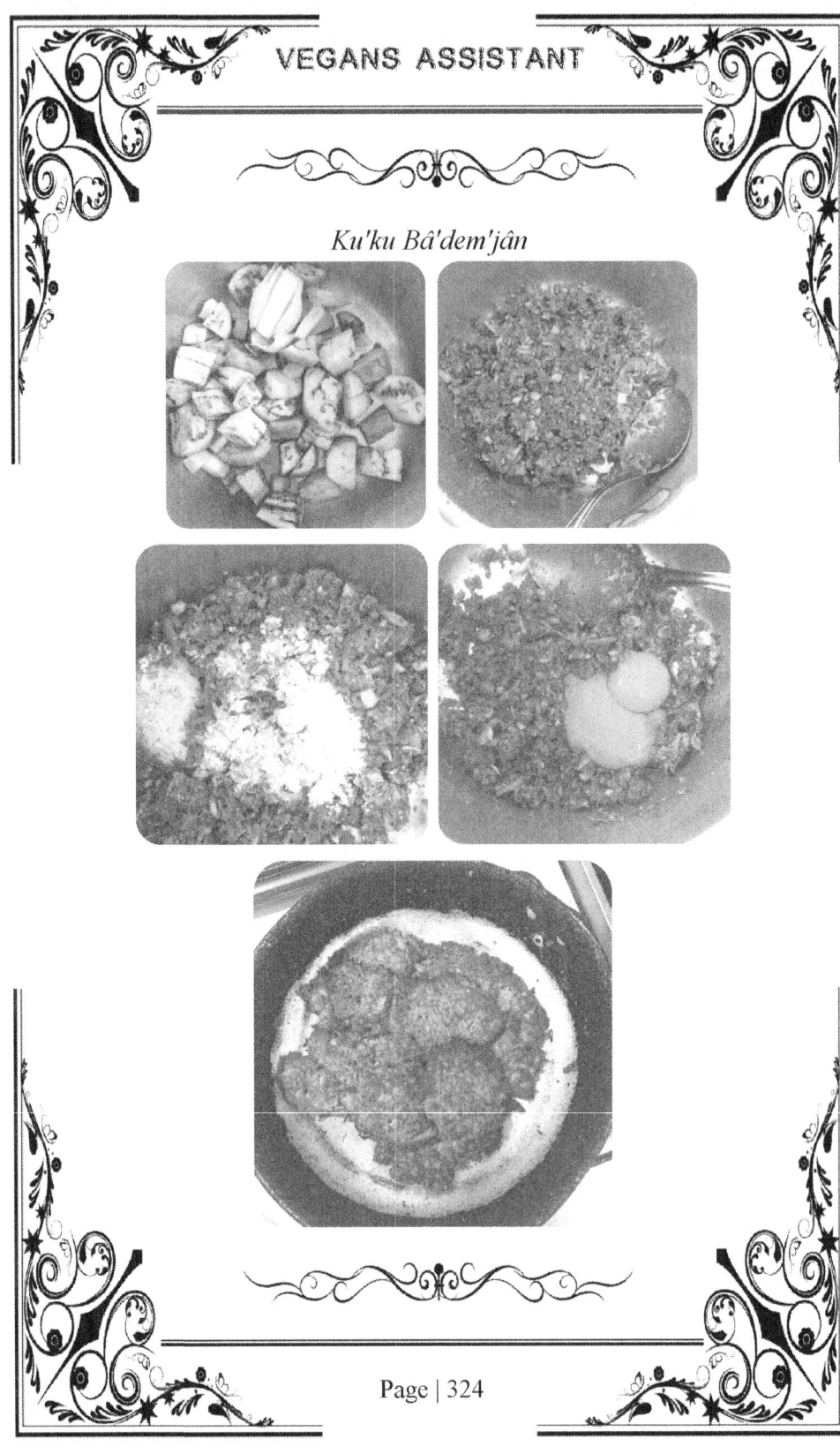

Ku'ku She'vid

Ku'ku Sir

La'gad Da'mo'jey
with lima beans

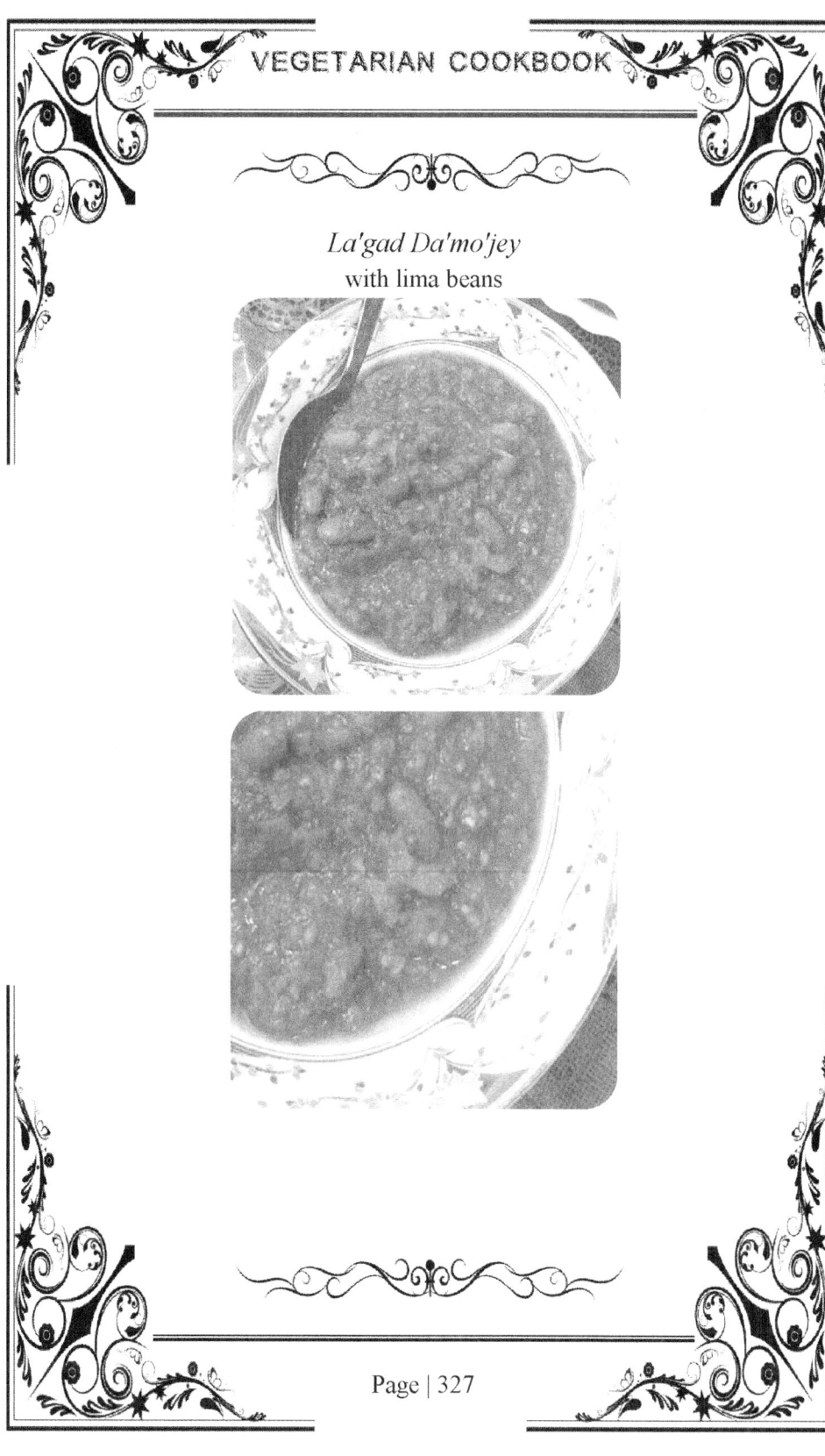

Mâ'kâ'ro'ni Bâ Ja'fa'ri Vâ'ram'bu

Mir'zâ Ghâ'se'mi

Mor'ju Vâ'vij
with lima beans

with black-eyed beans

Om'let Bâ Sir

She'vid Po'low Bâ Pa'nir Be'resh'teh

Sir Vâ'vij

Tah Bur'yân

Tor'sh-e Ta'reh

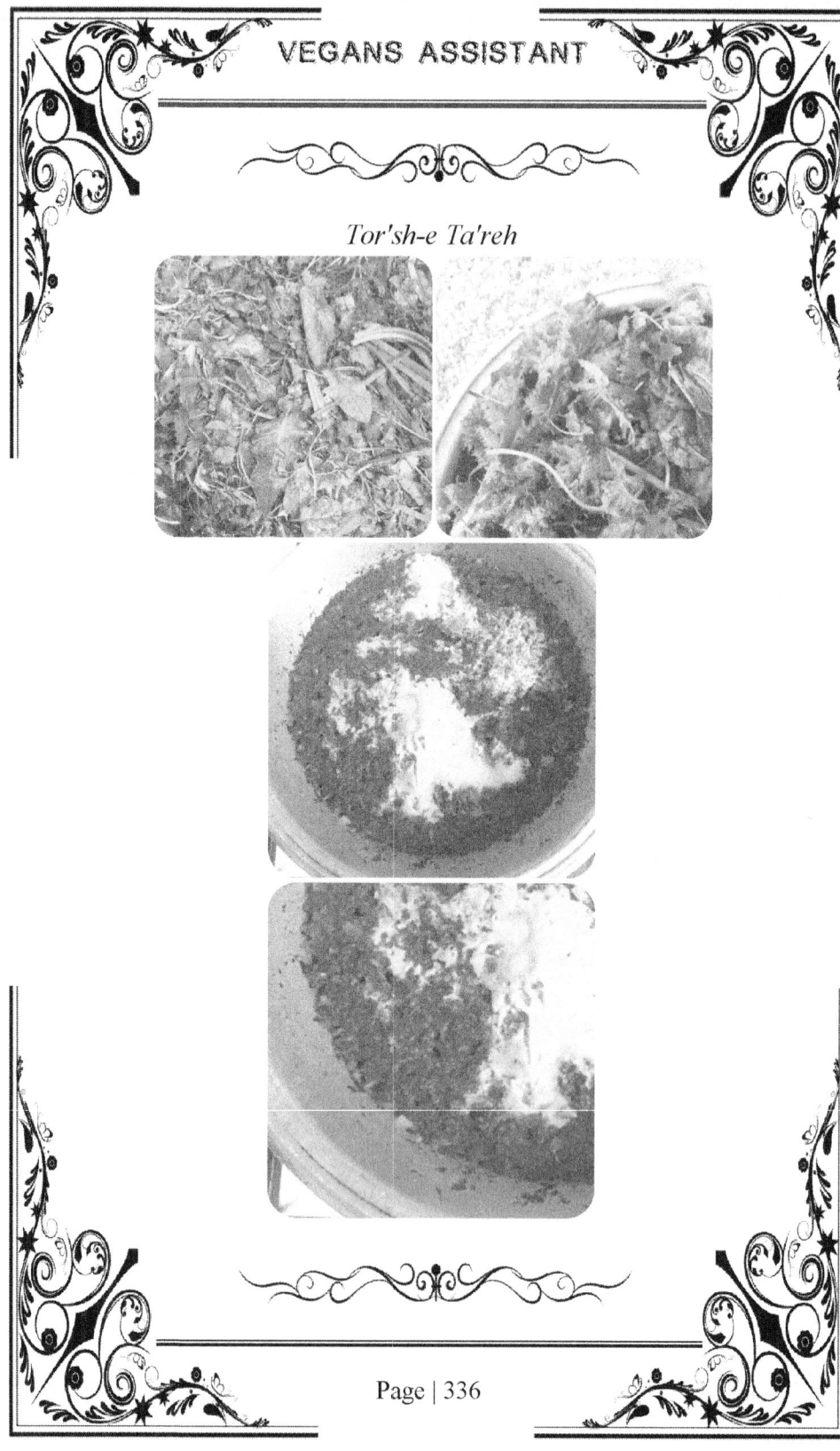

Iranian side item images

Bu'râ'ni-e Es'fe'nâj

Mâs't-o Khi'yâr

Sâ'lâd Shi'ra'zi

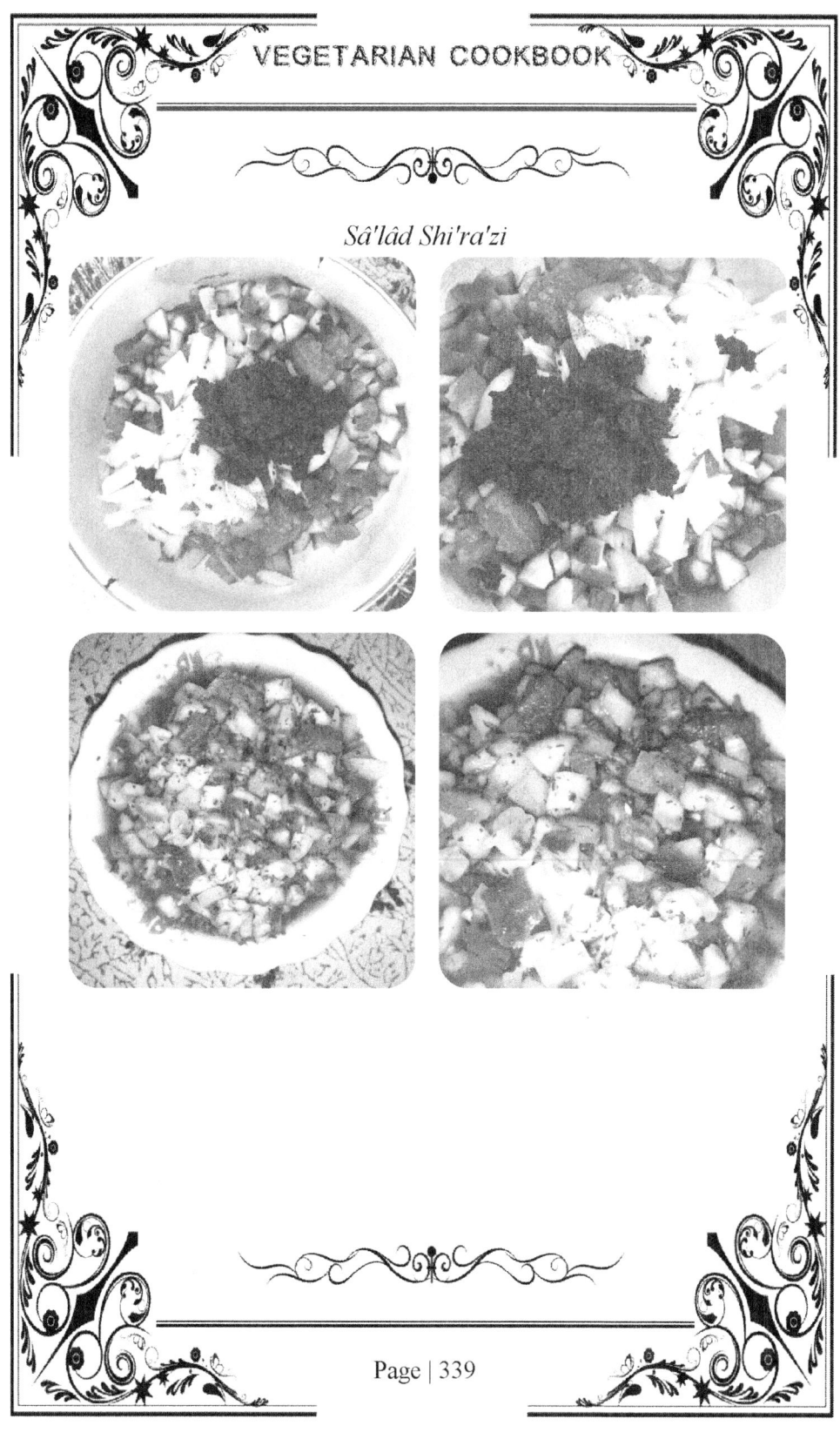

Sâ'lâ'd-e Fasl

Gilanian side item images
Bu'râ'ni-e Bâ'dem'jân

Kâl Ka'bâb

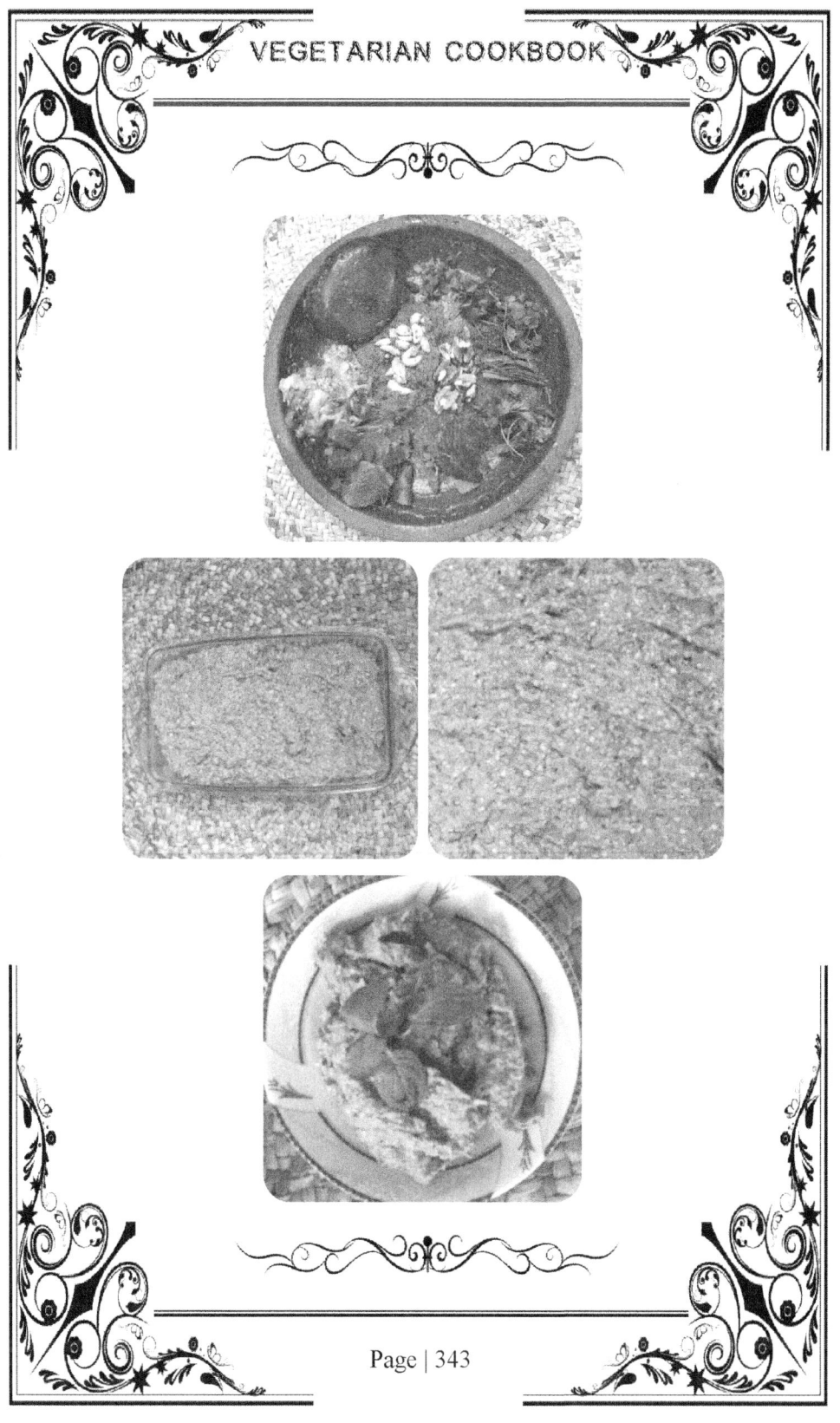

Zey'tun Par'var'deh

Pickle images
Tor'shi-e Bâ'dem'jân Chu'châgh

or ⟹

"Others"section images
Da'lâr

Ko'lo'bij Nân

So's-e Ger'du

More side dish images

Onion, tomato and sour cucumber (sliced)

Olives, raw fava beans

Olives, raw fava beans, white radish leaves and onion

Pickled cabbage

Pickled cauliflower

Pickled garlic

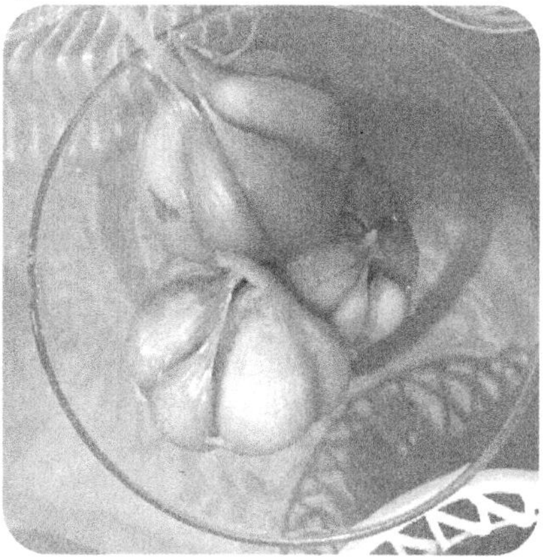

Vegetables

More related images

Angelica

(Ground Angelica)

Bâ'ghâ'li Po'low

Cinnamon

Dried apricots   *Dried prunes*

Dried limes

Ga'maj
(The local pot is made of clay)

Golden prunes
(Â'lu Bo'khâ'râ or Mash'had plum)

Local bread in Gilan Province
(Made by pumpkin)

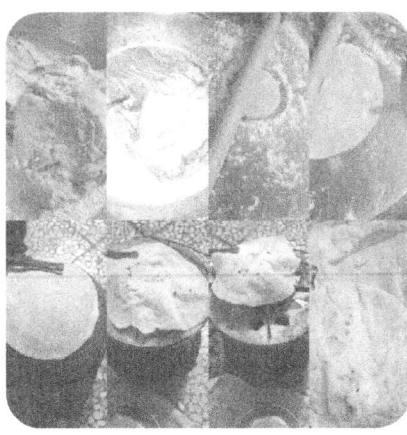
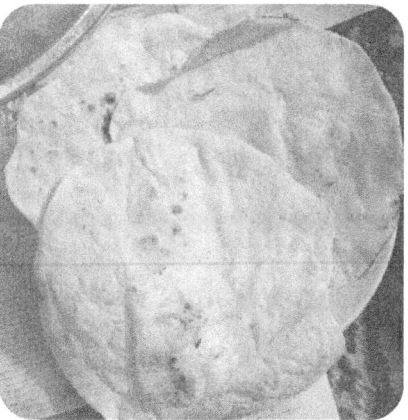

Persian bread (La'vâsh)

Persian bread (Bar'ba'ri)

Persian bread (San'gak)

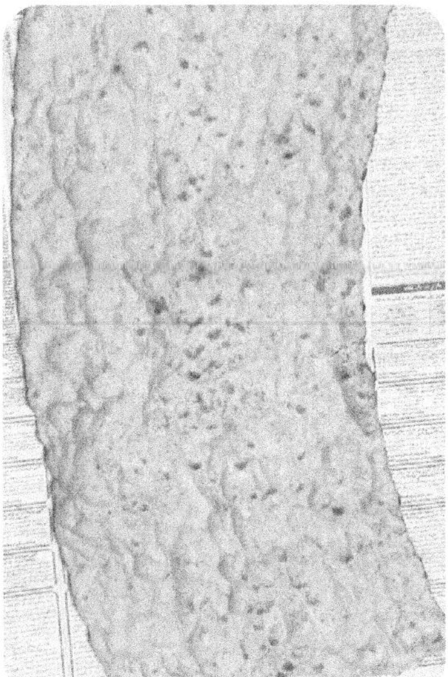

Pumpkin
(Pumpkins in the North of Iran)

Sab'zi Po'low

Saffron

ground saffron

melted saffron   brewing saffron

Sour orange juice

Stone and Nam'kâr
(Nam'kâr is made of clay)

Rice
(Persian rice)

Sour plum paste

Sour pomegranate

Sour pomegranate paste

Tah dig

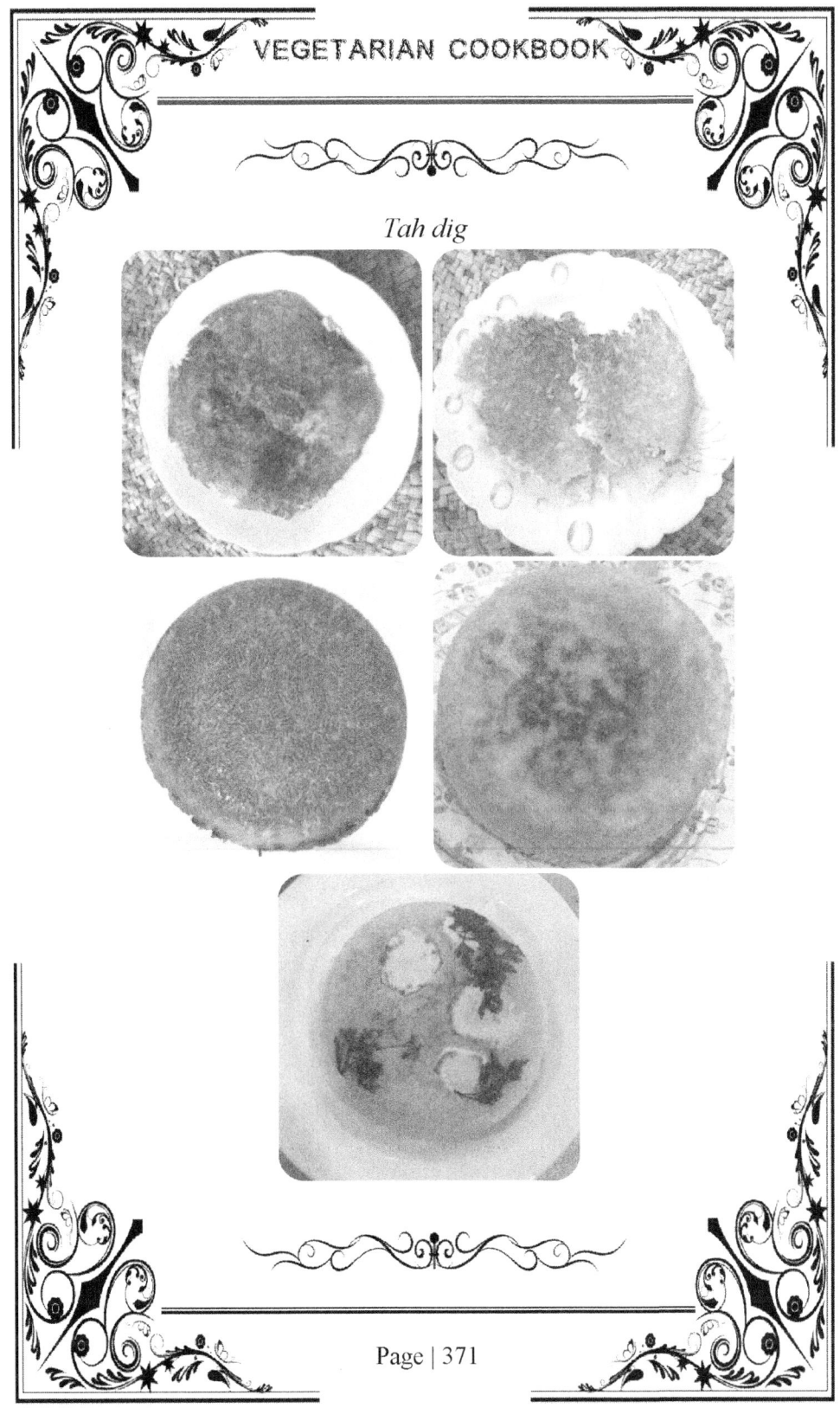

VEGANS ASSISTANT

Some of local herbs in the North of Iran
Alphabetical order

Name	Also Known As	Scientific Name	Family	In Farsi (With Phonetic)
Creeping wood sorrel	Procumbent yellow sorrel	Oxalis corniculata	Oxalidaceae	tor'sh-e wâsh or buyâ
Eryngium planum	Blue eryngo	Eryngium planum	Apiaceae	chu'chagh or shish shâkh
Pennyroyal	Sguaw mint	Mentha pulegium	Lamiaceae	Pu'neh
Ziziphora	-	Ziziphopra capitata	Lamiaceae	kâ'ku'ti

Herbs pictures
Ash'ke'neh

Beet greens

Coriander

Creeping wood sorrel

Dill

Eryngium planum

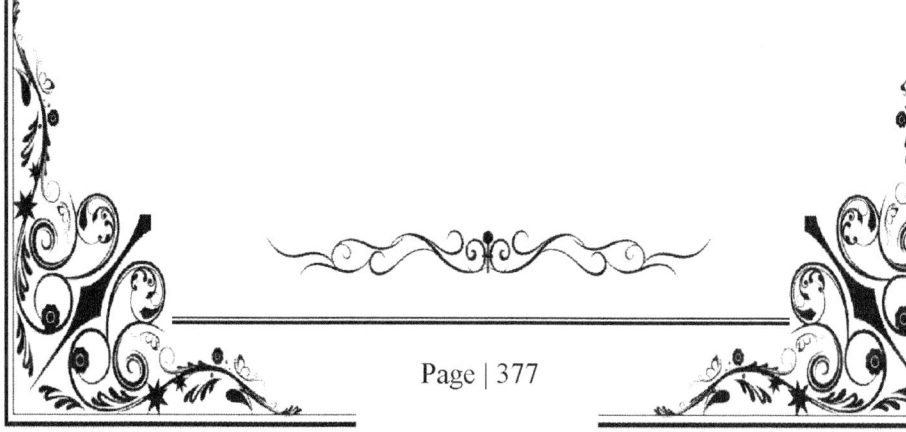

Fenugreek

Leek

Lemon balm

Mint

Parsley

Pennyroyal

Spinach

Tarragon and Savory

White Radish

Ziziphora

Dried herbs
Dried Dill

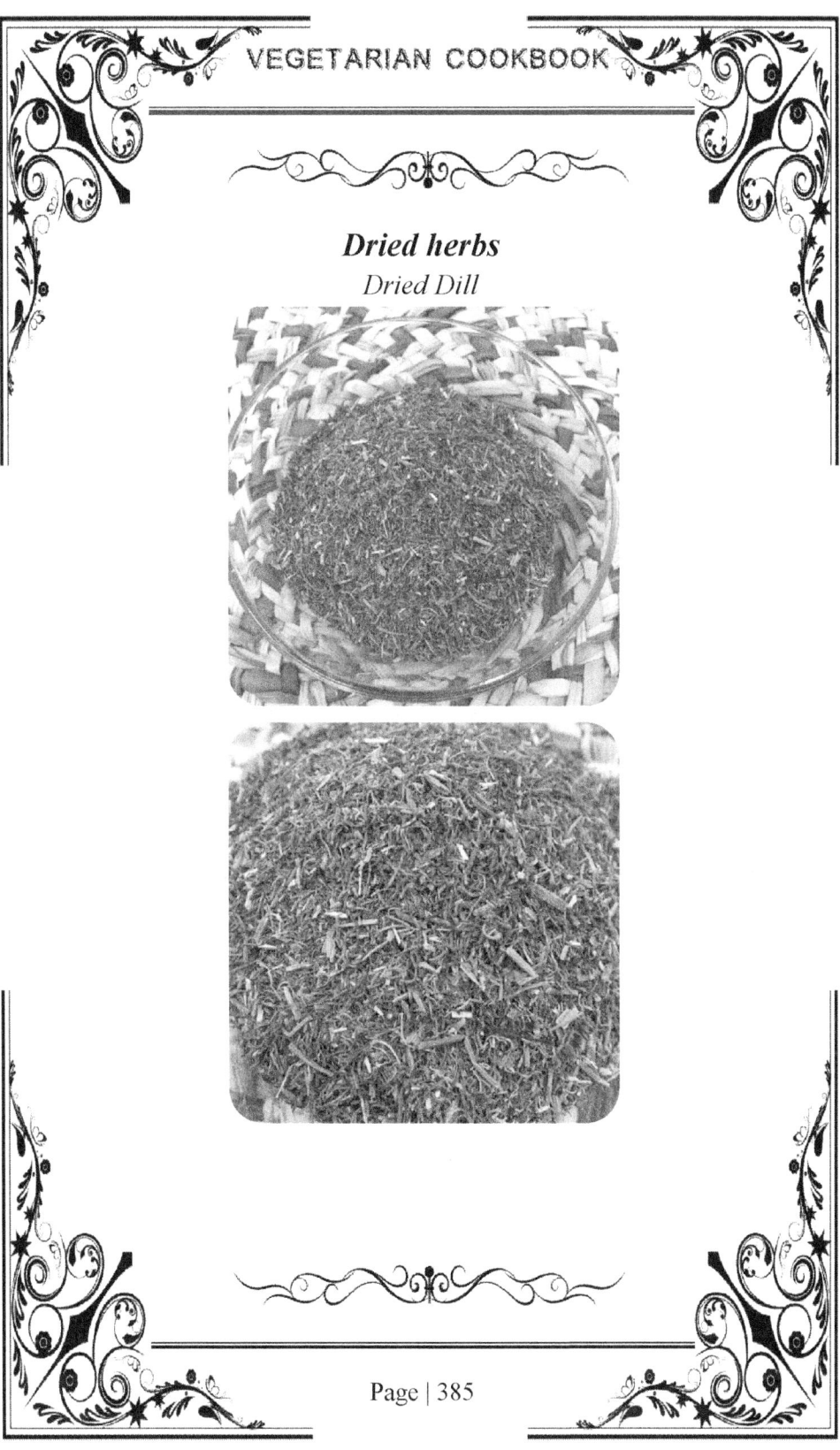

Dried Lemon balm

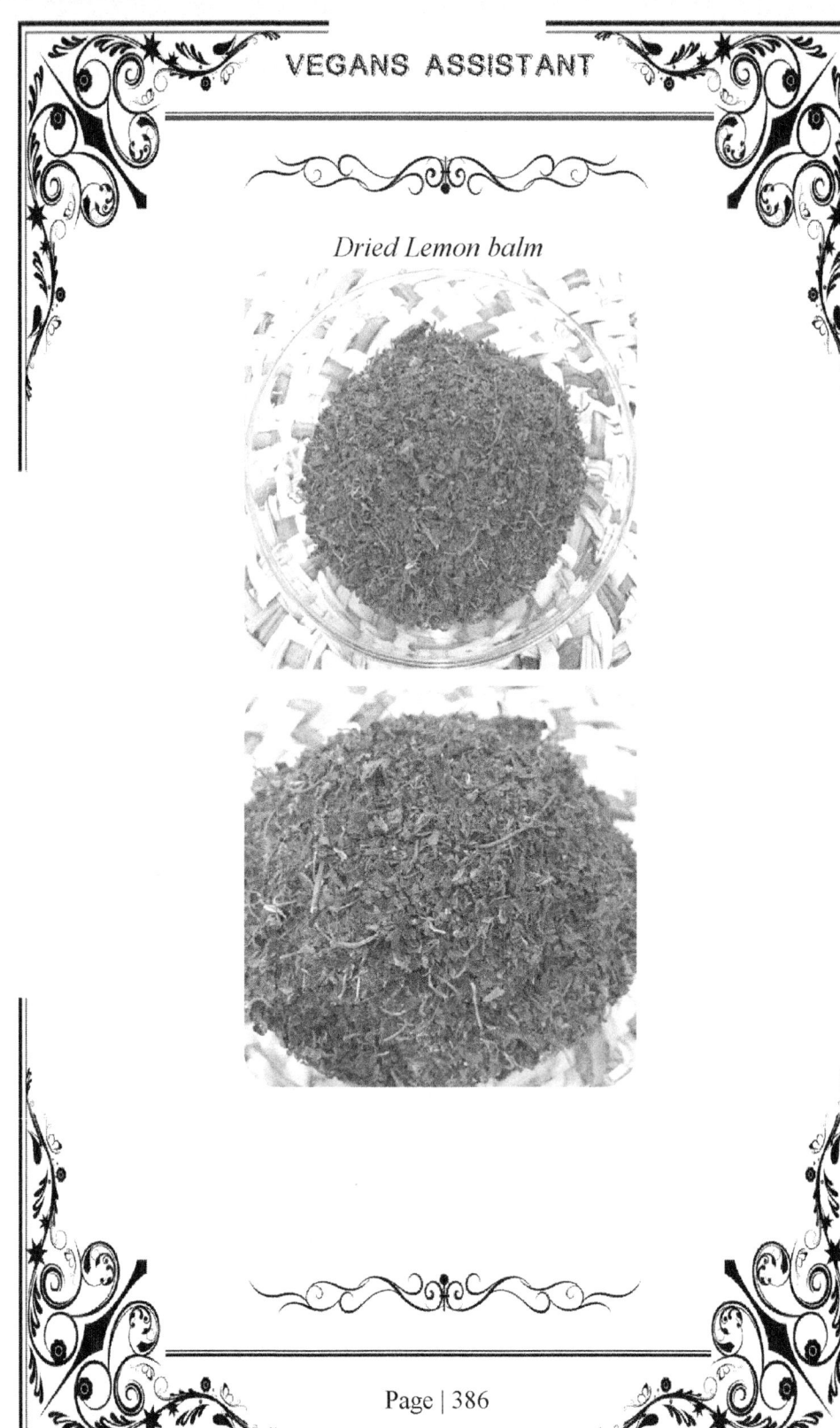

Dried Mint

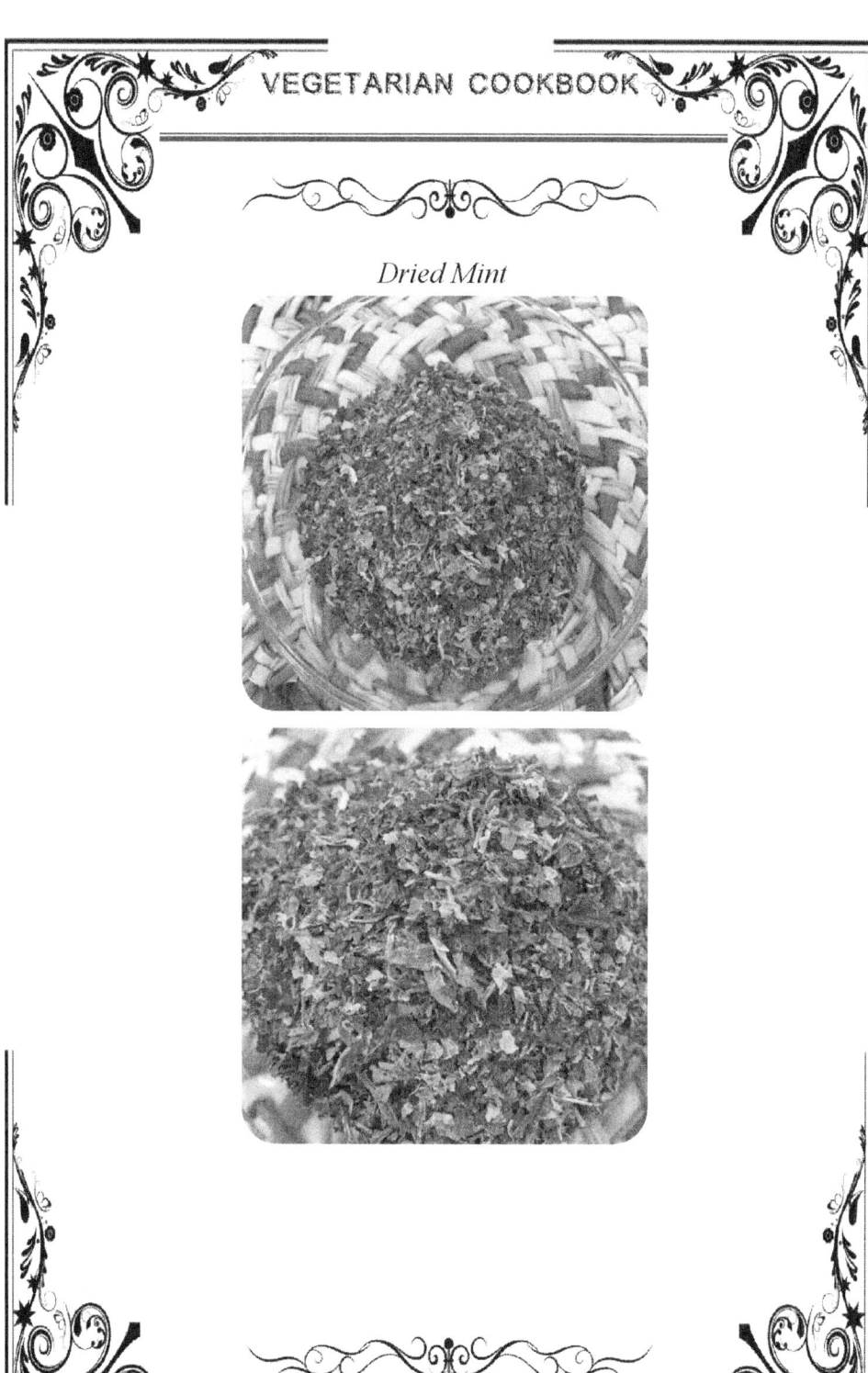

Dried Ziziphora

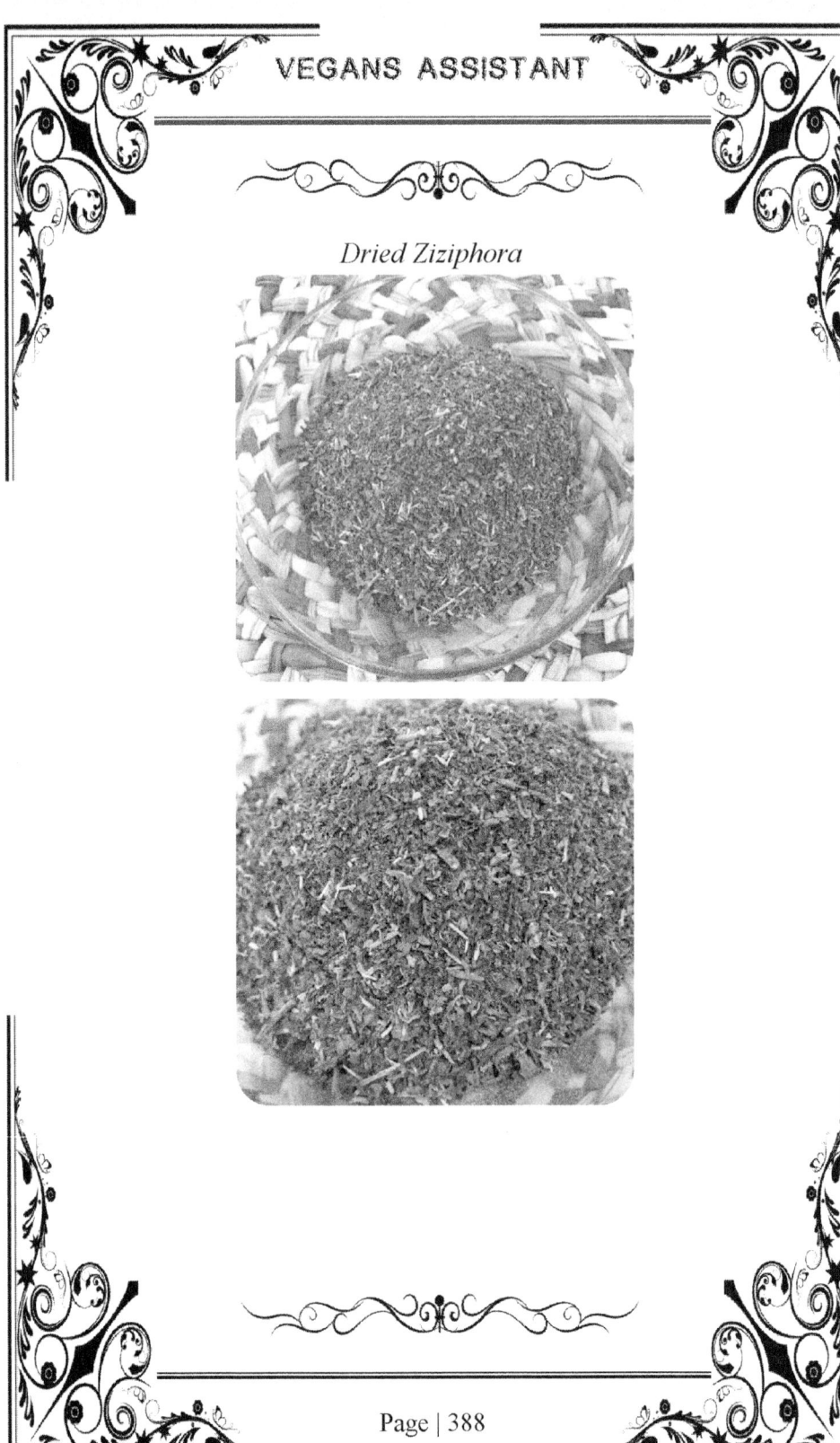

Other books of interest

Available in "Amazon.Com"

1. *202 Persian Idioms & Proverbs: For Advanced Farsi Learners. (Volume 1 & 2) (Persian Edition)*

The general objective of these books is to familiarize you with highly frequent Persian proverbs. For this purpose, among thousands of Persian proverbs we tried to select those that are essential and more frequently heard in spoken language for further description. Also, practical instances are offered for better understanding of proverbs beside of main descriptions, so that the reader could imagine the described conditions and states so as to understand the meaning of the proverbs and to easily use them.

In the end, it should be noted that these books could be used as a two-purpose collection because firstly, the reader has learnt Persian proverbs and terms which consequently makes it easier for him/her to understand the concepts and speeches in Persian. Secondly, because of carefully  selected words and verbs along with varied subjects used for better understanding of instances the reader will reinforce his/her reading skills. (These books are in Persian)

2. *Learn Farsi With Short Articles: Grow Your Vocabulary And Learn Farsi The Fun Way. (General Subjects) (Persian Edition)*

Organized by specific reading topics, "Learn Farsi with Short Articles: Grow your vocabulary and learn Farsi the fun way" is designed to help you improve your Farsi reading skill. The entertaining topics motivate you to learn more about Iran's history, culture and language. Dynamic passages present high-interest subjects for Iranian people.

In this book, the short articles represent wide variety of engaging topics about central interest to Farsi native speakers. Each of the book's topics is a simple one-page essay about Iran's history, geography, and culture. (This book is in Persian)

3. Persian Reading: 50 Iranian Main Food Recipes: For Intermediate to Advanced Persian Learners. (Persian Food) (Persian Edition)

Persian food is the ultimate comforting cuisine, full of robust and rich flavors. It shows you how to master the art of Persian cooking and illustrates how to prepare delicious, nice Persian foods from breakfast to dinner. The fresh and simple recipes will be available and perfect for everyday cooking. This book is for those who want to put a fabulous dinner on the table for their Persian friends or just kids.

Persian food recipes explain the Persian traditions and the history that defines the way Iranian's eat. Ranging from traditional foods such as "Ghor'm-e Sab'zi" (Persian Green Stew) and "Sab'zi Po'low bâ Mâ'hi" (Herb Rice with Fish) to local foods in the North of Iran. The Persian recipes in this book highlight the Middle East cuisines. Finally, with the help of this cookbook, you will not need to travel far to enjoy the authentic flavors of Persian. (This book is in Persian)

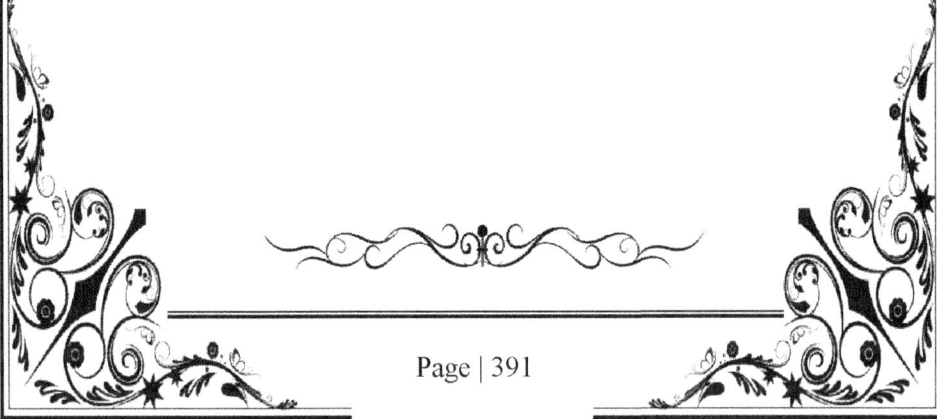

4. *Persian Reading: 50 Iranian Vegetarian Food & Dessert Recipes: For Intermediate to Advanced Farsi Learners. (Persian Food) (Persian Edition)*

"Persian Vegetarian Food & Dessert Recipes" are the ultimate comforting cuisine, full of robust and rich flavors. These recipes show you how to master the art of Persian cooking and illustrate how to prepare delicious, nice Persian foods from breakfast to dinner. The fresh and simple recipes will be available and perfect for everyday cooking. This book is for those who are vegetarians and interested in healthy foods. It's especially for people who want to put a fabulous dinner on the table for their Persian friends or just kids.

Persian Vegetarian Food & Dessert explain the Persian traditions and the history that defines the way Iranian's eat. Ranging from traditional foods such as "Mir'zâ Ghâ'se'mi" (a dish from Gilan Province) and "Sab'zi Po'low" (Herb Rice) to local foods in the North of Iran. The Persian recipes in this book highlight the Middle East cuisines. Finally, with the help of this cookbook, you will not need to travel far to enjoy the authentic flavors of Persian. (This book is in Persian)

5. *Fundamental Grammar Of Farsi Verbs: A Self-Study Verb Specifications Plus 202 Real Sentences Quizzes With Answers. (Persian Edition)*

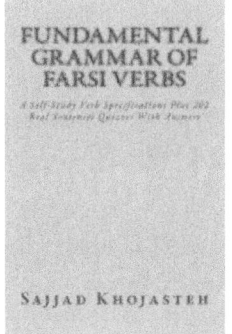

"Fundamental Grammar of Farsi Verbs" offers a solid foundation of major verbal and grammatical concepts of Farsi language. It will also give you 202 exercises for improving your Farsi language skills. This book offers an integrated guide to both Farsi verbs and the basics of grammar. Farsi verbal and grammatical concepts are illustrated in detail. Each topic is fully described and the explanations are supported by numerous examples to help you master the concepts. All examples reflect contemporary usage and real-life situations.

Fundamental Grammar of Farsi Verbs is the best reference source for verb usage in Farsi. This edition presents the most commonly used Farsi verbs.

Note: This book is
1- in Persian,
2- For Upper-Intermediate To Advanced Farsi Learners,
3- Based On 100 Essential Verbs.

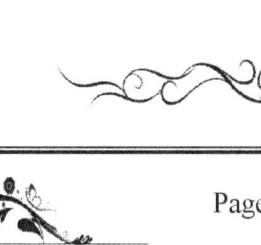

6. Persian CookBook: Let's Make Something Delicious with My Mom's Lunch and Dinner Recipes. (English Edition)

Persian food is the ultimate comforting cuisine, full of robust and rich flavors. It shows you how to master the art of Persian cooking and illustrates how to prepare delicious, nice Persian foods from breakfast to dinner. The fresh and simple recipes will be available and perfect for everyday cooking.

This book is for those who want to put a fabulous dinner on the table for their Persian friends or just kids. Persian food recipes explain the Persian traditions and the history that defines the way Iranian's eat. Ranging from traditional foods such as "Ghor'm-e Sab'zi" (Persian Green Stew) and "Sab'zi Po'low bâ Mâhi" (Herb Rice with Fish) to local foods in the North of Iran. The Persian recipes in this book highlight the Middle East cuisines. Finally, with the help of this cookbook, you will not need to travel far to enjoy the authentic flavors of Persian.

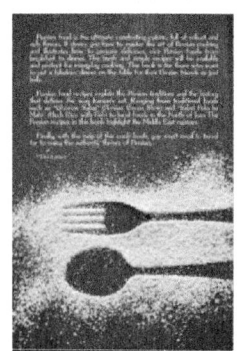

(This book is in English)

7. Hafez: The Complete Ghazals. A Treasure Of Truth And Divine Love. (English - Persian Edition with Phonetics) (Volume 1, 2, 3, 4 & 5)

Hafez (1325–1389), the great lyric Persian poet is known for his ghazals. He has published about 500 ghazals and 42 Rubaiyees. Themes of his ghazals are the beloved, faith, and exposing hypocrisy. His most popular book, Divan-e Hafez, is a pinnacle of Persian literature and is to be found in the homes of most Iranian people. Persian poetry lovers learn Hafez's poems by heart and still use them as proverbs and sayings.

Adaptations, imitations and translations of his ghazals exist in all major languages. All Hafez's ghazals are provided in this bilingual book in Persian and English languages. The translation appearing in this collection is by Henry Wilberforce Clarke (1840 - 1905).

This book can be useful for Persian and English language speakers and enjoyable for poetry lovers of any age. Not only will poems improve your understanding of Persian language and history, but they'll help improve your understanding of Persian culture. Since all ghazals are written according to the transliterated English spelling, reading the poems is easy.

(English – Persian Edition with Phonetics)

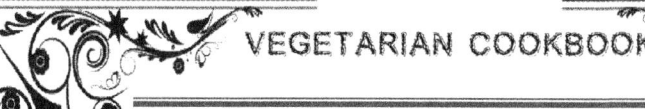

8. Learn How to Read Hafez Poems: The Best Guide for Reading Hafez's Ghazals with Phonetics (Hafez Poems with Phonetics) (Volume 1, 2 & 3)

(Persian Edition with Phonetics)

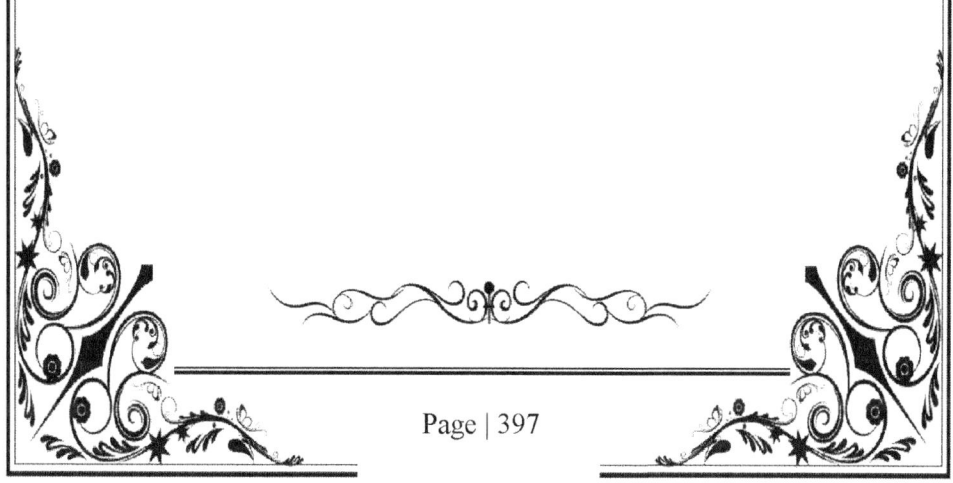

9. The Complete Book of Ghazals of Hafez: In Persian with English Translation (English - Persian Edition)

(English – Persian Edition)

10. *A Cup of Forbidden Wine: The Rubaiyat of Khayyam (English - Persian Edition with Phonetics)*

Omar Khayyam was a Persian mathematician, astronomer, and poet, who is widely considered to be one of the most influential scientists of the Middle Ages. He is mainly known to English-speaking readers through the translation of a collection of his Rubaiyat of Omar Khayyam (1859), by the English writer Edward FitzGerald.

All Rubaiyat are provided in this bilingual book in Persian and English languages. This book can be useful for Persian language learners and speakers and enjoyable for poetry lovers of any age. Not only will poems improve your understanding of Persian language and history, but they'll help improve your understanding of Persian culture. Since all Rubaiyat are written according to the transliterated English spelling, reading the poems is easy. Persian language students will have ample opportunities to enrich their Persian learning experience and extend a range of language abilities through exploring these poems.

(English - Persian Edition with Phonetics)

11. *Learn How to Read Rubaiyat of Khayyam: The Best Guide for Reading Poems of Khayyam with Phonetics (Persian Edition)*

(Persian Edition with Phonetics)

Follow us

Join the conversation on our social media channels to stay up-to-date with us. Furthermore, you can find all the latest news about our new books, ask us questions, send us your comments and many more by following us on:

E-Mail ⟶ Farsi.books@yahoo.com

Facebook ⟶ https://m.facebook.com/farsibookspublication

LinkedIn ⟶ http://linkedin.com/in/farsi-books-b7827563

Instagram ⟶ https://www.instagram.com/farsi.books

Twitter ⟶ https://twitter.com/farsibooks

Pinterest ⟶ https://www.pinterest.co.uk/farsibooks

Tumblr ⟶ Farsibooks

THE END

Printed in Great Britain
by Amazon

44807355R00231